DANCE PATHOLOGIES

WRITING SCIENCE

EDITORS Timothy Lenoir and Hans Ulrich Gumbrecht

DANCE
PATHOLOGIES

Performance, Poetics, Medicine

Felicia McCarren

STANFORD UNIVERSITY PRESS
STANFORD, CALIFORNIA 1998

Stanford University Press
Stanford, California
© 1998 by the Board of Trustees of the
Leland Stanford Junior University
Printed in the United States of America

CIP data appear at the end of the book

For my parents, remembering

Acknowledgments

This book began twice. The first beginning was made possible by my parents, who took me to dance and music classes taught by Trudl Dubsky and Herbert Zipper, who shaped my thinking about performance at an early age. The second beginning came in college when my teacher Richard Sieburth suggested that I read Frank Kermode's *Romantic Image*, and I realized that it needed a response. Many friends have listened to, read, and critiqued this project over the years, and made invaluable suggestions, not all of which I have been able to incorporate. For the shortcuts this book takes I alone am responsible; for the multiplicity of its branchings I have many people to thank. More than anyone else, Joe Roach engaged with this manuscript in 1996 and 1997 with wonderful intensity, and made it take its final form. For his exemplary criticism and intellectual camaraderie I am most grateful. For suggestions for revision of the manuscript I also thank Mark Franko and an anonymous reader. At Stanford, friends in literature, the history of science, and Humanities Special Programs created a great climate for exploratory interdisciplinary work. I count myself lucky to have had Pamela Cheek and Nicolas Rasmussen as readers and critics close at hand. At UCLA, my research assistant Seth Abelson was extremely helpful. At Tulane, among many others, my colleagues Valerie Greenberg and Vaheed Ramazani have read and talked with me patiently. In visits to New Orleans, Sander Gilman and Dick Terdiman responded to my work with enthusiasm and critical insight. In Paris, Claire Bustarret at ITEM has been a continual source of bibliography. Early versions of the chapters benefited from the teaching and reading of René Girard, Henri Godard, Philippe Lacoue-Labarthe, and Michel Serres. In Brassempouy, Santa Barbara, Washington, D.C., and

Gresford NSW, many—they know who they are—gave more immediate if less specific help by finding me a chair, a table, and an outlet. And at Stanford University Press, Helen Tartar's passion for books, biology, and dance has been a source of friendship. For their time and patience, I thank Pamela MacFarland Holway, Wes Peverieri, and Alisa Caratozzolo, also at Stanford University Press, as well as Stephanie Yang, for her help with the index.

Over the years, the explosion in the fields of dance studies and performance studies has brought me out of isolation and into contact with scholars working in the history of dance, drama, and cultural studies. I was able to meet many by participating in the 1992 MLA panel "Bodies of the Text," organized by Jacqueline Shea Murphy and Ellen Goellner, and the panel on "Exotic Bodies" shaped by Marta Savigliano at the 1997 Unnatural Acts conference at the University of California at Riverside, organized by Susan Foster, Sue-Ellen Case, and Phillip Brett. To the organizers of these rich exchanges I express my gratitude again.

For many inspiring conversations and for their support, I thank Tomiko Yoda, Katie Trumpener, Ruth Tsoffar, Hasok Chang, Hope Glidden, Madeleine Dobie, Wayne Klein, and Jacinto Fombona; and for new friendships and inspiration, I thank the faculty and students of the Department of Performance Studies at New York University–Tisch School of the Arts. During the final preparation of the manuscript, my graduate assistant at NYU–Tisch, Shane Vogel, was an extra set of eyes, arms, and legs, and an intelligently engaged reader, when I most needed all of those things. And all through the years of writing, the many dancers who taught and worked with me on three continents have remained with me.

Work on this book was supported by the Tulane University Committee on Research and the Newcomb Foundation, and facilitated by a leave generously granted by the LAS Dean of Tulane University and the Department of French and Italian. Portions of the book have been published elsewhere; for permission to reprint previously published material I thank the University of Chicago Press and Rutgers University Press.

Contents

Illustrations

DANCE PATHOLOGIES

Introduction

A history of dance pathologized may startle readers who find in dance performance all that is best in Western culture: beauty, grace, discipline, geometry, poetry, the body's transcendence of everyday bodiliness. In connecting dance performance to the medical, scientific, and negative social connotations of a "pathology," this book asks its readers to consider what has subtended dance's idealization in the West. It investigates a nineteenth-century response, in the intersections of dance, literature, and medicine, to the complex and long-standing connections between illness, madness, poetry, and performance.

When Boethius's Lady Philosophy banishes the muses of poetry from his bedside in the sixth century, disparaging them as the "Sirens" of a "chorus increpitus," these "whores of the theater" largely vanish from the scene of poetry and philosophy in the West. Boethius's text records dancers' fall from grace in a culture of institutionalized Christianity:

When she saw the Muses of poetry standing beside my bed and consoling me with their words, she was momentarily upset and glared at them with burning eyes. "Who let these whores from the theater come to the bedside of this sick man?" she said. "They cannot offer medicine for his sorrows; they will nourish him only with their sweet poison. They kill the fruitful harvest of reason with the sterile thorns of the passions; they do not liberate the minds of men from disease, but merely accustom them to it. . . . Get out, you Sirens; your sweetness leads to death. Leave him to be cured and made strong by my Muses." And so this chorus, reproached, shamefaced and with downcast eyes, went sadly away.[1]

Boethius's account of this ejection of the muses from the domain of metaphysics hints at a division between old and new conceptions of illness. For Boethius's particular sickness, Lady Philosophy introduces a new idea of cure. The thought that Sirens, dancers, actresses, performers might be imagined as comforting a bedridden man, distracting him from what ails him, is reversed when Philosophy takes over; in her regime, such women can only exacerbate the sickness, never contribute to cure. Boethius's allegory tells the story of the fall of performers within a story about the shifting locus of illness, from the body to the soul, and its need for metaphysical, rather than physical, cure. The separation of performers from the cure, and of cure from the body, suggests rich connections between theater and cure in ancient theater forms and in ancient medicine that are here—at least temporarily—terminated. But the female dancer will eventually return to cultural and even intellectual center stage with a vengeance. Described as a poet and metaphysician in her own right, she reappears in nineteenth-century Paris as the true muse of poets and philosophers, with her poetic and philosophical power reinstated, now reinforced rather than undermined by her meretricious and mystical qualities.

In the introduction to *Madness and Civilization*, Michel Foucault describes his project as an attempt to return to the "uncomfortable region" before the classical age, in which madness is an "undifferentiated experience." A return to preclassical conceptions of madness is necessary in order to chart the history of that other form of madness that "relegates Reason and Madness to one side or the other of its action as things henceforth external, deaf to all exchange, and as though dead to one another."[2] The classical age's separation of madness and nonmadness is in some ways reminiscent of Lady Philosophy's banishment of the muses from the domain of Christian life. Relegated by her to the "other side," dance has no choice but to line up with death, devilry, and illicit ecstasies. The *danse macabre* teams living, paralyzed partners with the dancing dead.[3] Dance figures prominently in accusations of witchcraft and descriptions of the witches' sabbath in European witch trials from the fifteenth to the seventeenth centuries.[4] The Christian tradition classed female hysterias both in the domain of witchcraft and in the realm of mysticism, but links between possession and dance, and later between possession and hysteria, make dancing suspect well into the nineteenth century.[5] Charcot and Richer's *Démoniaques dans l'art* reestablished the link between hysteria and behaviors the medieval church had deemed demonic possessions largely through iconography that underlined their resemblances to dancing. But the significance of dance's representing madness, hysteria, or possession changes with the medical climate of the nineteenth century, one in which the alienist, Jan Goldstein has argued, becomes the new priest.[6]

Dance has been closely connected to the history of madness in the Christian era; but is there a connection between the dances of death or of Saint Vitus, the hysterical dances of repression, and the later flowering of theatrical dance in the bourgeois capitals of Europe? This book argues that dance's popularity and its power in nineteenth-century Paris came from just such a connection. In the West, dance has largely been considered either a representation of madness (as in the dances of possession of the middle ages) or a manifestation of order, through individual or social control of the body (as in the baroque *ballets de cour*). Images and conceptions of madness have arguably always been in the background of dance interpretation, and it is precisely this subtext that has lent dance the powerful social, cultural, and political significance it had, for example, in these two historical contexts.

Legitimized as if by royal decree, instituted—and made fashionable—by the dancing Louis XIV, dance became a social and political strategy at Versailles. The baroque ballet staged the resolution of chaos, undoing its unseemly past in its ordered choreographies, which not incidentally feature male performers.[7] But the deviance ascribed to women of the theater by Lady Philosophy and the mainstream European Christian tradition she represents will return to haunt the image of the professional female dancer who emerges after the baroque ballet. This is the ballerina who will become the focus of nineteenth-century romantic ballet and the female dancer-choreographer of early modern dance.

The moment when the power of the ancient *chorus*—dance or dancers—became "increpitus" may be impossible to fix; but in nineteenth-century Paris, *chorus* is feminine, simultaneously idealized and closely connected to practices of prostitution and conceptions of hysteria. In the course of the nineteenth century, theater dance becomes an art form uniquely attached to the female form, an art in which the female body, an essentialized femininity, and feminine sexuality become the subject of dance. It may well be because of its "femininity"—as construed in both female and male performers—that these forms of dance theater have remained until recently largely insignificant in academic study, no matter how preponderant their role in the cultures studied in the academy. With the exception of performance studies and anthropological studies, contemporary critical discussion has frequently idealized or fetishized rather than problematized dance, even when describing its idealization and fetishization. Such work comments on dance from a literary perspective but does not take into account aspects of the production and reception of the real dances witnessed and recorded in texts. With some knowledge of both—derived from literary texts but also from archival and visual evidence, and using dance historical approaches—more can be said about how and what dance means in particular historical contexts and how texts about dance shape that context for their own purposes.[8] Cultural historians now affirm that "images and music" are objects of study as valid as texts, but dance is continually passed over.[9] Neither image nor music, neither film nor theater, but a synthesis of kinaesthetic, rhythmic, visual, and dramatic form, dance in its reference to all of these arts poses its own set of technical and analytical problems, intensified by its location in, and transformation of, the body. Nineteenth-century dance's essential femininity, as well as its physicality, its overlapping idealization and denigration, have made it problematic for writers, critics, and scholars alike.

The theatrical dancing whose written records are studied in this book has been idealized by its public since it took shape as romantic ballet 150 years ago. Writers have envisioned it as free expression, as ideal expression, as expression of what they have called "idea" itself. Yet idea or ideal— whether a philosophical, psychological, or physiological notion, Platonic, Hegelian, Charcotian, Freudian—when embodied in the dancer, proves problematic. Examining the other side of dance's idealization requires investigating the mechanics of such ideal embodiment.

It necessitates looking at the obverse of dance's literary idealization in French romantic texts influenced by German philosophy. It requires an understanding of bodies, in particular female bodies on public display, as the subject not only of projected ideals but also cultural anxieties. It necessitates investigation of how dance performance expresses, and addresses, profound questions about how the body signifies, and how we understand its signifying in our culture through a study of the nineteenth-century development of a genre of dance performance—first the romantic ballet and later modern dance—featuring women and excluding words. It requires looking across disciplines and practices to understand the contexts in which the body's gestures and movement, its somatic code, are read and interpreted.

The argument of this book depends on a view of culture in which writers are not taken literally. Their admiration of and identification with dancers are interrogated. Here, disciplines and domains often considered far removed from one another are seen to be in close conversation. Latent connections between writing, poetics, theories of expression, theories of mental illness, interpretive traditions, and performative practices are re-forged. Idealizing dance texts are read against the critical histories of their production and reception. Medical theory is read as both leading and resisting the current of medical practice. The performance arenas of the theater and the medical amphitheater are set against each other to better see how each features the female body. This book depends upon a view of culture that does not take culture at its word, even as it attempts to understand cultural products as discourses. This is an understanding of culture that looks beyond cultural intentionality to its less apparent, per-haps even unconscious motivations, and finds in the construction of its ideals a culture's pathology. It depends upon a view of history that con-siders not the perfecting of epistemologies but the conditions of their ex-istence. It depends as well upon historical and theoretical approaches in-formed by Freudian psychoanalysis: the depathologization of dance per-formance made possible in the development of the talking cure; and the analyses of the links between the body and language made possible by psychoanalytic literary theory in the wake of Freud. It depends upon a Marxian revalorization of the work that is dance; and a feminist revision-ist history of this female art that challenges social stereotypes of feminin-ity and the female body even as it plays to them. It depends as well on a literary history that considers not only the master texts of literature but all kinds of texts: from the daily newspaper account read by a vast audi-ence to unpublished pornography, unperformed libretti, the dancer's per-sonal account. And it depends upon the recent explosion of work in dance studies, performance studies, science studies, and cultural studies that have made arguments like mine possible.

CHAPTER 1

Idealism, Pathology, Idiopathy: Chorus, Chorea, and Chora

Chorus

In *The Natural History of the Ballet-Girl*, first published in London in 1847, author Albert Smith sets out to classify that newly discovered yet already much-talked-about species, the ballerina. Study of the ballet-girl, he believes, will prove to be both worthwhile and enjoyable:

After the unceasing labours of Cuvier, Linnaeus, Buffon, Shaw, and other animal-fanciers on a large scale, had surmounted the apparently impossible task of mar-shalling all the earth's living curiosities into literary rank and file, a worthy old clergyman, at some little out-of-the-way village in Hampshire, put together his observations of several years in the Natural History of Selbourne; and its spar-rows, grubs, and tortoises. And so we follow with this our Social Zoology, after more elaborate essays on different varieties of the human race. We have disposed of The Vermin in the Gents. Let us hope in the Ballet-girl we may now take up a more agreeable subject—The Butterflies.[1]

Smith informs his reader in the Preface to his "Social Zoology" that he will not repeat the "commonly-circulated notions of this class we are about to write of," that the work will contain no improprieties that might "exclude it from the drawing-room table." The author intends "to touch but lightly upon pink-tights and gauze-petticoats" and instead to "knock over theatrical romance for common-place reality."[2] In the man-ner of the social realists, Smith's account of real ballet-girls promises to focus on their everyday lives, hard work, tastes, and talent. It announces itself as (seriously) against the kind of gossipy brochures that it says men would gladly pay a shilling for and as (light-heartedly) a pseudo-scientific study of a fascinating type.

That there would be a market for little books detailing the private lives of chorus dancers suggests that by 1847 the ballerina—Italian, French, German, or English—whose greatest following was in Paris, had become a significant player even in London society. It suggests too that the ranks from which she emerged were of general interest. Perhaps most significantly, at a time when French writers were praising dancers as otherworldly creatures even as worldly patrons negotiated for their favors, *The Natural History of the Ballet-Girl* sketches a very different picture. Smith observes that the ballet-girl's love of dance gets her into a lifetime of hard work in which she submits to the rigors of training, the abuse of the body in performance, and the poverty of the profession. Because of this, ballet-girls look sick. It shows already when they are very young: "Their night's work only commences when the night is far advanced; and the effects of this artificial existence are usually painfully visible. Their lips are parched and fevered; their cheeks hollow and pale, even in spite of the daub of vermillion hastily applied by the dresser; and their limbs nipped and wasted. To the audience, however, they are smiling elves, who appropriately people the 'Realms of Joy.'"[3]

This is only the beginning of a career in which the dancer is punished not only physically—by painful training, unhealthy working conditions, long hours, and late walks home—but also psychologically. If the ballet-girl looks sick it is not only from the physical exhaustion of her work, but also from the way her work overexercises her emotions. Smith remarks that these women, who face enough obstacles in their daily lives to overwhelm many a hardier type, are also manipulated emotionally by their roles. Their hardest work is often not dancing, but acting: the ballet-girl has "to express the most vivid interest in, and sympathy with, the fortunes, sorrows, or joys of the principal performers. Possibly, no other class of humanity is actuated by so many different sentiments in five minutes. Were the 'heart-strings' which poets write of, really bits of cord to pull the feelings into different positions, as the string makes the puppet kick its legs and arms, then you would see that those belonging to a whole Corps de Ballet are tugged at once."[4] The ballet-girls' minor roles do not permit them the cathartic expression, in speech or in action, of these extreme emotions. They are never allowed to take center stage. And as a result, ballet-girls feel too much: "the shock experienced . . . affects them all as rapidly as the one from the electrifying machine at the Polytechnic

Institution, when the misguided visitors on the bottom row in the theatre are beguiled by the persuasive eloquence of the gentleman who lectures, into forming a chain with their hands."[5]

Smith's sensitive and often amusing portrait of the chorus dancer raises many of the most profound questions surrounding her increasing visibility and popularity in Europe in the nineteenth century. His account, even as it gently mocks certain trends of the 1840s, reflects the popularity and proximity of what might seem to be two unlikely bedfellows—biology and ballet. Why is the ballet-girl everywhere associated with nature—animals, insects, flowers, fairies—and the sick? The romantic ballet, across the nineteenth century, will cast its female *corps de ballet* as both flora and fauna: otherworldly, magical, beautiful creatures, sometimes charitable, sometimes vengeful, sometimes sick, and often dead. Why should the ballet-girl be linked, in the age's imagination, to the subhuman and the superhuman, when ample proof of her humanity, health, and courage are given at every performance? Why should Smith imagine her as a puppet, a passive experimental subject? And why should the discourses of medical and natural science be called upon to diagnose and classify her? In addressing these questions, this book explores how, during the course of the nineteenth century, the discourse of science—even if, as here, somewhat parodied—creeps into the discourse of the poet, the social critic, the art critic, the theater critic, and how literature helps to shape it. It also explores how dancing itself addressed the authoritative discourses of literature and science.

Smith's pathology of the ballet-girl may be less startling if we consider his text in the context of the 1841 ballet *Giselle*, the starting point for this book. In no other ballet is the complex web of connections between woman and spirit, dancing and ill health, and illness and madness, so cleverly woven as in the story of *Giselle*, and in his diagnosis of ballet-girls Smith may have had it very much in mind, for reasons that this book will develop at length. He does assert that, in 1847, his ballet-girl's "pet" model was the Paris Opéra ballet star Carlotta Grisi, the original Giselle, who had danced the role in London in 1842. Although by all accounts a healthy, vibrant, charming dancer, Grisi was called upon, in this role, to dance the peasant girl Giselle's illness—vaguely associated with a weak heart—and her madness—brought on by the shock of heartbreak—as well as the otherworldliness of "hollow cheek" and "wasted limb" after her onstage death.

Smith's typical ballet-girl is ambitious, and hopes for a promotion, even for a bit part that would include a spoken line. Grisi herself, at the beginning of her career a few years earlier, sang as well as danced at the Opéra; but during her performing years the ballet would undergo a revolution in which it would become established as a genre independent of opera, and excluding all speech. Yet as the romantic ballet moved toward wordlessness, the ballet-girl would find herself more and more at the intersection of social, medical, and poetic discourses.

In *Choreography and Narrative: Ballet's Staging of Story and Desire*,[6] Susan Foster traces the emergence of the French *ballet d'action*, the precursor to the romantic ballet typified by *Giselle*, as a genre that developed to tell stories. Deriving from the mixed ancestry of baroque court ballets with their elegantly presented myths, and traditional fair and circus entertainments emphasizing pantomime and acrobatics, the action ballet, Foster argues, was novel in merging the two traditions, abandoning mythic subjects for the representation of "real life." The action ballet successfully brought together the previously disparate genres of ballet and pantomime, using gesture to tell stories while also inventing new choreographic genres, new technical styles, and new body types to execute them.

Choreography and Narrative documents the many ballets choreographed in the period extending from the eighteenth-century versions of the court entertainments to the birth of the romantic ballet in the 1830s, as well as the creation of the modern notion of choreographer, choreography, and ballet company at the Paris Opéra. The stories these ballets told often treated the themes of love and desire, sometimes reflecting social and political contexts, and sometimes the philosophical or medical thinking of their time. But they were conceived as entertainments and received as such, losing the power they had previously had at court, even as their market and audience broadened. Foster shows how the ballet, understood in Louis XIV's time as central to court life, power politics, and personal identity, became, after two revolutions, a public entertainment, a spectator sport rather than a participatory pastime, and a profession with a standardized training.

Foster understands the dancers who entered into this training as bodies submitted to the institution of the Opéra and the demands of the market that now controlled its artistic policies. She sees the development of the romantic ballet not as a "happy ending," not as a liberation through movement or a resistance to cultural repression, but as a continuation of dance performers' submission to silence and its cultural marginality.[7] Yet her book hints at another tradition within this history of submission and discipline. Beginning with Marie Sallé's 1734 choreography for *Pygmalion* and ending with the late nineteenth-century female pioneers of modern dance, some dance artists did practice a kind of resistance to such cultural oppression through the invention of new dance forms, creating a "choreographic agency."[8] My study attempts to investigate the ways in which an emerging agency of female performers was pathologized and the ways in which it responded to that pathologization.

Foster notes that dance history records ballet's popularization and narrativization as a series of losses: an end to the belief in the possibility of gesture possessing inherent meaning, connected to the romantic dream of a universal language; and a shift to the idea that dance simply translates stories that it essentially mimes. Dance history "records with regret the loss of physicality as discourse, the loss of respect for both male and female dancers, and the loss of status for dance." In her revision of this history, Foster points out, however, that "the early eighteenth century offered no utopian space where all bodies spoke freely and eloquently. Its massive hierarchies of status and protocols for behavior legislated every pathway, every gesture that a body could make."[9] Foster proposes instead to view this history as "the supplanting of certain aesthetic forms of subjugation and celebration by others." For Foster, the history of "ballet's 'fall' out of language and its enslavement to narrative" reflects "a series of cultural operations on and through dance."[10]

The ballet and modern dance forms developed in the wake of the action ballet tell the continuing story of the social, political, cultural, and medical mechanisms governing expression and repression: dance and dancers had lost status, yet they continued to fulfill certain expectations of the growing market. This book begins where Foster's leaves off, at *Giselle*; the moment when the ballet—for all that it may have represented desire, passion, folly, and mania before—becomes openly self-reflective, self-conscious about the way it tells stories with bodies. *Giselle* addresses what is at stake in ballet's use of the body without words, and how dancers' silence reinforces dance's ties to medical and cultural conceptions of physical and mental illness.

In this book I argue that, as ballet began to tell stories, it had to fall silent. It represented an idealized form of expression that writers and artists hoped to exploit for its potential to escape the censorship that written performance texts were subject to; daring to tell stories of love and desire, the body's stories, without actually having to "tell." With *Giselle*, ballet began to discover that, precisely because it did not speak, it could comment eloquently, self-reflexively, on the meaning of its own and other cultural silencings.

The nineteenth-century French dance writing studied here imagines dance embodying a literary "idea": bypassing words and moving freely; translating the abstract into the human physique; moving beyond censure or censorship in this ideally free medium. Literature dreams of a dance able to say everything while saying nothing. Dance's silence and dancers' malleability seem to promise writers an outlet for free expression. Moving beyond words, dance is visual form; situated in the female body, it suggests a freedom of expression that transcends sex, identity, or medium. Making thought visible, dance nevertheless creates a complex visual illusion in which it hides nothing and yet never shows—or "says"—everything.

Using the body to "speak" visually, and not speaking, nineteenth-century dance stands as the image of the unsayable—whether sublime or grotesque, ineffable or unpardonable. By not speaking, dance seems to offer to writers the ability to say what words cannot: it is imagined as free expression, bypassing censure or repression. In the three cases studied here, Théophile Gautier deems himself able to say "everything" through recourse to ballet. Stéphane Mallarmé thinks of dance as a coded, summary writing with no writing instruments to slow it down. Louis-Ferdinand Céline views dance as the kind of rhythmic expression that gives writing a visceral life. These three writers make a strange trio: the flamboyant Romantic and man of the theater; the radical erudite poet and English teacher; and the working-class doctor, prosodist of street slang. A connection between their wide-ranging literary projects seems unimaginable, yet all are fascinated by dance. Identifying writing with dancing, these writers ultimately identify themselves writing with the dancer dancing. All three conceive of the literary "idea" as figured by dance and attempt to emulate the way dance works in their writing.

What does it mean for dance to represent an ideal, for writers to think that dancers embody "idea" itself? The German idealist philosophy that influences French romanticism is apparent in Gautier's adaptation of Heine for the Paris Opéra. In *Giselle*, dance performance can be understood to stage not only the German folklore of forest spirits, but also a kind of pedestrian Hegelianism: dancers represent the fantastic spirits of women; dance represents spirit taking shape as matter, moving—as Karl Marx would say of German philosophy—from heaven to earth.[11] In a similarly literary-philosophical tone, Mallarmé describes dance as a form of coded writing that is the express instrument of "Idea," and he raises questions related to its materiality and visibility. For Céline, dancers' embodiment of an ideal hygiene has social and political ramifications.

In the writings of all three, the location of dance in the female body is ultimately problematic. The dance texts read in this book ponder the physical and metaphysical issues posed by dance's simultaneous presentation and representation of this female body: as an art form in which that body is artist, artwork, and instrument, dance raises questions of metaphor, embodiment, abstraction, and agency. These writers' formal interest in dance is tempered by the age's deep-seated ambivalence about the female body's social and cultural specifics. Despite their idealizations of femininity, dance texts frequently assert negative stereotypes of the female sex as deadly, as castrated, as the locus of hysteria. Because it stages the female body, dance touches the mysteries of femininity: the sexual freedom implied by freedom of movement, in public, by women, in an erotically charged context; the poetic sublime epitomized by this femininity but also the excesses of a physicalized language. Images of the female sex become important to this literary idea of dance, but in their stylization they tend to become detached from problematic female bodies. The idealization of dancers in texts is frequently accompanied by their unsexing: dancers are fairies, flowers, poems, poetry itself, always feminine but rarely real women. And yet in many of the nineteenth-century ballets, they must be killed.

Dance performance and dance writing offer interesting arenas for the exploration of gender as performance,[12] but this study will focus on a dancer constructed as feminine and identified as a woman. The dance audience of the mid-nineteenth century is broadly characterized as male, and my generalizations about the reception of dance, especially of the Opéra ballets, have largely relied on texts written by men. Although several chapters show how dance performance problematized gender, none speak about dancers' female audience. The history of the audience in general, and the female audience in particular—the women who watch their husbands courting dancers, the families of dancers, the *courtisanes* in the audience—deserve greater attention.

The three case studies that make up this book trace a male idealization and identification with female performers that illustrate the seduction of the dance, and of the dancer's artistic persona. The writing of dancers considered in this book sketches a particular subjectivity—perhaps uniquely feminine, perhaps more generally performative—in which the audience's admiration and the dancer's own investment in her person produce a positive image of femininity that counters the victimization or degradation of performers in the public eye. Redefining the realm of interpretation of this principally female art form also suggests redrawing the lines of gender definition; my study considers femininity as it is linked to spectacle and performance, but also suggests that some of the dances under consideration redefine gender—or sexual identity in general—as interiority rather than visible conformity to socially constructed roles. In their art dancers legitimize the semiotic code of the body and invest movement with expressive meaning. Making the female body into not simply a work of art, but the self-possessed tool of a working artist, dance performance by women makes the female body not simply a symbol but a symbolizing potential. The dancer expresses not "femininity" in its definition as lack, or manliness *manqué*—in the ancient tradition familiar from Aristotle—but rather, femininity as the ability to represent itself in images, through movement.

The idealization of dance as romantic image is based on the abstraction or erasure of the bodies that make it work, an erasure often accomplished in the male-authored texts.[13] But at the same time, the opposite tendency is at work in dance reception. In nineteenth-century Paris, a network of associations links dance performance to prostitution, to syphilis, and to hysteria, both on the level of practice and on the level of theory. The visibility of performers in the public eye, the history of prostitution at the Opéra, and the viewing practices of ballet *amateurs* all contribute to its sexualization. The sexing of dance theater, the perception of both prostitution and hysteria as expressions of sexual deviance,[14] and the theatricality of such "deviant" expressions of femininity are all part of the fabric of nineteenth-century dance production and reception. Eroticized in the popular and literary imagination, dance seems to offer writers and viewers a freedom of expression that bypasses censure. Yet at the same time, dance's freedom of expression is projected onto it by a repressed society, making dance performance symptomatic of cultural tensions surrounding women, the body, and the body's relation to the mind.

As dance theater began to stage "femininity," featuring the female body, it was open to the projection of cultural stereotypes, and it confronted them. Dance performance by women implicitly addressed questions of sex, gender, anatomy, pornography, the mind's relation to the body—many contemporary social, sexual, medical, and psychological issues concerning the body. While not asking the same kinds of questions that medicine asks—which have to do with the cause, etiology, and treatment of disease—and not answering the questions it does pose in the same way, dance enacts ideas of how the mind controls the body, of how the body produces meaning without words, and of how those meanings can be decoded. The interpretation of body codes becomes the province of new medical sciences throughout the nineteenth century, and their changing interpretations of the body parallel those in dance and the literature fascinated by it. These shifts indicate close cultural connections between performance, medicine, and print, indicating that changes in thinking in these domains might be caused by the same factors: nineteenth-century concern about the body as a site of meaning and about vision as a theater of knowledge.

As a particularly performative form of madness, with disputed origins and multiple effects, the group of afflictions labeled "hysteria" serves as the very visible complement, or mirror image, of nineteenth-century dance. In a culture that views dancers as vaguely "sick"—as Smith does—hysteria's myriad causes and symptoms seem a reasonable diagnosis. The romantic ballet stages hysteria as the centerpiece of its plots of transformation and death of the female lead; the plot of *Giselle*, for example, closely connects dancing, madness, and death. The early modern dance forms that followed, with their liberating movement and costumes, comment directly on the tradition linking freedom of movement in the female body to the lack of control over the body thought to characterize hysterias. The traditional link between dance and madness is reinforced in the terminology of nineteenth-century French medicine, in which various forms of hysteria continue to be called "choreas" because they look like dance; the term "St. Vitus' Dance" to describe movements imitating what had earlier been interpreted as possession also continued to be used by Charcot's circle.

This book explores and attempts to explain literary and cultural interest in women's dance theater in its connection to changing conceptions of mental illness. Dance's proximity to forms of mental illness gives it a cultural relevance in the nineteenth century that has shifted as clinical and theoretical conceptions of mental illness have changed. Considering dance in the context of symptom, rather than reducing dance's expressive potential and the conscious discipline of dance artists, is a way to explain dance's cultural power and to widen the cultural understanding of somatic expression. It is an attempt to explain dance's passionate following, immediate effect, and just as rapid oblivion; to suggest why dance is both so culturally and historically resonant and yet has been until recently left for the most part in silence.

Chorea

The embodiment of idea has medical as well as philosophical and artistic ramifications in the period studied here. In different languages, using different vocabularies, ballet and poetry speak of the relation between mind and body in terms of spirit and spirits, the religious, the philosophical, and the fantastic, whereas medicine speaks in terms of the normal and the pathological. Moving across medicine, literature, and performance, this book attempts to make connections between three different ideas crucial to my history of dance: the literary concept of an "ideal," staged in some dance performance; the medical-scientific concept of the "pathological" defined in contradistinction to a "normal ideal"; and the medical-psychological concept of "idiopathy," of illness created by "idea." Because it performs bodiliness, dance exists in close proximity to the idealism projected onto it, to the concept of the pathological that subtends it in the nineteenth century, and to the concept of idiopathy developed from it.

Medicine's discovery of "idea" manifesting itself in the body in mental illness strikingly parallels the literary fascination for nineteenth-century dance's ability to manifest "idea," suggesting that shifts in medicine and parallel shifts in dance might be paradigmatic shifts motivated by the same factors. The medical notion of idiopathic or idiogenic illness links medicine to nineteenth-century dance forms' unspeakable moves and the literature fascinated with its somatic translations.

In tracing the history of these concepts as they cluster around dance performance, it seems not simply that a certain philosophical-literary idealism of the body gives way, via positivistic medicine, to more cynical psychologies, but that these ways of thinking about the body and the mind respond to, rather than simply replace, one another. A new space for the interpretation of bodily expression was opened by medical theories in the nineteenth century and was inhabited by new forms of theatrical dancing, such as early modern dance; and at the same time dance performance can be understood as participating in that opening up, redefining bodily expression as something other than pathology. Nineteenth-century medicine developed ways to read the body that might be called "semiological," depending as they did on what was called a "semiology" of signs, symptoms, and behaviors. The history of dance asks to be read in this medical semiological space, not only because of its cultural connection to madness, and not only because of medicine's cultural influence, but also because dance, as an art of the body, necessarily speaks about issues that concern medicine in its attempts to unravel the relations between body and mind.

Dance and medicine also resemble one another remarkably in their histories of "discovering," or constructing, new realities for the body, new understandings of what the body does, and especially, how it means. Both depend on the idea that the body means inherently, without language, but that the meanings of its movements, signs, or symptoms can be interpreted as a language. In the face of the long-standing link between dance and madness, this book considers the production and reception of nineteenth-century dance forms in a climate in which medicine becomes a major cultural index by which the body's meanings are measured.

Medical history records a century of explosive developments in medical science, and in particular in the philosophies and practices governing what would become mental medicine. During this period, and in a range of disciplines, medicine attempts to come to grips with how the body deploys "idea" somatically. French nineteenth-century medicine was marked by the development of thinking about how the body expresses itself in and through illness, how that illness can be caused by, or can reflect, the mind, and about how medicine itself should organize and approach the problem of mind-body relations in illness. Perhaps the tightest knot that medicine tried to untie was the knot of illnesses grouped under the heading "hysteria."

The performative nature of hysterias in the theatrical atmosphere of Charcot's clinic—its nineteenth-century capitol—the visual emphasis of the medical science of the period, and Charcot's and Richer's interest in artistic representations of hysteria are well known.[15] Like the dancer, the hysterical patient is almost always gendered female in the medical literature, and despite statistics of male hysteria and medical developments in the understanding of the illness, hysteria remains, in the cultural imagination of the century, a feminine illness, still linked conceptually to the womb from which it gets its name, and still frequently treated as a sexual disorder.[16] Defined and understood in its resemblance to dance, hysteria is very clearly not only in the background, but actively in the foreground of nineteenth-century dance production and reception. To suggest that dance and hysteria are linked beyond their visual resemblance or thematic coincidence is not to view dance from a perspective of antitheatrical prejudice,[17] reductively typing it as madness, or to diminish the sites or kinds of discipline that distinguish it from performative hysterias. Rather, it entails deeper consideration of how visuality works onstage and in the clinic at a particular historical moment; what the audience—dance aficionados or medical practitioners—are looking at, how they look, and what they see.

It also involves reading dance's visuality in relation to its silence. Dancers are not patients who have been silenced or disenfranchised. Yet in choosing not to speak, dance displays a special affinity with hysteria and with the production of symptoms. Though the conditions of the dancer's silence are quite different from the hysteric's—whose words, in the nineteenth century, are ignored or invalidated by medical institutions—it is the dancer's willful witholding of speech that makes her art enigmatic, multivalent, and thus not only apt for the projection of signification onto it, but also rich in signification. In my reading, this silence is one that has the power—in some contexts—of validating the mute expressiveness of the body, allying it to and thus commenting on contemporary symptomatology. Not by championing hysteria as a kind of artistic expression as Surrealism did, but rather by redeeming as art what is "lost" in hysteria, dance expresses nonhysterically what only hysteria had been able to express—what had been labeled "hysteria" when expressed: the somatic translation of idea, the physicalization of meaning.

Medical texts, practices, and practitioners are part of culture, always reflecting popular opinion, stereotypes, and social codes and at times leading them. In *Approaching Hysteria; Disease and Its Interpretation*, Mark S. Micale writes: "In late nineteenth-century Europe, medicalization was proceeding apace and included among its facets the application of descriptive disease imagery to the social and political world. The use of the language of nervous and mental pathology in particular became a common feature of French social, cultural, and political commentary between 1870 and 1914."[18] Micale ascribes the growth of interest in medicine among laity during the Third Republic to the secularization of French thought and society, to rising rates of literacy, popular medical and scientific press, and reading of medical books by lay people as a popular pastime.[19] Both medical texts and dance texts participate in print culture as well as the culture of body codes and images. Historians have teased out the many complex ways in which medicine and culture interact late in the nineteenth century, in what Micale terms a "culture of hysteria"[20] in which authors, medical figures, dancers, patients, and others participated, if not equally, at least across disciplinary boundaries. My study, like many others, shows that print culture, body culture, representations, disciplines, and institutions influence each other multidirectionally.[21] This is not to say, however, that disciplinary differences—for example, between medical texts and literary texts on hysteria—are ever completely erased in such a culture. Although medical texts must be read in their literary historical context, they must also be read in the context of medicine's real interventions with real bodies.[22] Nor is it to suggest that these domains are always consciously in dialogue. Rather, I argue that the permeation of medical thinking promulgated in medical texts and practices can be found not only in literature but in choreography as well, and that choreography can be analyzed not simply as an illustration of modes of popularized medical thinking about the body, but also as commentary on it. I am suggesting not only that medicine is shaped by culture (doctors go to the theater, and read poetry), or that cultural forms speak about cultural practices such as medicine (theater and literature constantly represent illness, madness, and doctoring). I am also suggesting that dance performance interrogates, represents, and comments upon mind-body relations, as does medicine.

In ritual cultures, dance is often closely linked to medicine and religion, to possession and cure; I will argue that even in the cases I am considering here, dance need not be marginalized by the historical authority of medicine, because it is in fact implicated in it. Reading dance in the context of the history of medicine offers an opportunity not simply to assert medicine's tremendous cultural authority, but to reflect on and contextualize that authority. It would be quite a different project, and one that remains for historians of medicine, to research a history of medicine that would investigate medical historical views of dance.

It is crucial, also, to point out that although I am considering the "high art" of medical theory and the cutting edge of medical practice in nineteenth-century France, I am not dealing with a single discipline (medicine) nor a single disease (hysteria), but with a richly woven fabric of practices and representations. I have chosen to focus on the particular disease entity called "hysteria" because it designates a range of afflictions typified by performative gestures or choreiform movements. It would be pointless to argue that medicine holds the key to dance interpretation or that any single medical idea dominated dance reception. Nor is it possible now to speak of hysteria per se, as we know the disease took many forms, featured a range of symptoms, and became, during the course of the nineteenth century, a catch-all diagnosis. Rather, I am looking at a few selective medical theories and practices that seem to me to be crucial for my study of dance texts, and I am interested in *representations* of hysteria, as constructed onstage, in print or in the clinic.

Each of the three case studies in this book presents a differing relation between literature, dance, and medical thinking, and each case examines dance manifesting—representing—different symptoms of the afflictions associated with hysteria: hypnotism, locomotor disturbances, convulsions, aphasia, mental degeneration. Medical history indicates that symptoms of disorders such as tertiary syphilis and epilepsy were often recombined in the various hysterias and in their medical classification. Medical uncertainty about hysteria, the difficulty of its definition, its broad array of symptoms and causes, and its cultural folklore all come into play in the dance representations of hysteria studied here. In that sense, dance reflects medicine's sporadic lack of authority and loss for words in the face of psychogenic disorders, the continuing challenge mental illness has posed for neurology, neuropathology, histology, physiology, and psychiatry: the mystery of the mind's hold on the body.[23]

The history of psychiatry in France, of mental medicine and its connections to experimental medicine, have been mined by historians of science and medicine whose work is referred to throughout this book. This volume cannot offer the detail that a thorough history of the medicine of this period demands or capture the complexity that such histories have illustrated. Instead of tracing the history of psychiatry, or of any single branch of mental medicine, this book attempts to situate dance texts and performances in their various medical contexts, reading them against the medical developments that they most directly addressed, or that most affected their reception. Briefly outlined, the story told by the medical texts considered here would be relatively straightforward. Shifting philosophical currents in French medicine in the first half of the nineteenth century steer it from hygiene toward what will be called clinical or hospital medicine, and experimental or scientific medicine. The statistical science of Alexandre Parent-Duchâtelet, whose work on Paris prostitution and its connection to dance and disease in the 1830s will be discussed in the second chapter, overlaps with the rise of a new wave in French medicine, the decline of system and the rise of the hospital.[24] In France, these changes allow the implementation of the experimental medical science led by Claude Bernard. This medicine, working with scientific theory and experiment, elaborates a concept of the pathological which it attempts to define in contradistinction to a normal "ideal" state. The medicine of experiment, instrument, and clinical observation come together in the work of Jean-Martin Charcot, who, via the study of the physiology of the nervous system and of locomotor functional disorders, ultimately elaborates a concept of idiopathy to explain what pathology could not explain, a pathology of "idea" itself. The final chapter of this book considers how twentieth-century hygiene returned to a medical model of the so-called social pathologies that understands mental illness in ideological rather than idiopathic terms. A parallel mini-history of hysteria to be sketched within this larger medical framework would see folkloric connections between hysteria, the womb, and feminine sexuality preserved in uterine theories of hysteria even as Charcot develops a more sophisticated symptomatology and neurophysiological explanations for hysterical behaviors.

But the medical history that serves as a background to my dance history is not nearly so simple or sequential. Within this story the complex histories of instruments, diagnostic approaches, experimental procedures, pathography, and terminology all blur the narrative I have just sketched. Medical history records no clear narrative of progress, even when diseases are diagnosed and cured. Medicine is, to use Bruno Latour's term, a "hybrid"; a collection of practices, instruments, institutions, and practitioners. Medicine is fluid: never exclusively scientific in its practice even when applying scientific method, neither fully objective nor completely subjective. Many cultural histories of medicine insist on the cultural construction of disease and see medicine as a series of creations or inventions— not discoveries of truths.[25]

The medical history under consideration here tells complex stories of disciplinary chaos. Members of the scientific academies changed sides in crucial debates, disciplines branched and then regrouped, practices previously thought to be useless were recuperated or justified, and techniques previously thought to cure were abandoned. In the 1840s, at the moment when my study opens, French medicine was in a period of intense debate and change that the case of *Giselle* perfectly reflects.

Gautier's ballet represents various kinds of dancing as illness or madness, and represents madness as profoundly dancelike. Chapter 2, "The Madness of *Giselle*," reads the ballet's text and first performance as commentary on contemporary connections between dancing, madness, sex, and syphilis. In a climate in which the dance world intersected with the domain of prostitution, public health concerns in that domain naturally devolve onto dance. Alexandre Parent-Duchâtelet's 1836 *De la prostitution de la ville de Paris*, ascribing the greatest risk of syphilis to casual prostitution, implicitly links dancers to the illness. Openly prostituted by the Opéra administration at the time, dancers were widely associated with the kind of unregulated prostitution outside of brothels that was deemed the greatest single cause of the spread of the disease. Parent-Duchâtelet's statistical evidence relied on a pre-Pasteur logic of contact and contagion, and on the idea of visual appearance as an indicator of risk. This thinking implicated dancers and the casual prostitution that flourished in the dance world, not only because dancers were prostituted but because they appeared to be prostitutes. The very visibility and popularity of ballet prove to cement this connection to prostitution; the chorus of Wilis in the ballet is linked to prostitution both in theory and in practice, and thus to syphilis and its ravages.

But shortly after the publication of Parent-Duchâtelet's study, and his early death, major shifts in medical philosophy and practice were influenced by scientific theory very different from his. In "Medical Philosophy 1836–44,"[26] Lester S. King considers how, during these years, the question of medicine as a science and the related philosophical questions about the nature of science were raised, particularly in France. For King, 1840 marked a pivotal change in medicine, which he calls "the decline of system."[27] Although Parent-Duchâtelet's copious research would not fit King's dismissive definition of "systematists," the scientific and experimental medicine that would develop after his death would set very different goals for observation. As King summarizes it, the hope of medical philosophy was that "with new technical developments, with more and better observation and a more critical attitude, it seemed as if the eye of reason might at last effectively join the corporeal eye in discovering the secrets of disease."[28]

King sees the medicine of 1840 poised for a great leap forward based on the developments in microscopy, anaesthesia, biochemistry, physiology, and microbiology in the preceding forty years—and not only in France. But because medicine was slow to adopt a critical attitude, the scientificization of medicine did not happen smoothly. Throughout the 1840s, disciplinary chaos reigned; debates on all subjects raged; Paris medicine began to change its mind about madness and methodologies.[29]

Giselle's sudden madness and mysterious dancing death illustrate medical and cultural confusion about what might be wrong with her. What Giselle dances looks very much like hysteria; yet *Giselle* manages to say nothing at all about the death of its heroine, staging it as a terrifying *chorea* inflamed by jealousy. Although old traditions were revived, and hysterias like Giselle's continued to be linked to disappointment in love, sexual complaints, and other afflictions hinted at in Gautier's libretto, one outcome of this "methodological chaos" was to connect hysteria's somatic manifestations less to organic cause and more closely to the mind. Giselle's madness is brought on not by physical causes but by psychological ones, although its effects are immediate and deadly. Giselle's inexplicable madness thus condenses into a few minutes of performance an entire history of hysteria: the tradition of the theories that connect it to the womb and to sex; the loss of motor control typical of locomotor ataxia, syphilis's tertiary stage; and psychological theories depending on idiopathy.

The development of a medicine more closely connected to the sciences after 1840 is a crucial element in the development of mental medicine and in the dance history I am tracing here, because of the influence that scientific medicine would have on medical and cultural understandings of madness. The figure in France whose thinking is most important for my study is Claude Bernard. His 1865 *An Introduction to the Study of Experimental Method* speaks very directly of the place of "idea" in experimental science, and brings discussion of the "ideal" out of the philosophical sphere into the arena of medicine: "Ideas, given form by facts, embody science. . . . Reasoning merely gives a form to our ideas, so that everything, first and last, leads back to an idea. The idea is what establishes, as we shall see, the starting point or *primum movens* of all scientific reasoning, and it is also the goal in the mind's aspiration toward the unknown."[30] For Bernard, "The object of the experimental method is to transform this *a priori* conception, based on an intuition or a vague feeling about the nature of things, into an *a posteriori* interpretation founded on the experimental study of phenomena."[31]

Bernard's terminology, and his thinking about "idea," sound less surprising when we consider that, undoubtedly under the influence of Victor Hugo's *Hernani*—also a crucial part of the French culture explored in Chapter 2—Bernard himself arrived in Paris in 1832 "with almost no paraphernalia except a tragedy which had never been acted and a farce-comedy which had had some success at a small theatre in Lyons."[32] Bernard himself, in *An Introduction to the Study of Experimental Method*, states that he makes "no claim to philosophy."[33] He can perhaps be seen as moving from a youthful passion for theater influenced by romantic ideals to an attempt to understand science as the embodiment of the ideal and to use it in medicine to understand the body. The ideal is crucial to the definition of both pathology and experimental medicine in Bernard's work. For the branch of biology concerned with pathology and disease, Georges Canguilhem points out, the ideal is the normal state ("the notion of this ideal which is the normal");[34] perfect health is a normative concept, an ideal type, the normal state is both the habitual state of the organs and their ideal, and the goal of therapeutics is to return the body to a "habitual ideal."[35]

Bernard's work is important for my study not only because of the language of its tenets, but also because his thinking was crucial in debates about how the pathological (and thus illness in general) was to be defined. As summarized by Canguilhem, Bernard's question was: "Is the concept of disease a concept of an objective reality accessible to quantitative scientific knowledge?"[36] And his response was to conceive of "the pathological phenomenon as a quantitative variation of the normal phenomenon."[37] In other words, Bernard argued that the difference between physiology and pathology was merely a difference in intensity, and not in nature. Significantly, arguments that the pathological was different from the normal only in intensity, and that it was not a different state, could be shown not to hold for infectious or nervous diseases, both of which, as I will show, are implicated in *Giselle*. Yet such an argument, that understands the pathological as homogeneity and continuity,[38] would be consonant with a certain pathologizing of performance. Such a view could, in theoretical terms, allow doctors and spectators to see the dancer's work as close to pathology, understanding her particular "sickness" as a more intense emotional state. Bernard's view of the pathological as differing in degree but not in kind from the "normal" is consistent with an understanding of dance as exaggerated emotion, in which dancers are jerked around like puppets.

But what connection does this particular medical history have with the history of dance and the dance texts considered here? What was the effect of this medical theory on practice and on dance reception? It is, after all, not medical logic that is uppermost in the minds of dance spectators, librettists, choreographers, and performers. It is not medical theory or medical writing that dance performance responds to, but a generalized medical culture. Such a culture, of popular images merged with medical ideas, existed in the "culture of hysteria" in nineteenth-century France, and it linked dance performance to the various afflictions associated with hysteria.[39]

The reasons for this close nineteenth-century connection between dance and hysteria are overdetermined: their long association in the popular imagination and the tradition linking dance to possession that is reflected in the medical terminology of *choreas*; the visual resemblance that is the source of this terminology; the motor and speech disturbances typical of many hysterias that can be understood partly to resemble dance. Hysterias have been understood to imitate dance, and dance has represented madness. But until recently, the mimetic circle of visual resemblance between them has been closed without considering the deeper connections between these two performative modes of expression.[40] Beyond the visual resemblance that partly explains their historical coincidence, this book stipulates a deeper connection: in its withholding of speech and its use of movement, dance functions as a form of symptomatic expression. The body's staging, in dance performance, of what writers called "idea" can be seen to connect it on the physical level, as well as the sociocultural level, to theories of mental illness that will come to elaborate the role of the mind in its etiology. Working like a symptom, translating idea into the body, and even sometimes looking like hysterical symptom, dance can also function as a commentary on symptomatology. Since epileptic movements, paralyses, and aphasias typify many hysterias that imitate the symptoms of these disorders, it can be understood why dance movement, with its controlled or convulsive movements and lack of speech, can be seen as the representation of such disorders, or even as their reenactment. Although they sustained high rates of illness and injury, in particular in the unhealthy conditions of nineteenth-century theaters, it can be argued that dancers were not de facto sick. But dance repeats in some important respects the mechanism of illness, externalizing inner states, translating ideas into the body as do psychosomatic disorders.

In the nineteenth century, the close connection between dance and various forms of madness, or their mastery, works principally through imagery: the visual resemblance between some forms of dance and some forms of hysteria; and the definition of both dance and hysteria as visible,

visual, phenomena. The contradictions between a visual science of diagnosis and a less visual but still visualizing neurophysiology are at the heart
of Charcot's Salpêtrière practice. Charcot's Salpêtrière work brought together often contradictory approaches, defining very differently the value
of observation and visualization. Charcot is famous in the history of
medicine for having established both an iconography and a symptomatology for hysterias: the famous photographs of the *Iconographie* and the cat-
aloguing of the classes and stages of hysterical attacks, the "tableau sémi-
ologique méthodique."[41] Yet Charcot's medicine ultimately resulted in a
reconception of the relation between mind and body as it malfunctions in
mental illness that facilitated the detachment of madness from visually
oriented diagnosis and etiology.

The third chapter explores one early modern dancer's response to the
tradition of visual resemblance of dance to choreiform hysterias, as staged
in *Giselle*. Mallarmé's dance texts on Loie Fuller record a shift away from
the spectacular and toward the specular as Fuller's dance offers its spectators not simply sight, but insight. Mallarmé describes Fuller's performing
persona as facilitated by the "absolute gaze" created by electric light, a
gaze that can be identified with what Foucault refers to as the "absolute
gaze" of the nineteenth-century physician newly armed with instruments. Mallarmé's texts on Fuller describe her as a hypnotized and electrified subject; she deploys electric lighting of her own design, and perceives herself as self-hypnotic, in order to create a multiple, multivalent
performance identity—in direct contrast to the clinician's manipulation
of patients via electricity and hypnosis in an attempt to collapse multiple
identity. Her use of the clinical apparatus used to diagnose and treat hysteria functions as a critique of Charcotian psychology, and reveals to what
extent technological agency imposes a hierarchy of well and ill. But her
performance practice also paves the way for the abandonment of these
technologies in psychoanalytic treatment.

Histories of hysteria have charted a trend in nineteenth-century medicine's move—through its well-documented professionalization and instrumentation—from materialist or physicalist explanations of hysteria as
a purely somatic illness to mentalist or psychological explanations that
have reigned throughout the twentieth century.[42] The notion of idiogenic
or idiopathic illness did not originate with Charcot, nor was he the first
to suggest that somatic illness could have psychological causes. Earlier
physicians who had attempted to define hysteria had come to similar

conclusions, even if they had not expressed them in the same terms. In *Approaching Hysteria: Disease and Its Interpretation*, Mark Micale traces at length the gradual shift to mentalist or psychological explanations of hysteria from the seventeenth to the twentieth centuries. Micale considers Edward Jorden's 1603 *A Briefe Discourse of a Disease Called the Suffocation of the Mother* to propound what was in some ways the first idiogenic theory of hysteria. It is generally agreed that the first neurological and neuropsychological types of explanations for disturbances like hysteria were advanced by Willis in 1670 and Sydenham in the 1680s and 1690s. Perhaps the clearest formulation of idiopathic illness prior to Charcot was Russel Reynolds's description in the *British Medical Journal* in 1869 of "paralysis dependent on idea."[43]

Foucault, however, argues that the early psychological explanations of mental illness were not in fact psychological. In *Madness and Civilization* he notes that, in the classical period—across the seventeenth, eighteenth, and nineteenth centuries—what might be thought of as early "psychological cures" were not considered such because there was no distinction between physical and psychological treatments; physical therapeutics were not distinct from psychological medication.[44] For Foucault, psychology, like psychiatry, is born in a nineteenth-century rupture with preceding medical forms of knowledge. The nineteenth century, he theorizes, "pathologized" madness, radically changing its conception from that of the classical period.

Madness and Civilization charts the reconception, with the development of both psychology and pathology around the turn of the nineteenth century, of what the classical age had identified as madness's two primary manifestations: "passion" and "unreason." With Pinel and the development of the mental hospital, Foucault finds "the reduction of the classical experience of unreason to a strictly moral perception of madness, which would serve as a nucleus for all the concepts that the nineteenth century would subsequently vindicate as scientific, positive, and experimental."[45] In the hospital, "madness will never again be able to speak the language of unreason, with all that in it transcends the natural phenomena of disease. It will be entirely enclosed in a pathology."[46] At the same time, a "purely psychological medicine was made possible only when madness was alienated in guilt."[47]

When, in the years that followed, this great experience of unreason, whose unity is characteristic of the classical period, was dissociated, when madness, entirely confined within a moral intuition, was nothing more than disease, then the distinction we have just established assumed another meaning; what had belonged to disease pertained to the organic, and what had belonged to unreason, to the transcendence of its discourse, was relegated to the psychological. And it is precisely here that psychology was born.[48]

It is my hypothesis that the constellation of epistemological changes that Foucault identifies in nineteenth-century understandings of madness affected the dance history in question here. This book argues that what Foucault calls the "pathologization" of madness with the development of the psychiatric hospital and the profession of psychiatry across the nineteenth century parallels a "pathologization" of dance performance based on the long-standing cultural, performative, and visual connections between dance and certain forms of madness. Charcot's Salpêtrière solidified the connection with its public, performative lectures and demonstrations. The translation of what the classical age had viewed as "passion" into organic pathologies is matched in the pathologization, in Charcot's clinic especially, of the so-called choreiform hysterias.

I will also argue that the establishment of psychological theories of mental illness, taking root slowly across the century, created a changed cultural context for the understanding of mental illness that eventually allowed dance performance to become detached from its implicit and explicit connections to it. The assignation of madness to the realm of guilt rather than the realm of error (to which it had been assigned, according to Foucault, in the classical age), created a context for mental illness, the psychiatric hospital, in which, although the performance of passion continues to be of interest, other factors predominate in diagnosis and treatment. The growing current of mentalist explanations, and a more developed neurological science that relied less on the observation of behavior and more on the observation of internal function via instrumentation, created an environment in which dance performance's visual resemblance to some hysterias was less significant. Thus, although performance continued to be identified with hysteria in Charcot's clinic, Charcot's *science* set up conditions within which dance can be, and historically would be, dissociated from mental illness.

The rise of the medical profession, the authority of medical discourse, and the power of its prescriptions are due to medicine's acceptance in a cultural context; but it would be impossible to deny that much of medicine's power in the nineteenth and twentieth centuries in the West dates from its marriage with experimental and laboratory science. While cultural differences are a factor, the accounts of nineteenth-century medicine both in Europe and in the United States have generally described medical practitioners adopting scientific data, instruments, or practices in an increasing trend toward professionalization and erasure of the patient. It is often claimed that late nineteenth-century physicians in particular gained efficacy by allying themselves with laboratory science. Revisionist historians have argued that the medical profession gained as much from the culture of science as from its technology; that science influenced the rhetoric and not the content of medicine, or that science functioned as a cultural tool to use in the medical marketplace and not at the bedside. Within this debate, of course, both the term "science" and the term "medicine" can be placed within quotation marks.[49] Medical historians would point out that the development of a broad-based concept of hysteria as idiopathic illness is thus neither a story confined to the nineteenth century nor a story that moves unidirectionally, from medicine to culture. In hypothesizing that the branch of medicine that established hysteria as idiopathic may have been influenced by dance performance as well as influencing it, I assume that some shared cultural contexts made these changes in medicine and in dance possible. It is in these shared cultural spaces, the overlapping arenas of print, performance, and medical practice, and the movement of "actors" among them, that I situate my study.

The clinic of Charcot is remarkable for bringing together medicine informed by science with popular images of hysteria. Charcot's lectures at the Salpêtrière, sometimes attended by writers and artists outside the profession of medicine, have remained more famous than the variety of approaches and treatments developed by him and by his associates. Roselyne Rey has argued that Charcot's success derived from his ability to work in three major medical fields, combining the reigning pathological anatomy with rigorous clinical observation and the experimental medicine of instrument and laboratory.[50]

Alain Lellouch has claimed that Charcot developed "a new scientific theory in medicine." Trained in the tradition of the "hospital medicine" that reigned for a half-century without contest in France, Charcot, Lellouch argues, radically and profoundly revised the medicine that relied on the scalpel. Charcot defined this medicine as incapable of connecting internal lesions with their outward manifestations: "This first pathological anatomy, that I will freely call empirical . . . limits itself intentionally and systematically to verifying and describing lesions, without attempting to seize the mechanism of their production, nor the connections that link them to external symptoms."[51] For Charcot, pathological anatomy does nothing more than identify organic illnesses, and says nothing about their essence, cause, or etiology.

In Lellouch's account, Charcot was a leader in bringing a new kind of medicine to French practice. Between 1835 and 1840 the rhythm of discoveries of the Ecole de Paris slowed down, and between 1840 and 1850, a methodological chaos reigned. Some doctors went back to Hippocratic ideas and the doctrine of "crises" held by Laennec;[52] others, called *localisateurs*, rejected the whole of Hippocratic-Galenic thinking, wanting to explain everything by lesions (*lésions d'organes*). With the exception of François Magendie and his pupil Claude Bernard in France, it was German researchers who developed the laboratory medicine whose authority has remained unchallenged until the present day. As of 1866, Lellouch argues, Charcot recognized the advances of German medical institutions and methods over those of the French.[53]

It has been argued that Charcot's importance rests not in an importation of German medicine, but in the fact that he was able to incorporate new methodologies into his practice without abandoning older ones. Beginning in the 1830s, Lellouch notes, important developments modified the anatomical-clinical method. These included instrumentation, which improved the "traditional physical semiology (founded on percussion and auscultation)" by allowing the physician to observe internal cavities in the living patient.[54] This is the extension of the physician's local gaze that Foucault identifies, in *Birth of the Clinic*, as contributing to the elaboration of a medical "regard absolu" (to be discussed in Chapter 3). Lellouch explains further that Charcot merged various methodologies in his work without ever commenting on how he did so; he often used the old medical language to explain a new medical idea. For example, despite Charcot's visual gift for diagnosis, and his description of himself as a photographer, the use of vision and visual imagery in his clinic is far more complex than he himself suggested.

Although Charcot remained for Freud a *visuel*, a seer, his medical career followed, like Freud's, a trajectory from a medicine based on visual observation and instrumentation to a medicine concerned with the less easily visible: internal organic, and eventually invisible psychological, causes. It is important to note that this is not a distinction between a visual physiology and a nonvisual psychology, between visual "hard science" and nonvisual "soft science." From the public health that depends upon statistical data and appearance, to the pathological anatomy of clinical observation and instrumentation, to the psychoanalysis that concerns itself with psychic rather than physiological cause, the medicine considered in this book constantly refocuses its gaze from surface to depth whether it be conceived as anatomy, physiology, or psyche. Charcot's medical science made a connection between surface and depth, or body and mind, of which pathological anatomy had been incapable: understanding that symptom could be not only the outward expression of an inner lesion but also the physical manifestation of an idea. Recognizing hysterical symptom as both real illness and idiogenic, Charcot showed that hysterical symptoms are created by the imagination, but are not imaginary.

Charcot locates "idea" as the source, for example, of hysterical paralyses: "The idea of the movement is already the movement en route to its execution; idea of the absence of movement is already, if it is strong, a realized motor paralysis; all that conforms perfectly with the ideas of the new psychology. Motor paralysis can thus be called ideal, psychic, imaginative (but not imagined)."[55] Thus the symptom does not simply *externalize* an internal condition, but it manifests, for the eye, a mental state. This idiopathic explanation for mental illness is the approach that Freud will take up in his elaboration of the hysterical symptom as a somatic conversion of a repressed idea, experience, or memory, following his year of study with Charcot in 1885–86.

Carlo Ginzburg has connected Freud's symptomatology to the art historian's focus on visual details and the detective's use of clues, both processes of using what can be seen to find out what cannot. Like a detective, the doctor pieces together a picture of the patient from clues—signs and symptoms.[56] The metaphors of surface and depth that figure in Freud's model of the psyche can also be traced to his research work in the Brucke Institute in Vienna in the 1880s; in his biography of Freud, Ernest Jones argues that Freud's interest in connecting what seemed apparently disparate and unrelated bits of information dispersed by the patient in analysis, finding a hidden thread, dates not from Charcot's influence but from his earlier work in histology. According to Jones, Freud's ability to connect the hysterical story to the body came from his training in experimental thinking, in particular in physiology. More than an attempt to legitimize the scientificity of psychoanalysis, Jones's sketch suggests a profound connection forged in Freud's psychoanalytic method between the kind of laboratory science that broadened visual diagnoses of mental illness and the narrative focus of psychoanalysis. Jones's summation of Freud's method hinges on his early training in research—he had published recognized research work—and suggests that Freud's interest in patients' free association developed as an outgrowth of the scientific method he had previously practiced:

Freud was deeply imbued with the principles of causality and determinism, so pronounced in the Helmholtz school that had dominated his early scientific discipline. Instead of dismissing the wandering associations as accidental, unconnected, and meaningless, as others might have done, he felt intuitively that there must be some definite agency, even if not evident, guiding and determining the course of those thoughts. He would be confirmed in this by noting that every now and then a thought or memory would emerge that would reveal the meaning of the preceding train.[57]

According to Jones, patient narratives, unwinding in free association, were not revealed progressively to Freud, but were illuminated all at once by a particular remark, in the way that data would reveal a pattern or "agency" after experimentation and collection. The point here is not only the nature of scientific or narrative "truth"; it also concerns interpretation. Data get interpreted just as patients' stories do, as they unfold; Freud applied his training to the interpretation of patient narratives just as he had applied it to data collected in the laboratory.

My account of nineteenth-century shifts in thinking about the body and mental illness is not simply encapsulated in Freud's career; it is also shaped by his example. Like that of Charcot, Freud's career condenses into one life's work a half-century of changes in medical science and its conceptions of mental illness; and like that of Charcot, Freud's work merged laboratory science with mental medicine. Although in Charcot's clinic hysteria reached its theatrical peak, Freud's symptomatology of hysteria is crucial to my history of dance because it takes into account hysteria's narrative qualities. For Freud, unlike Charcot, the patient has a story to tell:[58] psychoanalysis enables the patient to tell it in words. Freud's symptomatology ascribes *narrative* potential to the hysterical symptom, and Freud finds in it not simply a forgotten past, a repressed memory, a trauma, but also—to use Josef Breuer's term—the "cathartic" potential of its retelling. The particular cultural history of dance I am writing here requires psychoanalysis's understanding of the confluence of the body and language in hysteria to unravel. As a psychoanalytically oriented history of dance, it necessarily depends upon a Freud-focused history of hysteria.

For Foucault, the radical break in Freud's work was not due to his early research in histology, aphasia, or neuromotor paralyses, but rather in his reintroduction of discourse into the domain of illness and cure with psychoanalysis. He sees in Freud's work not the development of nineteenth-century psychologies, but rather a return to the classical notion of madness as unreason:

> This is why we must do justice to Freud. . . . Freud went back to madness at the level of its *language*, reconstituted one of the essential elements of an experience reduced to silence by positivism; he did not make a major addition to the list of psychological treatments for madness; he restored, in medical thought, the possibility of a dialogue with unreason.[59]

Whether or not we accept Foucault's argument for an epistemological break marking the "great discontinuities in the *episteme* of Western culture"[60] at the turn of the nineteenth century or find such a break in Freud's development of psychoanalytic practice at the turn of the twentieth, Freud's return to—or development of—the discourse of madness will be significant to my argument here. But to arrive at Freudian psychoanalysis and its consequences for literary theory and performance studies, it is crucial to consider the history of its foundations in medical and clinical culture. The history of the shift to (now broadly accepted) mentalist explanations for some forms of mental illness is a long one, and its "liberation" of dance performance is not clearly demarcated. It is the aim of this work to tease out these complex connections between performance, pathology, and psychoanalysis, rather than to describe an epistemological break or to date a cultural change.

In *The Order of Things*, Foucault describes his project as "a history which is not that of its [an episteme's] growing perfection, but rather that of its conditions of possibility."[61] Foucault defines his archeology as a comparative study that "produces results that are often strikingly different from those to be found in single-discipline studies. . . . Frontiers are redrawn and things usually far apart are brought closer, and vice-versa."[62] In order to isolate what I am calling the pathologization of dance, and to bring it into proximity with what Foucault calls the pathologization of madness, as well as to trace its potential depathologization, it has been necessary not only to redraw and move across disciplinary boundaries but also to focus on a few exemplary cases that do not present a narrative of medical or social progress.

Despite the growing importance of physiological and eventually psychological explanations of mental illness, nineteenth-century connections between dance, sex, syphilis, and madness did not die out. The connections made by nineteenth-century public health reemerge in the twentieth-century case considered in the fourth chapter. Louis-Ferdinand Céline equates the body of the French classical dancer with the French social body, degenerating into dance forms representing the social pathologies. The concepts of degeneration evident in Céline's never-performed ballets suggest that medical thinking can be connected to particular dance forms as much as to the age. With Céline ballet once again becomes an arena for the expression of cultural idealism and social ills. Despite the general trend toward conceptions of dance as central to women's health in the twentieth century—a view that Céline himself propounded—thinking about dance forms as manifestations of sickness continued. The case of Céline disrupts the chronology traced in the first two chapters: despite the broader acceptance of idiogenic explanations for mental illness after Freud, the trend to pathologize dance continues in a particularly persistent form of medical thinking. Such thinking casts the pathological as difference not in degree but in kind, while promulgating medical science's mission to identify a "normal ideal." This is the medicine that would use a medical-scientific model for theories of race and degeneration, twentieth-century hygiene that would be part of Céline's early formation as Dr. Louis-Ferdinand Destouches.

Despite significant developments in twentieth-century dance and medicine, Céline's dance writing illustrates not only that medical and cultural thinking are, like dance, the products of their time, but that dance forms can absorb, and embody, particular medical modes of thinking across time. Several early twentieth-century dancers whose work could be seen to fit the mold of nineteenth-century dance pathologies, such as Isadora Duncan and Vaslav Nijinsky, have been left out of this study. The case of Nijinsky, who made dances utilizing movements of possession and convulsion familiar from the history of hysteria, and who declined into mental illness after a brilliant performance career, is well known. Before his institutionalization, Nijinsky's choreography for the Ballets Russes de Monte Carlo of the Mallarmé/Débussy "L'Après-midi d'un faune" in 1912 and Stravinsky's "Le Sacre du Printemps" in 1913 explicitly staged dance as akin to madness. Both ballets make reference to cultural traditions of madness by using turned-in feet and disjointed movements: in the first, through the Faune's intoxicating dream of desire and narcissism, against a backdrop of erotic mythology; in the second, through representations of frenzied possession, mass hysteria, and ritual sacrifice.

Nijinky's choreography for the Ballets Russes shows modern dance's influence, across the nineteenth century and especially in the twentieth, in recuperating behaviors, gestures, and bodily codes that hysteria cast as illness. Some of these forms of dance successfully valorize that body language (in the male performer's body as well as the female) not as illness but as the artistic expression of, or commentary on, contemporary constructions of madness. In these remarkable forms, dance sets itself up as an interpretive science of the body in response to medicine, both valorizing and critiquing medicine as another such interpretive science. Yet in spite of its recuperation of movements from hysterical iconography, modern dance has until recently participated in a twentieth-century cult of health, whose most visible early pioneer was dancer, choreographer, teacher, and activist Isadora Duncan. Isadora's dancing might—like Nijinsky's—have looked something like madness but was conceived as liberating the spirit of modern woman with the ancient spirit of the dance. In a similar way, Martha Graham's psychological portraits of Greek mythological heroines may be agonizingly convulsed, but her work was part of a feminist educational impetus in the United States in which dance became associated with health. In *Where She Danced*, Elizabeth Kendall details the liberating philosophy of modern dance as it was established in women's colleges in the United States in this century: its connection to dress reform, women's liberation, and women's education.[63] In "Torque: The New Kinaesthetic of the Twentieth Century," Hillel Swartz has described the link between some forms of dance and what the nineteenth century called the "movement cure."[64] With the fuller acceptance and broader development of mentalist explanations for hysteria, after Freud dance no longer signified either as madness or cure on the level it did in the nineteenth century. Although dance therapies and reeducation techniques such as the Alexander technique or the Feldenkrais method have given ample proof that dance and movement can function as cure, psychoanalysis makes the idea of dance as cure ineffectual. It is psychotherapy, and not physical therapy, which has held center stage in the twentieth century.

Twentieth-century dance history records dance becoming a tool of physical therapy, of women's education, of the liberated body, and of the expression of repression itself. But it also records dance theories that suggest the opposite: for example, in Futurist conceptions of dance, the body as a machine, the dynamic and violent force of the dancer, the woman as instrument, the body enslaved to technology. While some dance traditions continue to represent dancing as vertiginous passion, seduction, or posses-

Fig. 1. Second phase of the hysterical attack: the "grands mouvements" and "contorsions." From Paul Richer, *Etudes cliniques sur la grande hystérie ou hystéro-épilepsie* (1881). Collection of the Lane Medical Library, Stanford University.

sion, in particular social dances such as the waltz, the tarantella, and the tango, the affinities between madness and performance—particularly women's performance—are often commented on in contemporary feminist performances.[65] The shift toward mentalist explanations of hysteria lifts the burden of visual resemblance to forms of madness from dance, and allows twentieth-century choreographers such as Martha Graham to represent madness as tragedy; it allows Merce Cunningham to experiment with arbitrary, unconventional, or self-absorbed movements that sometimes look like psychological experiments. Medicine's move away from purely physical explanations for madness, connecting somatic manifestations to mental ideas, allows dance to be read as commenting on the conception of hysteria as theatrical, rather than simply enacting it. It allows dance to separate from what it represents and to challenge cultural notions about what the body means, and how.

If the rise of women's dance theater coincided with a nineteenth-century rise in the hysteria diagnosis—or at least increased medical attention to it—the decline of such diagnosis and of the existence of the disease entity "hysteria" in the twentieth century have coincided with dance's relative liberation from its earlier association with social and mental pathologies. The four historical explanations that Mark Micale gives for the decline of the hysteria diagnosis no doubt contributed to dance's liberation: "de-Victorianization," "psychological literacy," "paradigm shift in diagnostics," and hysteria, by 1900, having "exhausted its metaphorical potential."[66] Changes in social mores, in thinking about the body and about madness, and changes in medicine and medical representations, certainly contributed to the detachment of dance from illness. But the case of Céline indicates that the history of this medical and cultural shift does not end in 1900, that technical or scientific advances in medicine are not immediately absorbed into medical thinking or medical culture, and that certain kinds of nineteenth-century medical thinking, as well as hygiene-oriented social pathologies, have continued throughout this century.

It is also possible that, just as the shift in medicine permitted a revalorization of the body's role in art, a changing economic theory revalorized the kind of physical labor that dance may not have resembled, but certainly constituted. Although I do not make it here, there is no doubt an argument to be made about the influence of Adam Smith's and Karl Marx's economic writings on the cultural reception of physical labor, and Marx's redefinition of it as "physiological expenditure."[67] The popularization of such economic theory could be understood as facilitating the disconnection of dance from what Foucault calls *désoeuvrement*, the absence of work that, for Foucault, ultimately defines madness in the nineteenth century. As performance, as physical labor, and most significantly as art, dance can never be "désoeuvrement": "*where there is a work of art, there is no madness.*"[68]

But both the beginning and the end of this century offer counterexamples that suggest that dance, in some crucial ways, has never been depathologized. In 1900, Freud's description of a "symptomatic act"—his name for Dora's gesture as her fingers crawl in and out of her reticule during analysis[69]—ironically pathologizes gesture as overloaded with meaning, in particular sexual meaning, even as psychoanalysis frees up the realm of dance performance by shifting pathology into the realm of talk. As 2000 draws near, the continued association of illness with the performing arts in the culture of AIDS reproduces social stereotypes that pathologize performers. Such examples suggest that even if the medical history and the performance history of this century are characterized by moments of epistemic rupture, old ways of thinking about the body and its performances endure.

Chora

One of the oldest ways of thinking about the female body uses its reproductive capacity as a figure for the production of meaning itself. In Aristotle's famous example, when a woman has milk, it is a sign that she has given birth. Thus the body produces somatic signs that record its experiences; but woman's body in particular, producing life, signifies signification. To give birth is to have milk, to have milk is to have a sign; thus birthing is signifying.

Although dance performers are traditionally dissociated from motherhood, the signifying potential of the female body in maternity is always implicit in the dance writing studied here. And at the same time so are the uterine theories of hysteria, in more or less sophisticated formulations. Even as nineteenth-century medicine moved away from uterine explanations for hysteria—and the cultural folklore of what was called "suffocation of the mother"—the association of women with hysteria continued to influence hospital treatment and medical thinking well into the twentieth century, as Elaine Showalter has shown.[70] In such a culture, performing women, whether onstage or in the clinic, would inevitably be seen as speaking about the female body—the female sex—and its significations.

Another tradition interprets the female sex as a symbol of castration. This tradition associates the female genitalia with "nothing," as Hamlet does in the bawdy exchange with Ophelia before "The Mousetrap." The legacy of Ophelia is directly confronted by the dance performance considered here. It might be argued that women's performance since Ophelia has often resembled her mad scene: often taking on extra-verbal elements to say what cannot otherwise be said. One of Hamlet's remarks to Ophelia predicts the male-dominated critical reception of women's performance in the last four hundred years: "Be not you asham'd to show, he'll not shame to tell you what it means."[71] Ophelia speaks and sings, but her meanings are coded, symbolic; her scene is more "show" than "tell" and thus not so distant from the dance this book will discuss.

Ophelia's mad scene is in many ways a precursor to modern dance performance; the play-within-the-play she choreographs sets up an alternate theater to the "antic disposition" Hamlet puts on—both responses to the death of fathers. Ophelia's scene, like the play itself, has generated many interpretations, but there has been no debate, as there has been in Hamlet's case, about whether her madness is real or contrived. By positing a theatrical, improvised madness in Hamlet and "real" madness in Ophelia, the play reflects the tradition linking female performance—especially that in which words are not the main matter—to forms of hysteria.

As the banter before the play continues, Hamlet makes the further remark that the female sex, as expressed in Elizabethan slang, is "nothing." In this famous exchange, Hamlet mouths a series of popular ideas, ranging from the simply misogynist to the more complexly psychological: that women don't think, that they have no sex; that maids' minds are as empty as the space between their legs. The dance performances I will look at here—through texts—respond directly to these ideas: revalorizing the "empty" space, making it the site of theater. In dance forms developed in the nineteenth century the female sex gets linked to dance's silence or not saying; audiences at the ballet, for example, focus on dancers' legs and skirts. But dance also represents this saying-while-not-saying or this saying-through-not-saying. It is not simply the expressiveness of the body, or silence, or gesture, but the expressiveness of censure itself.

Thus the female body that the dance presents and represents has traditionally figured both expression and repression, creation and nothingness. Though it looks as if what dance offers is spectacle, the visualization of writers' ideas, it is not so much about showing (since it does not show unequivocally, completely, or unproblematically) as about showing-instead-of-telling. The attraction of the dance is just that: it will never "tell" what it means, nor even exactly how. And what it shows is very much part of—even an illustration of—that not-telling while telling.

What is it that the dance manages to say, via the female body, without words? On one level, the unsayable that dance stages seems at times to be "femaleness" itself: the radical difference of the female body from the male that is read in the Freudian tradition as an image of castration. Yet in many male-authored accounts, the female body, lacking the signifier that the male sex constitutes on the male body, functions as a cipher with a freer range of expression onstage. This female body possesses the power of self-transformation crucial in the expressive use of the body. For some authors, it is this very "lack" of signifier, of male genitalia, and the "invisibility" of female genitalia, which appears to make the female body a richer site of expression in dance.

On another level, the dancing female body represents madness and its mechanisms; what is socially unacceptable, individually unutterable, censored or censured. Dance represents that fullness of expression—possession, trance, embodiment—that writing can only mime. All three writers studied here are interested in dance as an art that recreates *possession*: for Gautier the frenzy of passion, for Mallarmé the arcane, for Céline mass hysteria. Dance can represent, or even realize, a literary fantasy of expression without words, the dream of expression without repression. Yet in dance these writers also find the recognition and dramatization of repression's role in symbolic expression. The literary interest in dance explored here is attuned to dance's practice of censure, the discipline that allows the body to speak. Dance offers a body that seems to move freely and yet speaks of repression more powerfully than words can by dramatizing its very functioning.

Both of these traditions, the view of the female body as figuring signification either as reproduction or as castration, come together in the concept of *chora*. From linguistics, poetics, and feminist psychoanalytic literary theory, Julia Kristeva has developed a literary theory that defines a presymbolic, semiotic element in literary texts that she calls "chora."[72] Developing a literary-linguistic approach from the psychoanalytic terms of Melanie Klein, Kristeva identifies a "semiotic" element in literature, a current within poetic language like Mallarmé's, which floods the texts of writers like Céline. In response to the Freudian tradition in which the female body is understood as castrated, Klein focuses on the rich relations between the infant and the mother in the pre-Oedipal phase. Like dance performance, the theory of chora elaborates a female body that is a site not of castration but of multivalent signification. Kristeva takes the term "chora" from Plato to name the maternal space of this pre-Oedipal phase characterized by the drives (*pulsions*) and organized around the infant's relation to the mother. Chora, for Kristeva, describes the rhythmic and poetic "drives" in language associated with the body of the infant before it acquires symbolic language, drives that are then present as a layer or current of signification within some literary texts.

French nineteenth-century medicine depended upon what it called a *sémiologie*, suggesting to what extent medicine is one of the traditions of body interpretation, reading and decoding the body's signs and symptoms. By connecting the semiotic level of symbolic expression to a maternal space and a pre-Oedipal phase, Kristeva nuances the role of the female body in these traditions. Chora is also a pathological poetics. In more recent work, Kristeva has broadened the domain of the "semiotic" to include not only revolutionary poetic language, but also language that represents the somatic and enunciates affect, that expresses abjectness, melancholy, hysteria, and depression.[73] Kristeva's formulation suggests just how closely the body has been associated with the unconscious, and yet how linguistic structures of meaning have been applied to its expressions.

The body's productions of meaning have always been available for medical as well as artistic, religious, and social interpretation; but I have chosen not to consider the latter two, traditions that would require work on etiquette, moral behavior, and ethics.[74] The body has also always been implied in rhetoric, both suggested by figural language and physically deployed in the gesture that is part of persuasive communication.[75] Many literary theories have described action, gesture, and dance as a language or a writing.[76] Dance has also come to figure signifying practices: signification is imaged *as* a dance. A history of theories of the symbol, such as that compiled by Tzvetan Todorov in *Théories du symbole*,[77] charts the recurrence of conceptions of the symbol in which the symbol itself is represented by or as a dance. In many traditions, poetic theory explicitly defines poetry as a dance of words, as the rhythmic embodiment of images; dance or dancer often represent the way the symbol or sign work in poetics. Some dance forms are easily allegorical, others are less literal, more coded; some do not seem to "signify" at all, coming closer to what anthropologist Dan Sperber calls "symbolic" meaning, a richer field of meaning that cannot be reduced to "signification."[78] It is striking that both linguistic and extra-linguistic theories of meaning can find, and have found, models in dance.

But it is difficult to perceive the dance performer simply as a sign, or to do a "semiotic" analysis of dance theater. The dancer works; her body is a means of production, but it is also the product. Unlike the word and the thing it represents, the body of the dancer and the content of the dance do not represent exclusively signifier or signified but can be either. Like the ideogram or pictograph, the dancer often looks like what she represents; like the cratylistic sign, dance can be a "motivated" language in which there is a resemblance between signifier and signified. But at the same time, the dancer often represents abstractions, emotions, or images through "unmotivated" referential gestures.

Thus it is not so much that form and content are fused in the dance in an ideal embodied language, as that they are constantly in a shifting relation in which it is impossible to assign to either a specific place. Because of the nature of the dancing body, because of the complexity of the way dance works, sign theory—although it provides a framework for understanding the relation of dance's constituent parts—fails to describe dance as a signifying practice. The dance's images, birthed from the body, are simultaneously the signified content of the dance, as well as the signifiers of that body; and in the same way, that body is itself both signifier and signified. Because the sign that the dancer is cannot be dissolved into its constituent parts (there is no "dance" without a "dancer"); because the dancer's labor cannot be separated from the glories of performance (the work does not disappear in the performance, but it is not seen as work), dance has been perceived as an ideal image of the unity of signifier and signified. But this unity is easily unravelled by historical or anthropological research examining the technicalities of the dance—how the dancer prepares, what she does to be able to perform, and what she does while performing. In fact it seems that dance's structure relies not on fusion, but on the simultaneity of its overlapping and inseparable constituent parts: work and pleasure, body and soul, absence and presence. Sign theory can be useful in helping to understand the ways in which dance represents, but because the dancing image is a living body, its usefulness is limited to the sphere of theory, and complicated by the arena of practice.

. . .

In other cultures, in other times, dance's silence and the use of body code may signify differently; but in nineteenth-century France this silent code signifies illness, signifying as illness does. This connection depends not on the "image" of dance but on the visual aspect of its imagery, the way that dance works to create its images. Speaking through silence, revealing and concealing, the dancer acts out the censure or division that marks all symbolic expression.[79] The production of dance movement repeats in some telling ways the process of symptom production as defined by Freud. The symptom of neurosis is what Paul Robinson has succinctly called a "compromise" "between the demands of a repressed impulse and the resistance of a censoring force in the ego."[80] Dance stages, in its movement, the simultaneity of impulse and censure, the insistence and resistance of meaning. It is thus not simply a superficial representation of madness, but models the complex push-and-pull mechanism of repression itself. A tacit cultural understanding that dance reveals this bodily "truth," the truth of repression and its relation to the symptom, has fueled both its power and its marginality.

As the choice not to speak, dance aligns itself with what Freud calls the "symptomatic act"—the production of meaning on the body that is part of the process of "hysterical conversion." It is precisely this silence and its use of body code, I suggested above, that has contributed to dance's pathologization by referring to symptom formation. By communicating "symptomatically," dance not only addresses "medical" social questions, but also challenges literary form: dance functions at the limits of symbolic expression. Because dance—even abstract modern dance— is often understood as telling a story, it has often been read as a kind of sign language, miming its allegorical meaning.[81] But dance's wordlessness is as much a part of its language as its deployment of narrative, poetic, and semiotic structures. Dance's silence thus makes possible both its idealization as free speech and its pathologization. Without words, it gets connected to the somatic and the unconscious; as bodily expression it is viewed as symptom. Nineteenth-century literature and medicine both collude and confront each other in the cultural frameworks they shape for dance interpretation.

Literature and medicine come together in Freud's psychoanalytic method, which concerns itself with the overlapping of language and the body, with the physical and mental workings of expression and censure. Psychoanalysis can be understood historically as an outgrowth of the thinking about the body and mental illness that dance performance had staged. The process of free association, drawing the repressed material out of its (often somatic) hiding place, like dance allows the body to tell its story. And like dance, psychoanalysis realizes the nineteenth-century desire for the kind of intimate or internal theater, the stage for the unsayable, which permeates nineteenth-century French literature. The very idea that dance could speak in ways that writing could not, offering fuller expression, is itself symptomatic of tensions and anxieties of the age, of concerns about the body, knowledge, and vision. For some writers it is as if the dance, bypassing words, can bypass censure itself. If dance mimes symptomatic expression it is also because it maintains a close relationship to the unconscious, and to the role of the body and of repression, in expression.

Richard Terdiman's work on nineteenth-century France has developed the idea of the century's—and the culture's—crisis of hermeneusis. In *Present Past: Modernity and the Memory Crisis,* Terdiman argues that Saussurian sign theory fails to describe accurately the formation of memory and its expression in the symptoms of hysterics who "suffer from reminiscences," in Freud's early formulation.[82] In his exploration of Freud's association of hysteria with remembrance, Terdiman has reformulated Freudian mnemonics and its Lacanian poststructuralist interpretation to suggest that it is consciousness, and not the unconscious, that is structured like a language:

Denying the character of signs to the content of the unconscious emphasizes the impression of irreducible "foreignness" that Freud regularly attributed to it. To press the image, the unconscious does not simply speak a different dialect from the other agencies in the psyche. . . . Rather, in some mysterious sense . . . the unconscious must somehow not use language at all.[83]

Terdiman notes that for Freud, hysterical conversion brings derivatives of the unconscious to consciousness as symptom.[84] Thus the somatic is one field in which (with or, more frequently, without language), the unconsious is translated and brought to expression. "In psychoanalysis, I want to say, it is *consciousness* that is structured like a language."[85]

Inasmuch as dance legitimizes the body's expression, it can be seen as a "condition of possibility" for psychoanalysis, giving a stage to the "private theater," as Breuer's patient Anna O. called the inner life of the psyche.[86] Psychoanalysis under Freud gave the hysteric an alternate stage for self-expression: the body translates repressed memory or desire back from symptoms into words within sight and hearing of the analyst. Though this approach leaves for movement no real significance as cure, some forms of dance, this book argues, validated the body's "hysterical" forms of expression, suggesting that experiences that cracked the mold of speech could come to be expressed in analysis. Nineteenth-century dance was concerned with bodily experience, women's bodies, and the subjectivity shaped through them. This experience finds its place in the feminist psychoanalytic theory developed by women analysts working in Freud's wake.[87] This art of the body is part of the culture that makes psychoanalysis possible, carving out a space in which to listen to, and to tell, the body's story.

In its silence dance is what Foucault calls a "discourse." Foucault's work argues for the understanding of cultural silences *as* discourses:

Silence itself—the things one declines to say, or is forbidden to name . . . —is less the absolute limit of discourse, the other side from which it is separated by a strict boundary, than an element that functions alongside the things said, with them and in relation to them within overall strategies. There is no binary division to be made between what one says and what one does not say; we must try to determine the different ways of not saying such things, how those who can and those who cannot speak them are distributed, which type of discourse is authorized, or which form of discretion is required in either case. There is not one but many silences, and they are an integral part of the strategies that underlie and permeate discourses.[88]

Foucault's formulation that "Language is the first and last structure of madness"[89] suggests that what culture silences, what is suppressed, repressed, censored, or ignored, can be read and understood itself as a culturally produced and received discourse. Even when dance tells a story, stages a libretto, or is accompanied by narration or programmatic music, its "discourse" is constituted not simply by a verbal content but also by its gestural and expressive silence.

Dance's silence must be understood as a cultural discourse, listened to and interpreted like the silence of madness. This study attempts to do for the language of dance what Foucault does for the language of madness in several ways: by reading dance texts with performance history in mind; by reading texts written by dancers, in which their active participation in culture and language is evidenced; by considering dance itself as a language and revalorizing its code; and by considering its influence on and interactions with writing. Recent feminist scholarship that investigates the *writing* of hysteria in nineteenth-century French literature, medicine, and history tends to support the view that the hysteria diagnosis was manipulated by a patriarchal power structure to control its female victims.[90] Yet, without contesting that such manipulation took place, looking at the *performance* of "hysteria," or references to it in dance, produces another reading in which a more complex view of culture, medicine, and performance can be elaborated.

Nineteenth-century dance gives a different perspective on hysteria from histories that look only at text because dance mobilizes the female body, allowing it to respond to the culture of reception, critique, and diagnosis. Reconsidering dance's written record, rather than its historical marginalization, can facilitate its reevaluation. Reading dance texts—libretti, reviews, poetry, theory—with performance history in mind can help in reconstructing the mobility of that historical body. Many of these texts reconnect dance to its philosophical, aesthetic, spiritual, and physical roots. Text can turn over the spectacular side of dance to ponder its specular inside. And text can show how dance moves beyond its visual commodification, expressing freely by staging censure, symptom, repression. As an unrecorded art, nineteenth-century dance relies on text for its history; but even in the nineteenth century, text was integral to the experience of dance. Within the Parisian culture of spectacle, print diffused dance performance and broadened its audience. Written records of dance, especially reviews in the daily papers, widened its "readership" significantly. The only record of dance other than static visual representations, dance writing captured its life and movement, the dynamism that visual representations—poses or portraits—often missed. The prescription and description of dance movement in the range of dance writing from libretti to reviews gives it a certain life. The broader formal influence of choreography on other forms of writing, including narrative; the conception of dance as a poetics; and the use of dance itself as a form of "theory" applicable to writing reveal the rich relations between dance, writing, and literary theory.[91]

It seems natural, then, and even necessary, that a book that treats the history of dance in the context of the history of hysteria should make many of its points via literature and literary theory. In a world where men were more frequently read and heard than women, the silencing of female patients, for example, in Charcot's clinic, and the institutionalization of women without their consent, are particularly significant. Often the early cases of hysteria, such as Dora's, include loss of voice or speech, in her case prolonged aphonia; a loss of voice which is itself a metaphor for her predicament of "not being listened to" or of "having no voice" within her family social life. But hysteria, like metaphor or allegory, is another way of saying.

Against this background, the nineteenth-century dancer effected a revalorization of silence and of the body's meanings, even when performing in the public eye. Though dancers' existence in public linked their art to visually coded and regulated prostitution and hysteria, dance theater, because of the complexity of its form, escaped purely visual definition, problematizing visuality and its promise of free expression. Reading dance against the background of medicine and literature reveals the possibility that dancers, despite their association with prostitutes and clinical patients in the cultural imagination, were not simply victims of a regulatory or repressive gaze but managed, with some particular forms, within their institutional bind, through the development of an alternate identity, to escape complete "institutionalization." The writers whose work is considered in this book were not interested in a facile idealization of dance and dancers, but in the particular mechanics of their expression.

A nineteenth-century site of problematic femininity, subjectivity, and illness, as well as idealization, the dancer's body can serve as a special site for twentieth-century critical debate on these issues. In dance, the female body exists outside of language but within a symbolic system of self-representation or self-expression. Presenting as well as representing the female body, women's dance performance expresses the doubleness that marks the signifying subject, dramatizing in its particular technical structure, its production and diffusion of images, the overlay and interplay of presymbolic and symbolic systems. Bringing to public view what is culturally repressed, but requiring forms of repression in its own production, the dance dramatizes the difference that the body makes in expression, as well as the difference of the female body. It locates femininity within a theatrical realm inhabited, on the one hand, by the hysteric in the clinic whose dramatic illness is a kind of "unsuccessful" theatricalization, and on the other by the dancer who recuperates much of the "hysterical" movement or drama of the female body in a "successful" self-presentation on the stage.

Through the three case histories presented in this book, I will argue that the development of new dance forms paralleled medicine's move toward mentalist conceptions of mental illness across the nineteenth century. I will suggest that it is not coincidental that the rise of this art form, dominated by women, occurred in tandem with the rise of psychological theories of mental illness. It is clear that dance, as a culturally central art form in nineteenth-century Paris, and medicine, as a professionalized science of the body, interacted in complex ways: shifts in the medical conception and treatment of psychological disorders were played out in dance theater, and dance theater may be seen to have helped to shape the thinking that made such psychological, rather than purely somatic, explanations of hysteria possible. Dramatizing its connection to some forms of madness, nineteenth-century dance also shows that bodily expressive movement need not be pathologized.

Freed from the significance of its visual resemblance to hysteria by these mentalist explanations, dance could be perceived as commenting on, rather than simply representing, this long-standing resemblance. As its images were no longer implicitly bound up with images of hysteria, the public face of mental illnesses began to look less and less like dance. In the late twentieth century, resemblances between dance and hysteria can be read as choreographic commentary on their long liaison. Modern and postmodern dance's reshaping and restaging of themes and images of possession, sexuality, and madness are often explicit. Dance forms have recuperated or reproduced images from the Salpêtrière iconography. It could be argued that dance has never stopped representing, emulating, or staging madness. Recent sociological interest in dancers' diets and eating disorders suggest that dance has continued to be connected with notions of illness. And a mutated popular dance form, aerobics, now vehemently promotes itself as the foundation of health when—not unlike ballet—it is a well-known site of injury and illness. Performative forms of madness related to hysteria have not disappeared. Modern psychiatry and psychotherapy have not prevented the diagnosis of mental disturbances as a woman's disease related to feminine sexuality. The mad scene of *Giselle* continues to play before moved audiences.

The peculiar theater of hysteria in Charcot's clinic and its close connection to dance are fixed in history; the identification of dance with that particular illness has disappeared. Significantly, it has once again been replaced. Just as dance was connected to syphilis during the nineteenth century via prostitution, in the age of AIDS the milieu of dance has again become sexualized and connected to a sexualized disease that brings with it both physical and mental degeneration. In the late twentieth century the arena of dance is again pathologized, seen as the site of contagion, with a shift of focus from the female to the male homosexual performer. The cultural conception of dance performers and the AIDS illness is matter for another study; but its contemporary history reveals again the cultural presence of dance pathologies.

Although modern dance is often about possession, mysticism, sexuality, or madness, it did, for a time in the twentieth century, cease to be confused with it in the cultural imagination. With modern dance forms and their influence on ballet, and with female choreographers shaping movement for their own bodies and writing their own choreographic positions, a new social understanding of dance as liberating the body, and a new intellectual understanding of dance as an experimental art form, seems to have taken hold. Twentieth-century dance history records dance becoming a tool of physical therapy, women's education, and sexual liberation, and the artistic expression of repression. But it also records examples of nineteenth-century dance pathologies prolonged in twentieth-century thinking.

Dance is not a primitive gestural language. It is neither the failure of expression nor the perfect union of body and mind. Without words, dance will always express "symptomatically"; and in its ambiguity, open to a breadth of interpretation, taking all kinds of meaning, dance can be associated with the *mal de siècle*—as well as the idealized health—of any century, the body's short-circuited communication as well as its imagined freedom of expression. In its silence, it can always be read as the ideal and the pathological, showing the body functioning at maximum, and never telling at what cost.

CHAPTER 2

The Madness of *Giselle*

The beginning of a century of theater revolutions in Paris is usually dated from Victor Hugo's 1830 *Hernani*.[1] The outrage surrounding *Hernani* is well known; the backlash against the play by conservative critics was clearly provoked not simply by Hugo's tampering with the rules of classical drama, but also by the ostentatious behavior of the play's supporters. Hugo's statements in *Hernani* or the earlier *Préface de Cromwell* about what kind of theater the modern age demanded pale in comparison to the theatrics of the *Hernani* premiere itself, for which the young Théophile Gautier in particular became famous. After his appearance at the premiere in a red waistcoat, with long hair flowing down his back, Gautier was most famous in his lifetime as the author of the ballet *Giselle*.[2] The first moment, a decade before the ballet's debut, serves as a springboard for the second.

The debacle of the *Hernani* premiere shows the great divide between the literary theory that some of the century's writers were developing about theater and the state of theater practice at the time. A remarkable number of nineteenth-century French writers dreamed of writing for the theater, often with little knowledge of theatrical practice and even less taste for it. As a result, nineteenth-century French literature is full of plays difficult or impossible to perform, some of them prefaced by apologies or explanations, some claiming to be written by someone else. Hugo's *Cromwell*, Musset's *Spectacle dans un fauteuil*, Mérimée's *Théâtre de Clara Gazul*, and Mallarmé's "Scènes" are among the best-known examples.[3] Literary history has kindly forgotten that many now-canonical writers of the century considered themselves *hommes de théâtre manqués* in an age in which the idea of theater was inseparable from their literary theory.

Although Hugo was more at home in the theater than many, his theater was far less innovative than the wild carryings-on of his young supporters. In contrast to the conservative plot of *Hernani*, with its ultimate victory of the traditions of chivalry, patriarchy, and Christianity, the *Hernani* gang produced a far more interesting, and more radical, performance. To the modern reader, it is evident that Gautier threw himself into the *Hernani* battle with more passion than Hernani himself displays in the play. While the play's supporters seemed to embrace the same values as the play's hero, and the debate over the play lent its name in one recorded case to a duel, their bravado made *Hernani* into theater that was as significant offstage as on.[4]

The performance art of Hugo's band suggests that in some cases it was the playgoers as much as the plays themselves who were responsible for many of the century's theatrical upheavals. The nineteenth-century French theater is the arena where writers' private dreams for the theater met its very public, popular face; the myriad literary ambitions to have unperformable texts staged suggest the power of that popular form in making or breaking writers. This literary tendency in theater—even the failures it produced—were not without influence on popular forms. Although success in the theater promised money and fame to struggling poets, many were at odds with theater traditions and acting styles and hoped to remake them from the ground up: Hugo's clashes with Mademoiselle Mars, the veteran actress playing *Hernani*'s young Doña Sol, are one famous example. Gautier, idolizing Hugo and imitating him, like Hugo a graphic artist, poet, and novelist, would prove more adept at selling theater to its public, creating popular theater that conveyed romantic literary ideals.

With Gautier the ideal form of theater becomes most realizable in dance. Gautier went further than Hugo or others in changing the rapport between literature and the stage by moving into and taking over the genre that Stendhal had simply admired as more Shakespearean—and thus more romantic—two decades earlier. Stendhal is hardly remembered as a *balletomane*, yet, delighted by the ballet in Milan in 1818, he equated its romantic potential to that of Shakespeare: "Neither Racine nor Voltaire could do that."[5] In the wake of Stendhal, and of *Hernani*, Gautier began to compose the ballets that would solidify his reputation as a writer. The ballet could do, or could allow Gautier himself to do, what Racine and Voltaire could not. Beyond moralist classical drama or Enlightenment social critique, dance offered Gautier a performance art with seemingly tremendous freedom of expression. Beyond the conventional theater, beyond the popular melodrama, nineteenth-century dance—a "high" art that was also extremely popular—offered to writers the possibility of realizing their literary ambitions for a poetic theater. Despite its showiness, the romantic ballet could bring to light the deeper, more disturbing, issues of French romanticism.

French romantic theater, in its high and low forms, set for itself the project of saying on stage what had not been or could not be said, even if it meant writing unperformable plays, or breaking the rules governing genre and performance. In *The Melodramatic Imagination*, Peter Brooks has pointed out that romantic drama relied on the popular melodrama, whose stage and acting conventions helped it to move from the Théâtre Français (where the "bataille de *Hernani*" had raged) to the *théâtres du boulevard*. *The Melodramatic Imagination* develops the connection between literature and popular melodramas of the day around the issue of the excessive expressiveness of the genre.[6] In Brooks's revalorization, melodrama becomes a model for the romantic impulse to speak the unspeakable. More than just the popular form noted for its expressive and gestural excesses, melodrama is, he argues, a moral power in post-Revolutionary France: insisting on the clear victory of virtue over horror and fear of punishment, melodrama is an expressionist form implementing Rousseau's and Sade's dreams of uncensored speech, staged now in a moral context. Reaching toward a full range of expressivity, the melodrama calls on other forms of expression—mime, music, scenery, in addition to gesture—not unlike the ballet, for greatest effect.

Yet in spite of its obvious affinities to contemporary melodramas, the romantic ballet, without melodrama's excesses of speech, stages the problem of saying the unsayable in a very different way, with different expressive gestural forms. Though the ballet represents the ineffable in both its sublime and profane aspects, its verbal restraint shapes its forms of presentation and representation which differ significantly from the melodramatic model. It is ballet's quiet revolution, in contrast to the expressive excesses of melodrama, that this chapter charts, using Gautier's most famous ballet as a case study.

Melodrama's multimedia excess comes with what Brooks describes as its paradigmatic handicaps; like tragic blindness or comic deafness, the generic fault of melodrama is epitomized by the mute who must rely on code to communicate. The silent signaling in moments of crisis which is typical in the melodramas, the reliance on ambiguous gesture to tell a complex story of danger or disguise—excess expressiveness that is both too much and not enough, and is rarely clearly understood—serves as a metaphor for melodrama itself. The romantic ballet, in some obvious ways, repeats melodrama's storytelling, but with this crucial difference: as a genre entirely avoiding speech, the ballet functions without the kind of constraint embodied by the archetypal mute. Rather than the mad signing that fails as speech, dance's gestures derive their elegance and ambiguity from the genre's willing refusal of words. Ballet's sign language—its gestures, positions, and steps—is richly, even if sometimes enigmatically, expressive.

The romantic ballet's gestural code stylizes ambiguity rather than fighting it, and is immeasurably enriched by it. Moralistic messages, such as Giselle's mother's, will continue to be communicated with a sense of urgency, but the genre incorporates mime as a form of poetry rather than a shorthand telegraphing. Berthe's gestures are very precise, as Cyril Beaumont notes in his choreographic script of the action: "*Giselle's mother warns her daughter that if she will persist in dancing she will die and become a Wili.* To convey this, she mimes: You will persist in dancing—you will die—you will become a Wili. That is, she arches her arms above her head and, wreathing one hand about the other, gradually extends and raises them vertically upwards; at the apex of the movement she clenches her fists and, crossing her wrists, lowers her arms straight in front of her, then, just as the arms fall vertically downwards, she unclenches her hands and sharply separates them; she then turns sideways to the audience, and, placing the backs of her wrists at the base of her spine, lightly flutters the hands."[7] Yet these gestures are received by an audience that must vaguely apprehend their dark symbolism rather than translate them literally. The ambiguity of these gestures proves crucial to what the ballet will not say, but will rather suggest, about connections among dance, sex, madness, and death.

Although, as Susan Foster has shown in *Choreography and Narrative*, the French action ballet developed to tell stories, by the turn of the nineteenth century there was an impulse for creating ballets that, even if they were literary, did not depend upon text for their comprehension. Neapolitan choreographer Salvatore Vigano stated that the public should be able to "see everything and understand everything [tout voir et tout comprendre]" in the ballet's gestures without needing information about the argument.[8] And yet ballet's ephemerality in the face of print culture was seized by Stendhal, writing in 1818: "If Vigano invents an art of writing gestures and groups, I maintain that in 1860 he will be spoken about more often than Madame de Staël, and thus I have been able to call him a great man."[9]

Ballet appealed to Gautier for many of the reasons that made melodrama and pantomime popular arts: its animation; its use of the body and gesture; its melange of music, decor, and mime. But dance's affinity to melodrama ends with its silence. As a spectacle that seemed to come without a moral message attached, dance was the ultimate midcentury entertainment. Although its plots often continued to preach of the dangers of evil, even at the Paris Opéra its popularity was largely due to its reception as legitimized low culture and its connection to the eroticized subculture of dancers. In such an atmosphere, the dancer's essential femininity, which becomes the subject *par excellence* of romantic ballet, raises issues of pornography as well as poetics. Whereas Brooks describes the melodrama as teaching a moral lesson through excitement, the evidence suggests that the romantic ballet was received as excitingly immoral by its impassioned spectators.

Gautier, like other dance reviewers of his time, tends to idealize the ballet, denying its erotic charge even while helping to create it. The simultaneous exploration and disavowal of sexual themes in the ballet by librettists like Gautier makes its incorporation of romantic poetics in the dancing body more complex than the black-and-white picture Brooks paints of the melodrama's Manichean quandaries. Ballet's silence, teamed with the eloquence of the bodies giving it life, raises issues about the link between language and the body in both a moral and an extra-moral context. Because the dancer of the 1840s is subject to the Opéra's institutional discipline, the ballet illustrates contemporary desires and fears about regulation of the female body. Yet to the extent that she is also an expressive subject—not simply the victim of her public, but also admired by them, inspiring not simply idealization but also identification—the ballet also addresses writers' issues of bodily freedom and freedom of expression.

It is precisely because of its visual aspect that the romantic ballet was viewed as a domain of free expression by romantic writers, in particular Gautier. Dance's potential for free expression depends upon its visual component: its ability to show without saying and thus to appear to bypass public and private censorships. But the visual sphere is not less complexly ordered by censure than the verbal realm, and dance's visual component is problematically, not simply, visible. In mid-nineteenth-century Paris, the ballet is front-page news: reviews of the previous evening's performance at the Opéra share the front page of the *Journal des Débats Politiques et Littéraires*, one of the leading daily papers in the 1840s, with the day's diplomatic news. Why this public mania for dance, simultaneously as popular culture and as high art? In a culture known for its spectacles, and during a century now famous for its intense visuality, ballet seems on the surface just one of many bourgeois visual entertainments.

It is in part the ballet's very visibility in nineteenth-century Paris, and its primarily visual presentation, which lent the form its freedom to express what might have been unsayable in writing. The visual component of the ballet attracted Gautier, choreography as "animated form [plastique animée]," in which the dancer's body could be molded to give shape to the writer's words. But the visual conditions of dance performance and the appearance of dancers at the Opéra were at the same time extremely repressive. The idea that ballet bypassed censorship in a dream of romantic free expression, and the dissimulation of its sexual connotation, are two sides of the same coin. The dance does not show all any more than it tells all, and yet it shows—and says—more than its nineteenth-century creators and spectators acknowledge. Its apparent freedom of expression, constructed by writers like Gautier and projected onto it by admiring fans, was of course at the mercy of the machinery that kept the wheels of its illusion turning.

It is the nature of this illusion, and of dance's complex and visible silence, that makes dance a site of literary or poetic issues, concerning expression, repression and the relation of language to the body. Beyond writers' and critics' idealization of the dance as free expression, the romantic ballet reveals tremendous repression: as a site of closely controlled expression of authors' or audiences' repression, projecting onto it both the poetic and the pornographic, the sublime and the deviant. At the same time, it is a complex structure expressing—without showing—the dancer's own repression, the discipline necessary to make the dance seem so free. In this way, the ballet is not simply an art form that gives expression to what is otherwise repressed; it is also a form that presents, or reenacts, the very workings of repression itself.

Baudelaire recounts that during his first conversation with Théophile Gautier—a conversation about words, the care a man of letters ought to take of his body, and the resemblance between dancers and racehorses— Gautier asserted that there is nothing that cannot be said, that the true writer never encounters an idea for which he lacks words:

the writer who did not know how to say everything, he whom an unusual idea . . . *found at a loss and without the stuff to give it shape* [*sans matériel pour lui donner corps*] *was no writer. . . .* Any man whom an idea, however subtle or unexpected we might imagine it to be, finds lacking, is no writer. The inexpressible does not exist [*L'inexprimable n'existe pas*].[10]

Hovering between this "inexpressible" and the romantic call for expression will be found the romantic ballet. If the "inexpressible" did not exist for Gautier, it is, first of all, because he did not restrict the notion of "saying everything" to the written word. To give material form to the feminine idea, he wrote for and about dancers. After training in the plastic arts, he was drawn to the ballet, launching a career as a dance and theater critic in the mid-1830s, and becoming a successful ballet librettist at the Opéra beginning in the 1840s. The attraction of the dance for Gautier was not only its visual form, but its living form: "Animated form, that is the real essence of choreography, and the literary man who writes a ballet libretto would do well to collaborate with a painter or sculptor whose silent art has habituated him to rendering thought visible."[11] The ballet attracted Gautier more than the contemporary theater of melodramas and well-made plays because it offered a poetic theater in which the visual image could come alive, animating in public, plastic form the text of Gautier's libretto. The ballet's ability to translate the word into the visual image was its greatest attraction; the best libretto, Gautier noted, would be a series of images without any text at all.[12]

An investigation of how ballet furnished Gautier's writing with "matériel pour lui donner corps"—with matter to give it shape, and bodies to bring it to life—immediately implicates more material bodies. The love of "animated form" is an oversimplification of the very specific attractions of the gendered body bringing aesthetic form to life in dance. But the repression evident in the construction of this ideal feminine, in the poems of *Emaux et Camées* as in *Giselle*, is belied by the very graphic and grotesque descriptions of the female body to be found in Gautier's erotica, and in what he describes as his frequent preference for the masturbatory "Veuve Poignet [Widow Fist]."[13] This poetic "inexprimable [unsayable]" as expressed in the ballets might be better described as the "inexpressible [unmentionables]," the contemporary epithet for women's underwear first adopted for use by ballet dancers.[14]

The dance's importance for Gautier is so closely tied to the role of women within the dance that questions about the relationship between dancing and writing must be framed as questions of gender at work in

Fig. 2. Carlotta Grisi in costume for *Giselle*, Act I. Collection of the Bibliothèque Nationale de France.

artistic creation and artistic performance. With the ballerina's rise in popularity at the Paris Opéra accompanied by the male dancer's fall from popularity in the 1830s and 1840s—engineered by Gautier and others—the romantic ballet becomes dominated by the female dancer. For Gautier, the ballet is not simply a showcase of femininity: it is an art whose subject is woman, an art that seeks to define femininity and is defined by it.

Being able to "say everything," then, depends not simply on a text, but on a body—the female body—moving without speaking. The problems of the text and its meaning multiply onstage in the dancer's performance; the *Giselle* to be studied here is not entirely a product of Gautier's pen, but of the collaboration between writer and dancer, one that Gautier thinks will enable him to say what cannot be written: the subtle ("subtile"), the unexpected ("imprévue"), the feminine "idea." On one level, Gautier's belief that the real writer is capable of saying everything can be put down to writerly machismo; on another, it is romantic poetics, the desire to find the means to say everything, even and especially what is conventionally thought to be unsayable. It is largely the ballet's visuality which lent itself to the expression of what Gautier calls the "inexprimable." The dancing Giselle promises to bring to the eyes of her viewers what Gautier's text cannot say outright; by showing, it seems, she will tell all.

The body that gave form to Gautier's second ballet, *Giselle*, when it premiered at the Paris Opéra on June 28, 1841, was that of a young ballerina, Carlotta Grisi, dancing the title role. Gautier presented *Giselle* to the Opéra administration as a vehicle for Grisi, who danced most of his ballets and was for many years his friend, his muse, and possibly his mistress.[15] Although Gautier's first ballet libretto, the 1838 *Cleopatra*, had been a failure, *Giselle* was to be a great success: it gave Gautier an income and an audience to match the reputation he had made since *Hernani*; Grisi's success in *Giselle* established her as a star of the first order at the Opéra, and though other dancers performed the role, Gautier imagined Giselle as inseparable from her.

Yet Grisi was neither an undisputed star when Gautier created the ballet for her, nor was she its primary inspiration. Gautier was not immediately taken with her dancing. In March 1840, he reviewed her performance in lackluster terms: "her dancing has some spark, but not enough originality; she lacks her own style; it is good but no better." His descrip-

Fig. 3. Fanny Elssler dancing "La Cachucha." Collection of the Bibliothèque Nationale de France.

Fig. 4. Marie Taglioni in *La Sylphide*. Collection of the Bibliothèque Nationale de France.

tion of her beauty is also lukewarm: "from what we can tell, under the makeup her complexion has a natural color; she is of medium build, svelte, with a nice enough figure, not excessively thin for a dancer."[16] But a year later, at her Opéra debut, he wrote: "Assuredly you remember this charming woman who sang and danced, two years ago . . . today she dances marvellously. With vigor, lightness, suppleness and originality that put her instantly next to Elssler and Taglioni."[17] Having lost track of the time, or wishing to distance his earlier criticism, Gautier here praised what he had earlier found fault with: Grisi's ability to dance neither one style nor the other, but both.

The two acts of *Giselle* were in fact intended as homage to the two most famous dancers of the decade: the earthy Fanny Elssler and the ethereal Marie Taglioni. Gautier was a fervent admirer of both dancers, yet he may have preferred Grisi not only for personal reasons, but for her ability to dance both styles. Grisi's doubleness allowed her to become Gautier's ideal combination of what he called Elssler's "Pagan" and Taglioni's "Christian" styles. Taglioni danced with an otherworldly spirituality and lightness; Elssler was best known for her seductive, vivacious *cachucha*. The role of Giselle demands a performer who can dance both the coquettish peasant girl of the first act and the virginal spirit of the second; who can go violently, hysterically mad in the final moments of the first act, and display purity of line and limpid grace in the second.

Just as the libretto constructs a double subject, or two-women-in-one, the librettist himself makes the living dancer into two women, a living legend who is both the character she plays and a performer with a mythic past. There is a perfect equivalence between the depersonalized dancer and her role: "What is Giselle? [Qu'est-ce que Giselle?]" writes Gautier. "It is Carlotta Grisi, a charming girl [C'est Carlotta Grisi, une charmante fille]";[18] and she takes on an identity—becomes a star—through her incarnation of this character: "From now on this role is impossible for every other dancer, and Carlotta's name has become inseparable from that of *Giselle* [Ce rôle est désormais impossible à toute autre danseuse, et le nom de Carlotta est devenu inséparable de celui de *Giselle*]."[19] Yet he also makes her into a literary heroine; in Gautier's *compte rendu* Grisi's biography reads like myth: Gautier has her born in an abandoned palace in Italy where François II had once stayed, in "the king's very bed," with mice eating at the table and bears roaming the streets. Her tiny foot could wear Cinderella's slipper on top of her own, and she needs no makeup. Her one pot of rouge "serves only to refresh her flesh-colored slippers

Fig. 5.   The death of Giselle. Collection of the Bibliothèque Nationale de France.

when they are too pale ... [ne lui sert qu'à raviver les couleurs de ses souliers-chair, lorsqu'ils sont trop pâles ...]."[20] In contrast with the earlier critique, writing here has become a double exercise of turning the dancer into a legend and making legend live through her.

Giselle is, in every sense, a story of duplicity. Act I tells the story of the charming peasant girl courted by the local aristocrat, Albrecht (or Albert, duke of Silesia), who visits her village disguised as Loys, a local peasant. Both principal roles demand a combination of nobility and earthiness: although she is a peasant girl who loves to dance, Giselle is frail and sensitive; and Albrecht's aristocratic lineage is not hidden by his modest garb and his participation in the country dances.[21] His rustic rival, Hilarion, suspects Albrecht's true identity; finds his sword with its coat-of-arms in the cottage where he changes clothes and personae, and when the nobles pass through the village on their hunt, he reveals Albrecht's alter ego before Giselle, the villagers, and the court. Face to face with Albrecht's other identity and his other (aristocratic) fiancée, Giselle goes mad. In a fit of hysteria, she seizes Albrecht's sword and after playing distractedly with it at first, tries to throw herself onto its point, when it is snatched from her by her mother.[22] The memory of her love for dance returns to her, and she begins to dance "avec ardeur, avec passion" when suddenly, she drops dead.

Fig. 6. Carlotta Grisi in *Giselle*, Act II. Collection of the Bibliothèque Nationale de France.

Resurrected in Act II as one of the Wilis, the spirits of women be-
trayed by their lovers before their wedding day, Giselle is sworn to entice
Albrecht to her grave in the forest during the night and to make him
dance until he falls dead. Approaching her grave, Albrecht sees Hilarion,
who has arrived there before him, hounded by the Wilis, driven by them
to fitful, wild dancing which exhausts him to death. Terrified by this
spectacle, the shaken Albrecht is seduced by Giselle's apparition and led
by her deeper into the forest. Despite her vow for vengeance, Giselle
pleads for Albrecht's life before Myrtha, the powerful Wili queen, who
replies by brandishing the rosemary branch, symbol of remembrance, to
exhort the Wilis to their duty. But Giselle manages to delay the dance of
revenge almost until daybreak, when the Wilis' power wanes. Albrecht's
dance is shadowed by death and, pushed to the point of exhaustion, he
stumbles and falls during his variations as the dawn and his rescuers draw
near. The frenetic dance is cut short as Albrecht's servant arrives with
friends from court who drag him away, nearly dead with exhaustion.
Giselle disappears in the light of dawn, urging Albrecht with her last gesture to give his hand and heart to his living fiancée.

The plot of the ballet was taken from a tale by Henrich Heine about
the folklore of the seductive and deathly figures of the Wilis, the "young
betrothed women who died before their wedding day."[23] Although the
predicament of these women will turn out to be more complicated, the
ballet's themes are common in Gautier's poetry and signal what would
become the staples of the romantic *ballet blanc*: the tragic results of a love
gone wrong; the subsequent transmutation of the woman into a white-
bodied natural or supernatural being, and her removal into a fantastic
realm of nature; her quintessential inaccessibility, and the solitude of the
man who worships but cannot possess her, who has distanced and idealized her.

Many of the dualities of *Giselle* resulting from its heroine's two-act
transformation are echoed in the imagery of Gautier's poetry. Several poems in his *Emaux et Camées* volume are portraits in which women have
been transformed into spirits, framed as works of art, or fixed as objects.[24]
The poetry focuses on the movement of the transformation or on its final fixity, and the color representing that transition or its final form is
white. In "Symphonie en blanc majeur," the "swan-woman"—an image
of transformation to be exploited in a later romantic ballet—descends to
torment the poet with drunken reveries of "des débauches de blancheur."
Mixing the cold terms describing her body—snow, granite, the host,

wax, marble, silver, ivory—with the poet's passion, the poem speaks of his desire to melt her icy heart, "to bring some color to this implacable whiteness [mettre un ton rose dans cette implacable blancheur]!" "Le poème de la femme" speaks of woman transfixed as a statue, and of her body as a poem. In these poems, the female body is marked by coldness, whiteness, or blankness; it is the raw material of art.

The white body also expresses a ghostliness which in Gautier's cameos links art to death. The body of the phantom dancer in the poem "Inès de las Sierras" is marble white against her black gown: dead, yet still dancing. The body's whiteness signals its removal to the realm of art or death; the whiteness functions both as the fixed color of the body's reification or resurrection, or as total lack of color, a blankness illustrating the body's vacillation between human and inhuman, subject and object, alive and dead.[25] "Inès de las Sierras" narrates a tale of resurrection which bears directly on the main theme of *Giselle*. The poem is dedicated to a contemporary nineteenth-century dancer, La Petra Camera, who appears at its end as the incarnation of Inès, a ghostly figure Gautier borrows from a Gothic tale by Charles Nodier:

> Nodier raconte qu'en Espagne
> Trois officiers, cherchant un soir
> Une venta dans la campagne
> Ne trouvèrent qu'un vieux manoir

> Nodier tells a story
> of three officers in Spain one night
> In search of a *venta* in the countryside
> Who found only an old manor-house.

Gautier's setting is loaded with references; in this Anne Radcliffe–like castle, haunted by Goyaesque creatures, in whose architecture even Piranesi would be lost, a "charming ghost" suddenly appears in a long moonlit hallway:"Peigne au chignon, basquine aux hanches / Une femme accourt en dansant [Comb in her chignon, basque petticoat at her hips / A woman appears running, dancing]." Gautier describes her dance in detail:

> Avec une volupté morte,
> Cambrant les reins, penchant le cou,
> Elle s'arrête sur la porte,
> Sinistre et belle à rendre fou.
>
> . . .

Elle danse, morne bacchante,
La cachucha sur un vieil air,
D'une grace si provocante,
Qu'on la suivrait même en enfer.

Ses cils palpitent sur ses joues
Comme des ailes d'oiseau noir,
Et sa bouche arquée a des moues
A mettre un saint au désespoir.

Quand de sa jupe qui tournoie
Elle soulève le volant,
Sa jambe, sous le bas de soie,
Prend des lueurs de marbre blanc.

Elle se penche jusqu'à terre,
Et sa main, d'un geste coquet,
Comme on fait des fleurs d'un parterre,
Groupe les désirs en bouquet.

Est-ce un fantôme? est-ce une femme?
Un rêve, une réalité,
Qui scintille comme une flamme
Dans un tourbillon de beauté?

Cette apparition fantasque,
C'est l'Espagne du temps passé,
Aux frissons du tambour de basque
S'élançant de son lit glacé,

Et, brusquement ressuscitée
Dans un suprême boléro,
Montrant sous sa jupe argentée
La *divisa* prise au taureau.

La cicatrice qu'elle porte,
C'est le coup de grâce donné
A la génération morte
Par chaque siècle nouveau-né.

With a deathly voluptuousness
back arched, neck bent
she stops in the doorway
Beautiful and evil enough to drive one mad.

. . .

Dejected bacchante, she dances
the *cachucha* to an old tune
with such provocative grace
that one would follow her to hell.

Her eyelashes flutter against her cheek
Like the blackbird's wings
And her pouting mouth
would drive a saint to desperation.

When she raises the flounce of her
swirling skirt, her leg in its silk stocking
gleams like white marble.

She bends down to the ground
And her hand coquettishly gestures
as if gathering the flowers flung from
the audience, grouping their desires into a bouquet.

Is she a phantom? a woman?
A dream, a reality
Glimmering like a flame in a whirlwind of beauty?

This fantastic apparition
is the Spain of times gone by
rising from her icy bed
to the shivering of the tambourine

And suddenly resuscitated
In a supreme bolero
Revealing beneath her silver skirt
the *divisa* taken from the bull.

The scar she bears
Is the coup de grace given
to the dead generations by each newly born century.

Here the ghostly body of Inès functions as an image for the writing of poetry; the dancer gives body to the past, reviving it, telling its story in dance. Both writing and dancing resurrect the dead, bring the past to life in a series of framings. As the poem moves from the *passé simple* of Spanish legend à la Goya to Nodier's contemporary retelling of the tale, to Gautier's own version, the dancer moves from a past life to present performance. Inès de las Sierras is resurrected from the grave to dance before the soldiers of Nodier's legend, which Gautier refers to in the opening line. This resurrection is repeated in the last two stanzas by the dancer Petra Camera, who reincarnates Inès on the Paris stage, bringing the initial ghostly vision to Gautier's own eyes:

> J'ai vu ce fantôme au Gymnase
> Où Paris entier l'admira
> Lorsque dans son linceul de gaze
> Parut la Petra Camera,
>
> Impassible et passionnée,
> Fermant ses yeux morts de langueur,
> Et comme Inès l'assassinée,
> Dansant, un poignard dans le coeur!

> I saw this phantom at the Gymnase Theater
> Where all of Paris admired her
> When in her gauze shroud
> La Petra Camera appeared
>
> Impassive and impassioned
> Closing her languorous dead eyes
> And like Ines assassinated
> Dancing with a dagger in her heart!

The incarnation that the dancer embodies—both in the original legend and in the doubling Petra/Inès performance, is reenacted in the poem's series of framings. The work of the dancer, resurrecting from death into life, from grave to stage, from legend to contemporary poetry, is the same as the work of the storyteller or the poet.

The dancer can execute this kind of transition through her capacity to embody contradictions. Petra/Inès is "impassible et passionnée": death-in-life; legend and reality; both empty of emotion and full of passion; both cold and fiery. An ardent will burns beneath her deathly pallor and languor, just as the Wilis' submissiveness belies their drive for revenge. The coexistence of these oppositions within the body of the dancer is what makes her a key image for Gautier's poetics, the model for a poetry that moves between realms. Gautier's interest in the living dancers of his era, and his creation of ballet libretti for performance, suggest that he used the ballet as a vehicle for this poetic movement away from the street to a distanced fiction. Inversely, Gautier admires the dancer's ability to animate the work of art, the way in which la Petra Camera or Carlotta Grisi realize legend before his eyes. Like the figures or portraits of women in the poems, Gautier's dancer is a fixed or fetishized work of art, an object on display onstage. Gautier's libretti try inexorably to fix the dancer in

roles familiar from the poems, roles suggesting that the dancer's movement between realms is controlled by her male creator; in Giselle's case,
the movement of involuntary possession, manic passion, and superhuman,
inhuman transcendance.

On one level, *Giselle* establishes the figure of the dancer as a paradigm for poetry; her dance can be seen not simply as the stuff of poetry,
but as an image for what poetry itself is trying to do. She is thus not simply the librettist's pawn, but also his muse and model. From the familiar
plot of rivalry and jealousy to the transformation between the two acts—
the transposition of woman into a figure of the fairy, forest world—the
ballet stages the theme of metaphor itself. In this ballet, the metaphor of
woman transformed can be understood as a metaphor for metaphor.

But in the realm of theater practice and theater history, *Giselle*'s plot,
the conditions of its production, the relationship of its star to its creator,
its instant success, and its continuing powerful presence in the ballet
repertory tell a different story. The ballet's movement from one realm to
the next, and the change in character it requires of its lead dancer, can be
seen to repeat the duality of the ballet's idealized narrative content and
the real conditions of its production, the duality of the idealized body of
the spirit onstage and her physical existence as a dancer. Beyond the view
of dance as the embodiment of what Frank Kermode has called "romantic image," the ballet's text can be understood as Gautier's commentary
on the ballet of his time.[26] Taking into account the history and conditions
of its first production, the text can be read as social critique: a state-of-
the-art review of ballet at the Paris Opéra of 1841.

Giselle's social commentary did not escape the contemporary parodists of
the press and the stage in Paris and London. Popular parodies of *Giselle*
played on the ballet's themes of sex and madness, turning its threats
into comedy. Within eight weeks after the premiere, the Sadler's Wells
Theater produced an imitation of the ballet, a "Melo-dramatic, Chore-
graphic, Fantastique, Traditionary Tale of Superstition," called *Giselle or the
Night Dancers*.[27] Two English parodies were created after Grisi and Perrot's appearance in the London production of the original *Giselle* in 1842.
One began while the ballet was still enjoying an enormous success at
Her Majesty's Theater. "Grizelle, or Dancing Mad," starred "foreign
artists Signor Oxberrini and Louisotta Fairbrotherini" (W. H. Oxberry
and Louisa Fairbrother) as Skyleisure and Grizelle, and ran for three
weeks. "The Phantom Dancers or the Wilis' Bride" a burlesque at the

Adelphi, opened November 2, 1846, and parodied Edward Loder's ballad opera "The Night Dancers," which had opened October 28, and was popular enough to be revived in 1850 and 1860. The Adelphi burlesque, based on a libretto by Charles Selby, featured Madame Celeste as Giselle pursued by two suitors: Count Whirligig and Duke Albert, the son of Prince Noodlehead. The production came complete with a Giselle who, on hearing of Albert's duplicity, "goes out of her mind and fairly gives up the ghost," a Whirligig who is "waltzed to death" and complicated scene changes which turn the Haunt of the Wilis into a Salon de Bal for all "the old Adelphi favorite characters: St. George, Tilly Slowboy, Norma, Pollio, The Mysterious Stranger, &c. who conclude the piece with a grand *Tarantella d'Extase*." Though most of the burlesques were short-lived, they continued as the revivals of the ballet continued, the last produced in July 1871 after revivals of *Giselle* in 1870 and April 1871.[28]

The contemporary parodies of *Giselle* illustrate popular attitudes toward dance and dancers, but, more important, they reveal a broad cultural awareness of *Giselle*'s hidden messages. By staging the tensions surrounding madness, sex, and women as comedy, these parodies point out and play up the social commentary couched in the ballet's apparently naive or idealistic narrative. Seen in this light, *Giselle* is a ballet not simply about dancing but about its own dancers. It is an allegory that stages the social and sexual issues surrounding the Paris Opéra of 1841.

The transformation worked by Giselle within the two acts of Gautier's ballet—the movement from natural to supernatural—is an image for the daily work of the romantic ballerina, in her movement from street to stage, from private life to her public, idealized image. The social history of its first performers illuminates much of the subtext of *Giselle*. The idealized white spirits of Act II, like the idealized dancers onstage, are only half of the total picture of femininity created by the ballet. The figure of marble whiteness has a less innocent resonance in the parlance of midcentury Paris; "fille de marbre" is one of the contemporary epithets for the courtesan.[29] The female figures in white take on an erotic resonance in the sexual metaphor implicit in their dangerous dance-of-death. They are not simply women who died before their wedding day, as the libretto innocently describes them; they are women who die because they are jilted, their weddings called off. Their dance is one of sexual revenge. As Gautier himself puts it, in a letter to Heine, "These dead bacchantes are irresistible." Gautier's comment suggests that death heightens rather than extinguishes the Wilis's erotic charge. In fact, the Wilis are not so much dead as hypnotized, somnambulistic, a chorus of Bacchae in thrall to the mimetic madness of revenge. The Wilis's drill-line choreography makes direct reference to the ballet's practice rituals, parodying the *corps de ballet* as a fleet of driven, ambitious, deviant, and vengeful women. The Wilis embody many of the popular nightmares about female sexuality made evident in contemporary attitudes toward prostitution.

The ballet's plot associates dance with sex and death throughout; the gestures of Giselle's mother, in the choreography by Coralli, warn that only bad will come of Giselle's dancing too much with Albrecht. Giselle's death at the end of a hysterical dance, and Albrecht's threatened death-by-dancing make dance a metaphor both for madness and for sexuality. In the libretto, Berthe tells Albrecht: "I am sure that if this crazy girl dies, she will become a Wili and dance even after her death, like all the girls who liked the ball too much!" Berthe's gestures suggest the superstitions underlying the Wili myth: that dancing leads to madness and death, via love, seduction, and betrayal. Yet the poetic connection between the pleasures of the dance, sex, madness, and death is concretized by the physical reality of syphilis. The Wilis' mythic power to dance men to their deaths identifies their vengeance with the sexual revenge of the pox. Syphilis forges the missing link between sex and death in *Giselle*.

Figured as the euphemistic dance of death in the ballet, this invisible killer can be read in the context of 1841 Paris as the killer hidden in the prostitute's body; well into the twentieth century, prostitution was considered the principal source of venereal infection.[30] The transmission of syphilis by the lower-class women in prostitution's ranks to married men of all classes, who would then infect their wives, was widely conceived of as a kind of revenge.[31] Gautier was of course no stranger to the pox. The pornographic *Lettres à la Présidente* include vibrant descriptions of its virulence among the French army in Rome in 1849.[32] Syphilis serves as the common denominator between the ballet's themes of sex and madness, and madness and death. Berthe's warning, as well as the madness of the Wilis' (sexual) revenge, can be connected to the madness brought on by syphilis's late stages. A contemporary hygienist specifically attributed prostitutes' deviance to the madness of syphilis. In the 1840s syphilis would have been understood, by a certain class of audience, as the thread tying together sex, madness, and death in a certain class of women. Giselle's decline is itself too rapid to be explained by syphilis, or by Berthe's sign language, but the ballet's haunting ghosts of women, the threat of their revenge, and the madness associated with that threat all illustrate that syphilis is a hidden theme of the ballet.

The sexual allegory within the ballet can thus be read as an allegory for the contemporary context of its production. Although it defines an essential, and essentially perverse, femininity, it is simultaneously a drama of male impotence. *Giselle* is an example of a ballet created for the *danseuse*, with the *danseur* relegated to the status of support; neither Albrecht nor Hilarion dance any considerable variations. Hilarion hounded by the Wilis thus represents the rejected male dancer of the ballet of the 1840s, his box-office demise precipitated by a desperate, menacing *corps de ballet*: "What is Hilarion," writes Gautier, "but one danseur faced with so many danseuses? Less than nothing."[33] Prince Albrecht, in this reading, would represent a dandy of the Jockey Club, who comes to the Opéra to choose a mistress as he would choose a race horse,[34] and he is not destroyed by his passion for the dancer, perhaps because someone must live to pay the Opéra's bills.

The typical dancer of the Opéra of the 1840s was a lower-class woman dancing for an upper-class, largely male audience, and angling for a wealthy patron; the Wilis, poor girls who died because they loved to "dance too much" are aptly represented by the lower-class urban "*rat*" of the Opéra, named for her impoverished existence as a parasite of the institution. It is important to note that the artistic successes of some of the greatest female stars of the romantic ballet, Taglioni and Elssler included, did translate not only into financial success, but into social advantage; both married into wealthy upper-class families. In such examples, the Opéra's hierarchical star system can be seen to parallel the system of social classes, especially one in which new money was rapidly elbowing the old at the Opéra.

In the ballet, Albrecht's social obligations to his own class make a legitimate liaison with Giselle impossible, and she dies from dancing, or loving, too much, in what is either a Jockey Club fantasy, or a moralistic warning for the ardent fans of dancers. The ballet's plot and its popularity raise questions about both the homosocial and homosexual male audience. The ballet public of the 1840s was constituted by a preponderantly male mixture of Albrechts and would-be Albrechts: those who had entrée backstage, in the famous *coulisses* of the Opéra, and those who wished they had. The competitive adoration of the dancer, tempered by misogynistic undercurrents, is apparent, in tandem with a *dandyesque* homosexual identification with her.

Homosocial competition for dancers depends on an economic system that tried to make the dancer seem inaccessible while making her available at a price. The old money of Opéra regulars could of course buy entrance backstage; but a newer, younger, ballet public who could not get in invested the *coulisses* with the mystery and charm of unfulfilled desire, and inflamed the *loges infernales* with their communal passion. The dancer Léila in Albéric Second's 1844 chronicle of dancers' lives, *Les Petits Mystères de l'Opéra*, when asked by the narrator "how would you characterize the real Opera backstage? [quelle est la physionomie réelle des coulisses de l'Opéra?]," replies:

It is bourgeois, the worst of characters. We aren't too virtuous, because that would be stupid, nor too perverse because that would become tiresome. Backstage at the Opéra the feeling is above all one of boredom. It has the spleen like a fat English millionaire, and it would be difficult for it to be otherwise. A large percentage of the patrons have been around the Opéra for ages. For them, backstage no longer holds any mystery, flavor, novelty or poetry. The ones who have just arrived limit themselves to looking, not being rich enough to touch. For the most part they are minor stockbrokers, unlicenced brokers, backstage hangers-on of no importance, poor devils, who when they want to seduce, are often obliged to apply to love the economic system of the omnibus box. Their reciprocal passions are paid by subscription.[35]

This new Opéra public was the creation of Louis-Désiré Véron, an entrepreneur who made the Opéra a successful commercial venture when it lost state funding after the July Revolution. Véron, whose directorship in the early 1830s effected changes that continued well into the next decade, conceived of his mission as purveyor of culture to the newly triumphant bourgeoisie: "The July Revolution represents the triumph of the bourgeoisie: this victorious bourgeoisie will want to hold court, to amuse itself; the Opéra will become its Versailles, it will run there en masse to take the place of the exiled *grands seigneurs* and the court."[36]

This bourgeois crowd made new demands on the Opéra which Véron was quick to anticipate. He undertook renovation of the interior of the building in the Rue Lepeletier to create more seats "whose reduced price would better accommodate the fortune and lifestyle of the new *grands seigneurs*" and augmented the lighting in the house, to help the newly rich and powerful see each other better. New communal seating in the *avant-scènes* was created which would serve as the *loges omnibus*:

Men were beginning to seek both luxury and reasonably priced pleasures from the spirit of association. Clubs in Paris were multiplying. The loges of the *avant-scènes* were like our *courtisanes du jour*, who no longer belong to a Prince de Soubise or a Marquis de Lauraguais, but who all at once replace their heraldic livery with a fantastic elegance and the often uncertain fortune of one man with the more dependable revenues of a clientele.[37]

Véron's strategy overall was to make available to a wider audience what had been exclusive, and to offer it—or some glimpse of it—at a lower price; Véron's Opéra, and by extension, its dancers, were now like courtesans frequenting a wider clientele.

The desire for Opéra tickets, as for courtesans, was fueled by competition; Véron employed on a large scale what René Girard has called the mimetic "stratégie de la coquette."[38] The larger the dancer's audience, the better both for the dancer and the theater; her artistic and economic success depends upon the sheer size of her audience, upon the number of admirers willing to pay to see her. Véron cleverly made more seats available at lower prices, but he heightened demand for seats, and desire for dancers, by making tickets difficult to get. For the first time in Opéra history, men waited in line beginning at ten o'clock in the morning, only to be told when they reached the box office window that no more tickets were available. A contemporary critic paints the picture of a Véron delighted by such box office schemes; with each customer turned away, Véron felt himself victorious: "Because he was sure to see them again, with their friends and their friends' friends: the crowd is a lover who attracts a crowd."[39] A current joke recounted in Charles de Boigné's *Petits memoires de l'Opéra* played on the contemporary fashion for tight trousers and the competition for seats at the Opéra: "—*If I can get in*, said the Young Man in front of us, *if I can get in, I won't buy it.—If I can get in*, echoes the crowd, *I won't go in*. The first is talking about his trousers, the other about the Opera."

Véron further fueled public desire for ballet and ballerinas by creating the Foyer de la Danse, an exclusive salon behind the stage where dancers were shown off to *habitués* at parties and informal performances before and after the production. By making the dancers accessible, the Opéra not only set up a patronage system for its *corps de ballet* based more or less on prostitution, but also guaranteed consistently large audiences of the ranks of the would-be rich. Those who could not get invited backstage seem to have constituted the most loyal and enthusiastic pub-

Fig. 7. The "Foyer de la Danse." From Albéric Second, *Les Petits Mystères de l'Opéra* (1844). Collection of the Bibliothèque Nationale de France.

lic, keeping the box office busy, filling the seats of the *claques*.[40] The knowledge that the merchandise which the Opéra offered—its ballerinas—was available at all, for any price, urged on those who could only look.

The Opéra engaged in rigorous institutional control of its dancers. Like the courtesan, who ignited and fanned desire through carefully controlled appearances and disappearances, —Dumas fils' courtesan Marguerite Gautier in the 1847 *La Dame aux Camélias* is one example—the dancer's public success depended upon a carefully controlled visual presence, as well as staged absences. The Opéra administration used all means at its disposal to force dancers to appear; in addition to their salaries, the dancers of the Opéra were paid *feux* or stipends for each performance, to guarantee their appearance. Carlotta Grisi's August 1841 contract, dated a little more than a month after her triumphant opening in *Giselle*, more than doubled her salary but required her to remain in Paris on the day of any performance, and to leave an address if she left the city on any other day, so that the Opéra would always know where she was. She was required to be ready to rehearse day or night, and to perform on unscheduled nights if asked.[41] Yet the best dancers exercised their rights not to appear, and seemed to know that choosing not to perform at particular times—perhaps when their performance might be less than was expected of them—was one strategy of stardom. The *rats*, in turn, imitated the stars and were often fined for missed performances.

If the dancer gives the writer the power to "say everything" it is, on one level, because her position in the institution allows her to say very little in the public eye. Gautier shapes Carlotta Grisi through his text much as the Opéra administration closely controlled her movements, both onstage and off. With such means of institutional control, it is little wonder that Gautier would claim, during the period when he was writing libretti, that the inexpressible did not exist. But the prostitution of dancers in this context at the Opéra is not only a result of cultural practice or social stereotype, but also, and more importantly, a result of the theoretical implications of their performance in the public eye, a further effect of the commercialization of the Opéra and the economy of performance. The prostitution of the dancer's image, her commodification in the public gaze, is an effect of the visual, as well as physical, nature of her work. Dancers did not belong to the group of prostitutes who were required to register with the police, and whose social, economic, and geographic backgrounds were examined in detail in the hygienist Alexandre Parent-Duchâtelet's seminal 1836 study, *De la prostitution dans la ville de Paris*.[42] Of a group of 3,120 currently registered prostitutes, only 16 gave their profession as actress or *figurante*.[43] Yet by midcentury, the habit of finding a mistress in the *coulisses* of the Opéra was common knowledge, if not common practice.[44] That the professional dancer would not have officially registered as a prostitute in 1836, though by midcentury her association with prostitution was widespread, suggests first that dancers did not belong to the category of registered prostitute—the prostitute practicing in the brothel or independently who provided the core of Parent-Duchâtelet's data. The prostitution engaged in by dancers might then be classified as casual, the sort of unregulated prostitution that most concerned Parent-Duchâtelet. Inasmuch as dancers' prostitution was controlled by the Opéra, and in some cases, by their families, they would be identified with the courtesans who served a wealthier clientele, and whom the law exempted from regulation, rather than with the *insoumises* who posed the greatest risk of infection and thus the greatest problem for public health.

It was not the mere fact of the dancer's theatrical employment which removed her from this category of common prostitution, since all of the registered prostitutes in the Parent-Duchâtelet study list some other, primary, occupation, such as laundress, barmaid, seamstress. The nature of the actual prostitution that ballerinas at the Opéra engaged in gave them, in legal terms, roughly the status of courtesans. Yet the very legal code that exempted them from governmental scrutiny and regulation set out the terms that equate dance performance with common prostitution. The rhetoric of the law concerning courtesans, cited by Parent-Duchâtelet, bases its legality on its private nature:

> Il est établi qu'une femme qui tire parti d'elle-même, non publiquement, mais ça et là, et en se livrant à un petit nombre de personnes, peut attaquer en justice celui qui la traite de prostituée. Mulier quae non palam, sed passim et paucis, sui copiam facit actio, competit adversus eum qui eam meretricem vocavit.

> It is established that a woman who turns her own person to advantage, not publicly but here and there and in delivering her services to a small number of persons, can rightfully attack any who would qualify her as a prostitute.[45]

This is the law that accords to the *femmes galantes* and the *femmes à parties*, the highest classes of prostitute in Parent-Duchâtelet's hierarchy, their special status as "private" rather than "public" women, and protects them from regulation and arrest. These women, mistresses of the wealthy and powerful, have their own domiciles, and pay their *impôts* as private citizens. Because of their limited practice, their reduced number of clients, they are not considered to pose the same risk as the general body of prostitutes; in fact, they are not included in the category of "prostituée" at all.

The ballerina who practiced prostitution in a similarly restrained manner, in similarly refined circles, would be protected by the same law. But ironically, the legal code that puts the ballerina's prostitution, along with the courtesan's, above common prostitution, simultaneously classifies her public performance as a kind of common prostitution. The rhetoric of this law locates the dancer between these two realms of public and private, that of the performer and that of the courtesan. The dancer earns her living not "here and there," but publicly. Her performance is a public act; in a theoretical sense, she earns her living by giving herself, bodily, to many people. Thus if one specific element of the dance reinforces the

Fig. 8. From Albéric Second, *Les Petits Mystères de l'Opéra*. Collection of the Bibliothèque Nationale de France.

ballet's close theoretical association with prostitution—here I am speaking not of the dancer but of the art of ballet itself—it would be its public visibility.

The Opéra of Véron prostituted not only its dancers but, more significantly, their images. Nineteenth- and twentieth-century ballet critics and historians describe the romantic ballet as a visual commercial feast. A joke contemporary with *Giselle* published in a humor magazine describes the vulturelike gaze of ballet aficionados who wish that "la voir" (seeing her) would be synonymous with "l'avoir" (having her):

During the interval, opera glasses peruse the theater and linger on one or two beautiful duchesses. . . . There is barely a duchess for every 30,000 men: but there is only one Carlotta Grisi for a million Parisians—this million wants to see her—to see is to have [—ce million veut la voir—Voir, c'est avoir] says Béranguer.[46]

The attendance of the ballet for a kind of music-hall entertainment seems not to have dropped off in the 1830s and 1840s, despite the more refined artistry of the new performers. As early as 1824, the then-Intendant of the Opéra, Viscount Sosthène de la Rochefoucauld, ordered dancers' skirts to be lengthened so as not to inspire "carnal thoughts" in the gentlemen who sat near the stage.[47] Gautier ridicules this rage of false moralism in the preface to *Mademoiselle de Maupin* ten years later: "I remember the jeers directed before the revolution (I'm speaking of the July Revolution) at this miserable and virginal Viscount Sosthène de La Rochefoucauld who lengthened the skirts of the Opera danseuses. . . . His lordship the Viscount Sosthène de la Rochefoucauld has been far outdone. Modesty has been perfected since those days and we have now introduced refinements that he would not have dreamed of." In the 1840s, the skirts were shortened once again.[48]

In the case of *Giselle*, Gautier conceived of openly seductive movements for the second act. In contrast to the innocent charm of Act I, Giselle dances with "such voluptuous grace, such powerful seductiveness that the imprudent Albrecht leaves the protection of the cross and moves toward her reaching forward with his hands, his eyes shining with love and lust."[49] The Wilis are described by Gautier as being as dangerous as real women: "these cruel night-dancers who have no more mercy than living women do for a tired waltz partner"; their mythic revenge is measured in real, sexual terms.[50] In some cases, the ballets seem to have been more openly suggestive, playing to the appetite for the erotic even more than did the *cachucha* or *Giselle*. Gautier's third ballet, *La Péri*, contained a variation danced by Grisi in which she was supposed to shed garment after garment as if tormented by a bee. The dance received rave reviews and Grisi was praised for her innocent execution of it. After several performances, however, she refused to dance this variation and asked to have another substituted for it.[51]

Giselle's erotic component, then, can be traced to many factors: the libretto's descriptions of movement, the coquetry of some dancers' styles, stereotypes of the dancer reinforced by social practice, the behavior of the dandy audience. This seduction is both created and disavowed by the libretto, the dancers, and the Opéra simultaneously. Yet the way in which its choreography was interpreted by its audience as seduction relies not only on the empirical evidence of how the ballet looked, but also on the function of looking for pleasure, the scopophilic nature of the audience experience, which complicates the nature of the Opéra's visual prostitution.

Through the dandy's looking glass, the dancer was not only a sylph, but an ordinary woman in an extraordinary position; a work of art whose mystery was diminished from poetic enigma to the minor secrets of underclothing.[52] Unlike the idealized painted nude, the dancer is a woman who has had to take off her usual garb to put her filmy costume on, as Zola describes Nana doing late in the century. Dance historians tell us that the imagination of the dandy audience a decade before *Giselle* had been gripped by an exaggerated scrutiny of the lower half of the dancer's body; it was an audience thought to live for the dancers' *bouffante* pirouettes, the simple turns that would lift dancers' skirts:

> The *bouffante* is a ruse from the old days of the dance, that is much used in our time and will be used for a long time for the edification of our youngest nephews. When a ballerina has been in the air and shown herself off all around . . . she finishes her attack with a pirouette en pointe. This pirouette begins in a lively way and then wanes, so that the tulle dress of the goddess balloons up; intense attention is paid to this by the orchestra boxes and the front rows of the parterre; it is this swelling up that I call a *bouffante*. The bouffante never fails to have an effect; it is usually followed by a murmur of approval, it saves mediocrity, it protects genius, it removes years and wrinkles, it is the goal of all ballet. . . . The bouffante is the drinking song of the ballet.[53]

If "voir, c'est avoir"—if seeing the dancer means having her—it is not only because in the context of midcentury Paris spectatorship has a fetishistic tone. It is also because belief such as Gautier's in the visible is already a belief in vision as a form of knowledge, in its exercise as power, and in gender as visible on the body, concealed and yet revealingly alluded to in the skirt's movement.

But what the dandy was able or unable to see under the dancer's costume is less important than the way in which he looked. Because of the exigencies of dance costuming, and Opéra policy, the audience did not see what some dance commentaries suggest they hoped they might. Audience looking-for-pleasure is more complex, and the nature of visibility at the ballet more tenuous than "possessive" spectating suggests, tending, at the time of *Giselle*, toward a destabilization of looker and looked-at. A closer look at the ballet's production of its images effectively undermines viewers' vaunting descriptions of their proprietorship of those images.

Charles de Boigne's description of Elssler dancing gives the tone of this crowd in the *loges infernales* who came to examine their "race-horses" armed with the Opéra equivalent of field glasses:

> These movements of the hips, of the behind, these provocative gestures, these arms that seem to seek out and surround an absent being; this mouth calling for

a kiss; this whole shaking, shivering, twisting body; this seductive music, these castanets, this unique costume, with its shortened skirt, and bare, décolleté top, and above all the sensual grace, the lascivious abandon, the plastic beauty of Elssler, were very much appreciated by the opera glasses of the orchestra and *avant-scènes*. The public, the true public, had more difficulty in accepting these choreographic temerities, these wide eyes, and one can say that this time it was the *avant-scènes* that brought on success. The French Cachucha is not a natural taste; it is an acquired taste.[54]

Though Elssler's talent and charm are well documented, and the dance steps surely seductive, viewers in the *avant-scènes* zooming in close to the body with their "télescopes" seem not to get a better view of the performance, only a more eroticized one. Opera glasses created a particular reading of Elssler's dance and costume, whose "half-open bodice" was most likely a trompe-l'oeil effect necessitated by the demands of dance costuming.

In fact, at the Opéra in *Giselle*'s time, the dancer's costume was considered to be revealing precisely in the way in which it was not revealing; that is, in covering the body without hiding its form. The translucent fabric which allowed the outline of the body to be seen against the stage lights heightened its perceived exposure. The composer of *Giselle*, Adolphe Adam, described the ballet's second act to Gautier's collaborator Saint-Georges: "There is nothing so pretty in choreography as the groups of girls which Coralli has designed with great talent . . . the naked women in the middle of a forest."[55] In *La Fanfarlo*, Baudelaire succinctly described the contradiction of the "ethereal dancer, always dressed in white, whose chaste movements leave everyone in good conscience [la danseuse éthe-rée, toujours habillée de blanc, et dont les chastes mouvements laissaient toutes les consciences en repos]" who nevertheless wears "these insipid tulle gowns that allow everything to be seen and leave nothing to the imagination [ces insipides robes de gaze qui laissent tout voir et ne font rien deviner]." The dancers' deshabille is not what makes her costume erotic; Baudelaire and others note the seductive challenge of women's formal dress of the day, considered provocative because it rendered the body inaccessible.[56] For Baudelaire, the dancer's costume undoes the desire generated by fashionable women's dress; her perceived state of undress becomes interesting for Baudelaire only at a distance.

Looking under the dancer's skirt at the Opéra, then, could be described as both voyeuristic and fetishistic, both furtive looking for what could not be seen, as well as fixed staring at what could. Describing dancers' relevance to photography, and photographic pornography, in Second Empire France, Abigail Solomon-Godeau has measured the viewing and valorization of the dancer's body in the empirical context of dress practices against a psychoanalytic context of spectating:

That the legs of the dancers are the focus of the fetishizing gaze of the male spectator is only the reflection of a far more generalized phenomenon which superimposes a map of (erotic) significance on the woman's body. . . . Certainly, the fact that European women did not routinely wear drawers until well after the mid-nineteenth century is relevant. Above the stocking, the leg was bare, under the skirts, underskirts, and petticoats, the woman's body—her sex—was exposed. Yet the persistence of the fetishism of legs as, in Kleinian terms, a part object is such as to trivialize attempts at an empirical understanding. . . . The salient fact is that until the twentieth century it was only the legs of dancers or entertainers that were publicly on display.

But the relationship between the relevance of historical cultural practice and the persistent fetishism of dancers' legs remains unresolved here; Solomon-Godeau's argument does not take into account the complexity of what "publicly on display" means in the context of the ballet. While this passage emphasizes that an empirical reading is trivialized by a psychoanalytic one, its conclusion merges the two points of view: dancers' legs were more easily, or more generally, fetishized because they were publicly visible; but because of their visibility, they served as the emblem of that fetishism. In the romantic ballet, empirical factors and historical practice coexist with often contradictory psychological criteria in the audience's way of looking.

The details of women's dress enumerated by Solomon-Godeau can be accepted as cultural history and as a viable resumé of the historical view of the ballerina. Yet these facts are contradicted by the recorded policy of the Opéra. Tights were de rigueur for Opéra dancers; a decree of Louis XV had made the *caleçon* obligatory for performers.[57] Philippe Perrot has argued that when French women adopted the *pantalon*, tellingly referred to as "l'inexpressible," in the second half of the nineteenth century, they were borrowing it from dancers, and gained greater freedom of movement in it, almost as if it were a pair of trousers: "this type of undergarment . . . can evoke that of dancers or actresses who for a long time rigged themselves out in it. As with them, it also allows for a far too lax deportment, and even encourages far too much freedom of movement."[58]

Albéric Second describes dancers' rehearsal clothes, in which "their thighs are chastely hidden beneath a thick calico *caleçon*, as impenetrable as any State secret,"[59] although there was one scandal at the Opéra, in April 1844, of a dancer appearing without tights. Lola Montez, who has remained famous not for her dancing but for—among other adventures—her liaison with King Ludwig of Bavaria, was fired, dance historian Ivor Guest reports, because she refused to wear tights at her debut. Montez's most recent biographer has described her throwing a garter to the audience at this performance.[60] Three months after the scandal, which Gautier did not mention in his review of her debut, he wrote in *La Presse* "there can be no choreography without tights [... sans maillots, point de chorégraphie]."[61] Although the assertion may reveal some general tension surrounding the issue, and the search for the odd Lola Montez may have driven the dandy to the *loges infernales*, such scandals did not constitute all the scopophilic pleasure derived from the ballet.

The general tension between empirical and psychological factors in the experience of the romantic ballet is aptly illustrated by the example of the dancer's version of the *pantalon,* the *caleçon* or the *maillot*. The tights' function was to cover and reveal at the same time—to be there in order to cover, but not to be seen as covering. Tights served to make what they covered more visible rather than less, and are described as serving a function similar to that of makeup in Baudelaire's famous essay "In Praise of Cosmetics" in *The Painter of Modern Life*:

what our age vulgarly calls *make-up* . . . has as its aim and result to make disappear from the face all the marks that nature has so outrageously planted there, and to create an abstract unity in the quality and color of the skin, which, like that unity produced by the dancer's tights, immediately brings the human being closer to the statue, that is to say to a divine and superior being.[62]

The wearing of tights, for Baudelaire as for Gautier, is not only a sexual question but an aesthetic one: the question of the "unité" produced by the *maillot* on the dancer's body, making that body into art. Baudelaire is less concerned with what the tights cover than with how they cover, smoothing out the female body into undifferentiated, nonspecific surface. Flesh-colored tights would create the appearance of a perfectly smooth, perfectly unified skin. Second describes dancers' tights not as "rose," but as "maillot-chair" or "leurs bas couleur de chair." The purpose of tights was thus to give the illusion that they were in fact flesh or leg; tights were to be seen and not seen—to be seen as what they were not.

This seeing-what-is-not-there characterizes the visual experience of the dandy scrutinizing the Opéra dancer, and suggests that the visual image created by the ballet is an artifice. Baudelaire's remark about the ballerina's costume, which belies her chaste dancing, can in fact also be applied to the dancing itself, seducing while denying its seduction. Giving the illusion of purity or innocence, some of the movements of romantic choreography carried an erotic significance that their execution seemed to deny. Carlotta Grisi's *pas de l'abeille*, contrived for her by Gautier, is one example. Another, less obvious, is the pose, which became an essential choreographic component after Taglioni capitalized on her ability to hold an *attitude*, balancing on one pointe, while counting to one hundred. The verb "taglioniser" was invented to describe this hovering quality, which many dancers sought to emulate. The second-act score of *Giselle* includes several *andante* variations before the final frenetic dances, and Perrot's second-act choreography for Giselle contains some slow passages with such poses.

Presenting herself to a public conceived of as her "husband," rotating arms and legs to diagonal and turned-out positions for maximum frontal presentational effect, holding poses as if for a portrait,[63] the romantic ballerina plays a game of seduction with the audience. Yet the difficulty of the movement, the great discipline of many of the dancers, and the physical risk inherent in stage performance made ballet far more than seductive sport. The eros associated with the romantic ballet is of course as much a production of its spectators as a strategy of its creators. Dance viewing in the public space of the theater, privatized within a box or within the boxed-in field of opera glasses, was itself an exercise of erotic power.[64] Even when surrounded by competitors in the omnibus box, the dandy sought, with opera glasses, to privatize his visual experience; one English ballet fan of 1843 recounts that when going to the ballet, "we white-waist-coat, pantaloon, and double-opera ourselves up to the hilt . . . so that nothing may interrupt our study and deep contemplation of the 'new gal's legs.'"[65]

Why the dandy audience sought to privatize viewing in a public place, to see without being seen, to be alone while in the crowd, and to exclude other male bodies—both those in the box and those onstage— from its sight, tells a story of visual "consumption" of the prostituted image; it also speaks of visual power. The visual experience of the dandy at the Opéra, shaped by concerns of power and pleasure, emphasized uninterrupted viewing and visual possession of the dancing image in conjunction with the homosocial atmosphere of the loges. The simplicity of recorded accounts of what dance amateurs were looking for, or at, is belied by the complexity of scopophilia at the Opéra.

The eros associated with such dance movement is thus not only an effect of intentional seduction by the librettist, choreographer, or dancer. It is more importantly an effect of the looking-for-pleasure or relocation of pleasure to the scopic realm, made possible by certain conditions of the spectator's viewing experience at the Opéra: the fixation of the dancing image in "téléscopes"; the dandy's Baudelairean solitude or privatized viewing amid the multitude; and thus the exclusion of other male bodies from the scene viewed occurring simultaneously with an implicit male bonding in the scene of the viewing.

As the Lola Montez scandal suggests, the ballet's ability to titillate depended not on striptease but on veiling; the erotic view was not the one that revealed but that infinitely promised revelation. The ballet was guaranteed audiences and patrons only when its dancers adhered to its carefully strategized seductions. Yet in this regard, the ballet dancer of the era seems less the victim of a voyeuristic crowd, and more a subject complicit with a gaze that is both fetishizing and identificatory. What we find in looking more closely at the lookers' commentaries is that gender definition, the line between possessed and possessor, is not so clearly drawn.

Nowhere is this blurring of gender clearer than in the contemporary audience's distaste for male dancers. Interrupting the dandy's contemplation and exclusive "visual consumption" of the dancer onstage was her male partner, who was viewed by dance aficionados with a more and more critical eye. Why should the exclusion of the man onstage order the dandy's visual experience when he watches the dance in competition with a theater full of men? Newspaper critiques of the period, as well as modern critics, have singled out nineteenth-century bourgeois gender anxiety as the motivating factor.

In the course of the nineteenth century, the ballet played out a tension between the masculine and feminine elements of the dance and its male and female dancers. Early in the century, a masculine athleticism reigned, and old followers of the ballet were disturbed to see female dancers trying to emulate the men's technical feats—jumps and bravura passages to show off sheer endurance and virtuosity rather than control or refinement. But by midcentury, when the reign of Taglioni had changed the nature of women's technique and relegated the male dancer to the status of support, the situation was reversed. The more gymnastic variety of male dancer had disappeared, and the male dancer most often seen, the *danseur noble*, was not well received. Gautier notes that "a danseur doing anything other than a character dance or pantomime has always seemed to us to be some kind of monster."[66] The *danseur noble* became a figure of ridicule for the reviewers, his demise engineered and celebrated by contemporary commentators such as Jules Janin:

> You know perhaps that we are hardly the partisans of what are called the grands danseurs. The grand danseur seems to us so sad, so heavy! He is simultaneously so unhappy and so pleased with himself! He corresponds to nothing, he represents nothing, he is nothing. Talk to us of a pretty dancing girl, who deploys at ease the grace of her face, the elegance of her figure, who shows us all the treasures of her beauty in such a fleeting way; thank God, I understand that marvellously well; I know what we all wish for this lovely person, and I would willingly follow her wherever she likes in the sweet land of love. But a man, a horrible man, as ugly as you and I, a vile empty rabbit, who jumps around without knowing why, a creature expressly made for carrying a musket, a sabre, and wearing a uniform! for this being to dance as a woman would do, is impossible! This beard-sporter who is the head of the community, an elector, a member of the city council, a man who makes and mostly un-makes the law for his own interests, to come before us in a sky-blue satin tunic, wearing a chapeau whose floating plume lovingly strokes his cheek, a frightful danseuse of the masculine sex, come to pirouette front and center, while the pretty girls stand off respectfully at a distance, this was surely impossible, intolerable, and thus have we done well to erase such great artists from our pleasures. Today, thanks to the revolution that we won, woman is the queen of the ballet. She breathes freely and dances at her ease. She is no longer forced to divide her silk skirts in half in order to dress her neighbor with it.[67]

The importance of this critique grows when considered in context. It appeared in the daily *Journal des Débats Politiques et Littéraires*, which often printed Janin's ballet and theater reviews on the front page with the day's political news. The readership of the paper thus included the "chef de la communauté," "élécteur," or "membre du conseil municipal," whom Janin mentions; the author himself was elected to the Académie Française a few decades later.

The reluctance of this male ballet audience to identify with the *danseur* seems on the surface to be a reaction to his femininity, a rejection of the threateningly effeminate man. Yet Janin's praise for Grisi's partner Jules Perrot, like Gautier's, lauds his feminine qualities, his lightness, his elegance: "Nowadays the dancing man is only tolerated as a useful accessory. . . . Well then, now that it has been proven beyond a doubt, you

Fig. 9. Jules Perrot in *Nathalie*, 1832. Collection of the Bibliothèque Nationale de France.

must believe me more than ever, that this Perrot is the most admirable dancer to be seen. He has an extraordinary lightness."[68] In a rare passage of praise for a male dancer, Gautier cites Perrot's feminine qualities, calling him "a male Taglioni," a danseur whose beautiful legs make up for an ugly face. What is disagreeable about the male dancer, then, to the audience member who sees himself as a member of the empowered male bourgeoisie, is precisely his "*membre*" or penis; the fact that the dancer is a man, identified by his phallic musket and sabre. It is the male dancer's sex, his "*sexe masculin*," which seems so unnecessary, or useless, onstage and which makes him "*une affreuse danseuse.*" It is his sex which so disturbs this audience who had thought to "erase the *danseur* from our pleasures." The critic claims that Perrot is an exception, because he is a man who dances like a woman, Taglioni: not a man who dances in an effeminate way, but a man who dances as if he were a woman.

Dance historian Lynn Garafola has argued that Janin "added another element to Gautier's list of characteristics unbecoming in a male dancer—power. No real man, that is, no upstanding member of the new bourgeois order, could impersonate the poetic idealism of the ballet hero without ungendering himself, without, in short, becoming a woman in male drag."[69] But when Gautier criticizes the *danseur*, it is for his gauche manliness—for a lack, rather than overdose, of feminine elegance: "Really there is nothing worse than a man displaying his red neck, his great muscular arms, his legs with beefy calves, and his whole heavy virile frame shaken by jumps and pirouettes."[70] For Gautier as for Janin, man's place is not on the stage, but in the audience. The performer should be female; not simply because the stage is an effeminizing place, but because it is a place where masculinity is out of place, where what is conventionally thought to be male power is seen as powerlessness, and where its conventional sign, the male sex, is deemed extra, unnecessary. Thus *danseur* and *danseuse* did not clearly define gender roles onstage; the male audience was reluctant to identify with the male dancer, and the *danseuse's* potential was not given free reign in her more restricted role with a male partner.

When aesthetic and popular concerns pushed the male dancer out of sight, the ballet was restructured in such a way that the audience member could perceive himself as the dancer's only partner, as he was backstage in the Foyer de la Danse. Strangely, Taglioni's preference for dancing without a partner created an image invested with more, rather than less, eros for her viewers: the poses she held by herself without the support of a *danseur*, and the *danseur*'s nearly total disappearance from the stage, heightened the ballerina's perceived seduction. "An actress' true husband," writes Gautier in 1838, ". . . is the audience; it is to the audience that she owes her brightest smiles, her tenderest looks. . . . The audience does not want a husband to see these lovely shoulders so pleasingly bare: this husband interrupts its amorous fantasy."[71] The dancer should not be an ordinary woman, wife, or mother, but an independant abstraction of woman:"the performing artist, as an artist, has no family."[72] The audience is "libertine as an old bachelor (nothing is as bachelor-like as the audience)"[73] and, although the teaching notes of some ballet masters from this period mention a female audience contingent, its bachelor tastes are clearly kept in mind.

The restructuring of male-female partnering was more complicated, as the male position had to be filled by someone onstage. A new female role in the ballet was created, the role of the *danseuse en travesti*. Wearing form-fitting trousers which were considered even more revealing than the bouffant skirts, the male costume seems to have reinforced the objectification of the female body onstage.[74] Yet the male audience could identify with this female *danseur* who assumed the privileged position of partnering the *danseuse*. The travesty gave expression to the "masculine" side of dance which had been bred out of the ballerina after Taglioni. The female body in male garb, dancing the male role, could be read as an image of castration; yet it was in fact read not as a male body feminized, but as a female body masculinized. The travesty's feminine elegance in masculine garb could easily be assimilated to a dandyesque, hermaphroditic ideal. Gautier reads the sexual doubleness embodied by the dancer *en travesti* as the kind of doubleness to be found in his 1834 *Mademoiselle de Maupin*. He writes of one of Fanny Elssler's *travesti* appearances: "Although she is a woman in the full acceptance of the term, the slender elegance of her figure allows her to wear male attire with great success. Just now she was the prettiest girl, and here she is the most charming lad in the world. She is Hermaphrodite, able to separate at will the two beauties which are blended in her."[75] The point of view Janin represents wants the *danseuse* alone onstage, not only in order to partner her from the audience, but to identify with her; when there is a male dancer onstage, the bourgeois in the audience is obliged to identify with him. If the male dancer onstage makes it clear that the male sex is useless or unnecessary, the female dancer onstage is phallic, powerful.

It would be difficult to chart the gender and power dynamics of productions of *Giselle* in which the role of Loys/Albrecht was danced *en travesti*; Cyril Beaumont documents one such production staged in 1884 in London.[76] What the ballet of the 1840s suggests is the fluidity of gender boundary lines and dancers' constant crossing of them. Albert Smith's 1847 monograph *The Natural History of the Ballet Girl* lists men's wear (the *débardeur*) as the ballet-girl's preferred costume, even though Carlotta Grisi is her most admired and most imitated star. An audience practice of seeing-what-is-not-there in the performance environment prefers a female body, considered to be less visibly marked by sexual markers than the male. Onstage, the female body, without the encumbrance of the male sex, is imagined as more multivalent, able to shift back and forth between sexes, playing at both, and broadening the range of the body's capacity to signify. Part of the practice of seeing-what-is-not-there then involves not-seeing-what-is, a certain blindness to the bodies under scrutiny. This is the blindness that allows Gautier or Jules Janin to excuse the encumbrance of male genitalia in certain gifted *danseurs*, to assign to the male body dancing the grace of the female form. It is this blindness or denial of the dancer's very femaleness that is the cornerstone of male identification with the dancer. A cartoon of Gautier in his middle years, with swollen belly exaggerating the extravagant gesture, shows him floating above the head of one of his dancers, demonstrating the airiness his libretto demands of her; teaching her to do what he himself obviously cannot.

The dandy's identification with the dancer that is manifest in the popularity of the travesty with a largely male audience, and in the cartoon of Gautier soaring, is explored in a slightly different context in Baudelaire's *La Fanfarlo*. First published in 1847, but written some years earlier, *La Fanfarlo* imagines the private relations between writer and dancer, describing what the writer finds in the dancer's body, art, and sexuality before which he falls helpless. Despite Baudelaire's respect and admiration for Gautier, the *maître* to whom he dedicated *Les Fleurs du Mal*, it is tempting to find in his dandy Samuel Cramer, the half-Creole poet, the great romantic, a caricature of what he imagined the young Théophile to have been. Gautier's early, critical reviews of Carlotta Grisi give way to mythic panegyric in much the same way as do Samuel Cramer's ripping reviews of La Fanfarlo, written as he falls in love with her. But the relevance of *La Fanfarlo* here is neither as quasi biography, nor as reportage; and La Fanfarlo herself is not a ballerina, but a music-

Fig. 10. Caricature by Cham from *Le Charivari*, August 1, 1858. "Monsieur
Théophile Gautier in person, demonstrating to Madame Ferraris various steps
from his ballet which she has only to interpret for the public."

hall dancer. The story's value is rather as a document, albeit a fictitious
one, of a dandaic identification with the dancer which is both sexual and
artistic, in which the writer's admiration for the female form parallels a
formal admiration of her art as masquerade.

The story describes both the writer and the dancer as hermaphroditic
doubles. Samuel writes under a female pseudonym, Manuela de Mon-
teverde, for a female public. La Fanfarlo dances like a man, for men. She
is Samuel's perfect match: masculine and feminine, actress onstage and
off; she is described as the antipodes of the romantic ballerina. La Fan-

farlo dances fiercely, wearing a saltimbanque costume, leaping, laughing, crying out to the *parterre*, accomplishing her feminine seduction with masculine bravado. Her body is neither masculine nor feminine, but both: the neck of a proconsul atop a curvaceous torso. Her fetishized leg, the object of Samuel's eternal desire, is such that "a man's real leg is too hard, and the women's legs drawn by Devéria are too soft, to give any idea of it." Her body represents the mélange of parts that makes a scandalous whole.[77]

Samuel identifies with the dancer's art via this hermaphrodite body; the dancer's art *is* her body; she is her own, and only, creation. Like the dancer, the dandy embodies his art; Samuel is one of those "demi-grands hommes" of *dandysme* who are themselves a better poem than they can write. But the dancer's other great attraction for the dandy is her doubleness, her artifice, her particular mix of contradictions. Expressing an aesthetic in his posture, his costume, his gestures, Baudelaire's dandy is also an actor; but by the end of the tale they have both become the established parents of a bourgeois household. They abandon the ideals of the dandy, the sterile artifice of self-creation and the poetry in which "the angels are hermaphrodite and sterile": Samuel for the labor of journalism and politics, and La Fanfarlo for the labor of sexual reproduction—"reproduction as love's vice, and pregnancy as a spider's malady."[78] Their descent into conservative conventionality reads as an ironic commentary on the artificer's lifestyle in general, and the impossibility of keeping it up.

An identification with the dancer like the dandy Samuel Cramer's with La Fanfarlo does not undo the objectifying power of the public's gaze on the dancer, but it does suggest the subtlety of its makeup, revealing an ironic subtext in the twin discourses of idealization and subjugation that surround the dancer of the 1840s. *La Fanfarlo* hints at an unexpected explanation for the fear of the feminine that lurks in the dance—beyond the fear of syphilis: it is male identification with the dancer (even if only on the part of dandy *amateurs*) that leads to the containment of the dancer's sexual threat—in this case, to what is described as the bourgeois confinement of motherhood. Although male identification with the dancer like Samuel's for La Fanfarlo blurs gender boundaries, it also attributes to the dancing female body the ability to transcend gender divisions. More than an impersonation of masculinity, La Fanfarlo's dance dramatizes the real physical prowess and sexual power typically associated with men. But male admiration for female dancers' gender flexibility is not unrelated to the regulatory gazes that attempt to define medically and constrain socially the deviance associated with dance in the era of *Giselle*.

The idea that the Wilis' dance kills—implicitly, through venereal disease—brings into *Giselle* the medical thinking operative in contemporary public health. Parent-Duchâtelet's pre-Pasteur medicine charts the likelihood of disease by relying on statistical evidence rather than bacteriological knowledge; his program for the registration and examination of prostitutes aims for the containment of contagion. The threat of contagion is to be combatted through a rigorous program of recognition relying on appearance as well as statistics. Visual recognition and acknowledgment play a large part in this life-and-death game with the Wilis of the streets of Paris whose sexual revenge, in the form of syphilis, could bring a man to madness and death.

Visual criteria remain uppermost in the syphilis diagnosis of this period: syphology is closely connected to dermatology through the end of the century. The disease is given away by its visible markers—chancres on the body—and deemed "cured" when, in what was later identified as syphilis's secondary stage, they disappear.[79] Brothel madams were experts in dissimulation of the disease's markers, using makeup and other means of masking infection; state doctors, overburdened with brothel visits, were less vigilant than Parent-Duchâtelet hoped. But after Philippe Ricord developed, beginning in 1838, a symptomatology for syphilis, it ceased to be the mysterious disease on which all kinds of afflictions were blamed by a medical science incapable of their cure.[80] Ricord's chronology of its symptoms and description of its characteristics—including the fact that it is impossible to catch a "double dose" of syphilis because it makes the patient resistant to a fresh dose—made syphilis less of a mystery. Yet the rates of syphilis infection rose with those of tuberculosis toward the century's end, and syphilis continued to be identified with madness in the theories of degeneration that became increasingly popular, in spite of progress in the understanding of syphilis infection and etiology.

The visibility of women in nineteenth-century Paris is closely connected to ideas about their sexuality or sexual availability. Visual codes governed in particular the practices of prostitution. Appearance was especially crucial for the midcentury courtesan who, according to Baudelaire, aped the dress and manners of the "honnêtes femmes." The only difference between the honest woman and the courtesan, Baudelaire argues, is distinction itself—a certain indescribable difference, the one that makes a difference. The prostitute can imitate the great lady, but she will never be the real thing. Baudelaire calls "presque rien" the artifice that separates the courtesan from the honest woman, the illusion of being what she is not: "this almost nothing, it is almost everything, it is distinction."[81]

Thus a complex program of seeming problematizes the appearance of women in nineteenth-century Paris and plays a role in cultural stereotypes of feminine sexuality. In the course of the century, two such stereotypes of women closely associated with the dancer and referred to in *Giselle*—the prostitute and the hysteric—are increasingly identified as the focus of investigating and regulating gazes. In Parent-Duchâtelet's 1836 study of prostitutes, the famous hygienist moved on, from Paris sewers, to consider the role of prostitution in the spread of disease and the role of visual criteria in the regulation of prostitution.

Despite the fact that more men carried syphilis than did women, its spread was deemed principally the result of unregulated prostitution.[82] By far the greatest risk of infection, according to Parent-Duchâtelet's statistics, was brought by the *insoumises*, those women practicing prostitution not only independently of a brothel but also undeclared to the police and thus uninspected by state physicians.[83] Since the clandestine prostitute was considered to pose the greatest risk, Parent-Duchâtelet's goal of recognition was instrumental to regulation.

Parent-Duchâtelet's ideal of prostitute recognition takes its place in a long-standing argument about the possibilities of regulation of prostitution. He argues at length against requiring a special costume or identification plaque for prostitutes; both because such measures had been found to be too difficult to enforce, and because they threatened the decorum of the street and the morality of the neighborhood. Parent-Duchâtelet's contradictory twin goals of prostitute recognition and prostitute invisibility, far from according the prostitute the individual liberty that he believes she has renounced any right to by her practice, recognize the impossibility of abolishing prostitution while attempting to limit its harm. On the one hand, not seeing prostitutes on the street is crucial to improving the city's moral character; but on the other, identification of casual prostitutes is necessary to halt the spread of venereal infection.

Parent-Duchâtelet's mission to gauge the risk of syphilis by identifying its sources indicates that the casual prostitute was less visible in 1836 Paris than after midcentury. In the second half of the century, Alain Corbin has noted, the public face of prostitution became increasingly visible in the visual culture "of what we call, somewhat inaccurately, Haussmannization."[84] The *police des moeurs* often based their arrests on purely visual criteria, and as a result, working-class women were frequently mistaken for prostitutes and arrested.[85] Prostitution, in its public form, entered a vogue of self-exhibition and theatrical self-presentation; the prostitute's visibility, like that of actresses, dancers, and singers, encourages both desire and competition:

> Never had so much been on show in the cities as in the second half of the century. There were exhibitions everywhere, and we know the role they played in relation to prostitution. The windows of the large department stores were themselves exhibitions. Paris had become "the city of food on offer." The prostitute in turn came to show and offer herself. All this explains the impression noted by all observers of an invasion of the street by prostitution, without anyone being too sure whether it was the result of an actual increase in numbers or of greater mobility and display. . . . The prostitute intended for the bourgeois male had also become woman as spectacle [*femme-spectacle*]. She paraded or exhibited herself on the terraces of the high-class cafés, in the brasseries, in the cafés-concerts and on the sidewalk. . . . It was then and in this way that the primacy of the visual in sexual solicitation originated. Such exhibition, more than anything else, expressed the failure of regulationism and at the same time gave rise to the fearful hyperregulationism already described.[86]

Crucial to the prostitute's visibility were not only an architecture and social milieu which now gave more space to public display, but also her built-in invisibility to those who would prefer not to, or ought not to, recognize her. To a degree, this development creates Parent-Duchâtelet's ideal prostitute—a woman whose availability would be instantly visible to men, but invisible to honest women and especially their daughters: "We will arrive at our goal of achieving the best that is possible in this manner, by obtaining that men and in particular those seeking [prostitutes] can distinguish them from honest women; but that these women and especially their daughters, cannot make such a distinction, or make it only with difficulty."[87]

Parent-Duchâtelet's theory declares, in effect, that what makes the prostitute recognizable to potential clients is *her* recognition of them—that is to say, her open or inviting look, her complicity with the male client's gaze. Ideally for Parent-Duchâtelet, the honest woman's gaze would be so uninformed by a life of not looking that she would be unable to see—to recognize—a prostitute in the street. The prostitute is, by definition here, a woman who looks back: the *femme-spectacle* is not only an observed object, but an observing subject.

Isn't the dancer also a woman looking back, complicitous with the male public's gaze on her? Gautier's critique of Manet's 1863 *Olympia* denies any connection between dancers and the infamous courtesan with her confronting stare. Gautier was personally involved in the art criticism that created the *Olympia* scandal. For him, the problem with the painting was its confrontation of the question of "seeing":

In the eyes of many, it would be sufficient to walk by and laugh; this is a mistake. Monsieur Manet is not unimportant; he has a school, admirers, even fanatics; his influence reaches further than we think. Monsieur Manet has the honor of being dangerous. The danger is now over. Olympia cannot be understood from any point of view, even if we take her just as she is, a worthless model stretched out on a sheet. . . . We would even excuse the ugliness if it were real, studied, heightened by some splendid coloring technique. Here, we are angry to say, there is nothing but the will to draw attention at any cost.[88]

In his discussion of *Olympia*, T. J. Clark has argued that the courtesan was the most visible or representable part of midcentury prostitution, and that in this painting she represents not only prostitution, the meeting point of money and sex, but nakedness itself.[89] Because, for Clark, the body of Manet's Olympia is the terrain on which class war is fought, because the body represented here is accessible, for sale, it can no longer be the glorified nude of classical painting. No longer contained in an idealized, painted space, the nude confronts the gaze of the public with her own painfully direct gaze. Olympia acknowledges her nakedness in the face of her clothed spectators.

But whose "will to draw attention at any cost" is Gautier condemning? Manet's? *Olympia*'s? Or Olympia's? Issuing from a former art revolutionary and defender of Manet, Gautier's anger is ironic, but it is important here because it is directed not only at Manet, but at the work itself, or more precisely, at the woman depicted in it. His critique collapses the work of art onto the woman it represents, confuses the perspective of the painting and the painter—as if they were necessarily the same—with the perspective of its subject. Gautier disapproves of the painting in the way he disapproves of its subject, in what he perceives as her desire to draw all eyes, in her confrontation of the public gaze, not only defining herself as subject by that gaze, but also announcing herself as the object of that gaze. It is this acknowledged subjectivity-as-object that seems so to offend Gautier's sensibility.

Is Olympia's "will to draw attention at any cost" so different from Giselle's? The hand that has moved to cover Olympia's sex while the rest of her body remains revealed, belies the gesture of the ballerina who is all modesty at the same time that she is all display; whose modesty, therefore, depends on her total inattention to or denial of her own body. Furthermore, the face of Olympia turned toward what Clark identifies as her potential market of consumers—her clients, her painter, or the viewers who stand in their place—offends the *amateur* of the dance. In the ballet, the female figure appears to offer herself to some distant abstract notion of Art, though she may also be offering herself to the real economic power of those present.

Despite its tone, it is difficult to read Gautier's critique as the kind of critical *pudibonderie* he had so vituperously ridiculed in the preface to *Mademoiselle de Maupin* thirty years earlier. Rather, his complaint is framed in aesthetic terms; he finds the painting, like its subject, not merely ugly, but pointless. Olympia is scandalous in Gautier's eyes not simply because she wants to draw eyes at any cost, but because she seems to understand that she is nothing but the eyes trained on her.[90] On the contrary, Georges Bataille's reading of *Olympia* finds in the painting's "nothingness" that directness of vision that Gautier had earlier on called half of genius ("Voir, c'est la moitié du génie").[91] Bataille writes of *Olympia*: "The harsh realism that the Salon visitors considered the ugliness of the 'gorilla,' is for us the painter's concern with reducing *what he saw* to the gaping simplicity of *what he saw*."[92] What Gautier calls the emptiness of the will to attract attention at any cost, Bataille calls Manet's simple, straightforward desire to paint what he saw: "He wanted this painting to be clear, he wanted the transparency 'that he saw.'"

Gautier is criticizing in Manet's work the very kind of seeing that Mallarmé praised Gautier himself for: "the mysterious gift of seeing with the eyes (remove mysterious) [le don mystérieux de voir avec les yeux (ôtez mystérieux)]." For Mallarmé, Gautier's gift was radical for his time: he was "the seer who, put in this world, looked at it, which one does not do" [le voyant, qui, placé dans ce monde, l'a regardé, ce que l'on ne fait pas].[93] Baudelaire's description of Gautier's uncanny vision also insists on his bent toward extro-spection rather than introspection: "It is a curious thing how much this man who knows how to express everything and who has more than any other the right to be blasé, has a natural curiosity and pierces with his sharp gaze the *not-I*" [C'est chose curieuse combien cet homme qui sait tout exprimer et qui a plus que tout autre le droit d'être blasé, a la curiosité facile et darde vivement son regard sur le *non-moi*]."[94]

At first glance, the quality of Olympia's gaze, which gives her the status of an object in Gautier's eyes, is comparable to the dancer's; though she is not a representation but a living subject, certain conditions of her performance at the Opéra create a climate in which her subjectivity is denied. But by appearing to return the gaze of a public she cannot see, the dancer maintains not only an economic but a poetic power, an aura, as she hovers between subjectivity and objectivity. The public appreciation of this aura depends upon the uniqueness and inaccessibility of her image in the field of opera glasses at the same time that her image is repeatedly reproduced in pair after pair of them.

It depends also on the uninterrupted space of the stage, the border separating spectator and dancer, which may be crossed before or after but never during the performance, except in the field of vision. Theatrical lighting, even in the time of gaslight stage lights and a well-lit house, would make it nearly impossible for the performer standing in the light to recognize specific members of the audience. Lit from the front of the stage, as well as from the side or above, the dancer would be effectively blinded to the forms beyond the footlights. Although the seating created by Véron in the *avant-scènes* at the Opéra in the Rue Le Peletier brought the spectators very near to the stage, it is unlikely that any dancer at the Opéra would have been able to locate someone in the audience unless she did not have to dance at all. Thus, while complicitous with the dandy's scrutiny, at least in some cases, the ultimate effect of theater practice, if not social practice, at the Opéra was to keep the dancer distant.

This highly charged distance is responsible for the creation and experience of the dancer's aura. Walter Benjamin finds this idea in Baudelaire: "Baudelaire insists on the magic of distance. . . . Does he mean the magic of distance to be pierced, as must needs happen when the spectator steps too close to the depicted scene? This is embodied in one of the great verses of the *Fleurs du Mal*: 'Le Plaisir vaporeux fuira vers l'horizon / Ainsi qu'une sylphide au fond de la coulisse [Vaporous pleasure flees toward the horizon / Like a sylphide slipping away backstage].'" In Benjamin's well-known definition, the aura of the work of art, "which withers in the age of mechanical reproduction,"[95] depends on transposing onto the work of art the human ability to return a gaze:

Looking at someone carries the implicit expectation that our look will be returned by the object of our gaze. Where this expectation is met (which, in the

Fig. 11. "Le binocle des coulisses" (The backstage binocular). Collection of the Bibliothèque Nationale de France.

case of thought processes, can apply equally to the look of the eye of the mind and to a glance pure and simple), there is an experience of the aura to the fullest extent. . . . Experience of the aura thus rests on the transposition of a response common in human relationships to the relationship between the inanimate or natural object and man. The person we look at, or who feels he is being looked at, looks at us in turn. To perceive the aura of an object we look at means to invest it with the ability to look at us in return.[96]

The dancer's aura depends upon her audience's perception of her as a woman looking back, and she helps to create that aura by seeming to see her audience.[97] But it is less likely that the dancer at the Paris Opéra in the 1840s really saw anyone in particular than that she gave the impression of doing so, with what might be assimilated to Benjamin's "look of the eye of the mind." Her ability to see her audience was limited by technicalities of production and performance; the dandy's experience of the dancer's aura depended on staging and lighting that in fact prevented her from returning his gaze. The dancer is a woman who can look back at her audience, while maintaining the distance that valorizes her work, moving between the seeing subject and the blinded object. Her ability to look back types the dancer as complicit in her own prostitution; not seeing types her as the victim of her audience. But the dancer's identity, framed by these two limits, takes shape in her movement between them.

For the "*rats*" of the *corps de ballet*, a kind of social freedom, however slight, can be enjoyed in this movement; in performance, however briefly, and however tenuously, they use their institutional framework and manipulate their audience to advantage. First, bringing to bear her offstage knowledge or experience, her understanding of where to look and how to look to convey a particular impression, the dancer manipulates her audience's gaze while in collusion with it. Opéra dancers onstage did often know toward which particular box, or in which particular direction, to turn their gaze. They were in fact able to verify, offstage, who was in the audience, and—according to some accounts—to communicate with them. This was the function assigned to two tiny windows from the *coulisses* out into the house, windows through which the dancers are said to have signaled complicated messages to members of the audience by a simple sign language. Second describes these two windows, known as "le binocle des coulisses," where

each evening, they engaged in a sign language of the deaf and dumb using these innocent apertures, a very telegraphic language, and yet quite explicit nevertheless. There are simple finger movements, perfectly understood by the Oedipuses in the orchestra or balcony seats, that signify: "Wait for me in the dark passage-way" or "It is impossible for me to have dinner with you."[98]

These windows serve a crucial dual purpose: using them as "binoculars," dancers could enjoy, like members of the audience, the power of seeing without being seen; using them to signal audience members, they established themselves as individuals with the power to communicate outside of the actual performance.

The gaze of the dancer onstage, then, is only a part of the economy of gazes exchanged at the Opéra; and it is a referential gesture. The audience member armed with opera glasses can perhaps assure himself that a dancer is looking at him. But she can, depending upon her place on stage, the angle of her head, and the direction of her gaze, give that impression of uniqueness to many spectators. Her gaze gives her an economic power, serving as a kind of guarantee for the spectator that he is directly involved with her, that he is an acknowledged, active part of the action onstage as well as its passive consumer. The dancer's actual inability to see, behind the lights highlighting and blinding her, serves to assure the spectator his privacy and his power; yet it also guarantees her own power as an artist working within the proscenium frame, establishing a subjectivity in the stage lights. Both styles of dancing which reigned at the Opéra in the 1840s paid particular attention to the power of the dancer's gaze: the tradition of Vestris who urged his pupils to seduce their audience, and the school of Taglioni *père* who taught that women and girls in the audience should be able to look at the dance without blushing.[99] Though the two styles are quite different, both invest the dancer with tremendous power, and both base the dancer's power on the creation of an illusion that the dancer is offering herself up—whether it be to the gaze of an eager audience or to the dictates of Art.

It is thus not only a dancer's real ability to look back at her audience, but also her ability to internalize the audience's gaze, that shapes her subjectivity as a performing artist who both depends on the audience and transcends it. This gaze is a built-in effect of performance and of performers' self-perception in classical ballet, a kind of third eye. The ballet emphasizes not only dramatic interpretation—the expression of inner emotion—but also precise positioning and execution, the satisfaction of an external visual standard. In ballet performance, the audience sits in the place of the dancer's mirror. Performance demands that the dancer divide herself in two: while dancing her role from the inside out, she must simultaneously see it from the outside in. When giving instructions to their female students, the ballet masters Vestris and Taglioni *père* do not simply tell the dancers what to do; they tell them how it should look from the audience's point of view. In the romantic ballet, even today, the ballerina is taught at every step to keep in mind how she looks in her audience's eyes.

The ballerina's autonomy, then, depends upon the idea of an audience perhaps even more than the audience itself. Even when rehearsing without an audience, the ballerina's inner eye—the "eye of the mind"—replaces their gaze. In this sense, the romantic ballerina's internalized gaze may be linked, via ballet's development from the court masques and baroque ballets, to the gaze of an idealized spectator, the king. The architectural and social structures of the Paris Opéra of this period illustrate how the ballerina's audience is made up of two components: people she does not know, and people she does; or put another way, the audience members she "sees" or knows are there, and those whom she does not. The mixed nature of this public gaze—coming from both known and unknown people, in a way both embodied and disembodied—or the way the Opéra dancer works with it, gives her a relative, if fragile, freedom. The Opéra dancer can achieve some independence and power onstage, simultaneously submitting to the Opéra's socially, physically, and artistically repressive structures and using performance to rise above them.

The inner eye created as an effect of ballet performance gives the ballerina an integrity or identity that results from her own satisfaction in performing. More than the sign of slavish submission to the institution, this "inner eye" is constitutive of the dancer's pleasure despite the sweat, blood, and poverty associated with her work. This internalization of the gaze prevents the dance from being nothing more than masochistic subjection to public taste or institutional discipline. Though limited to the temporal and spatial constraints of performance, and defined by the institutional, choreographic, architectural, and social structures of the theater, performance creates what might be called dancers' *jouissance*.[100]

The theatrical structures in place at the Opéra effectively deny dancers' hardship without really concealing it. Dance performance by its very nature recognizes such doubleness: without hiding the work, or the discipline, that makes it possible, dance presents it as something else. The work that goes into the creation of danced illusion is not seen as work, but as pleasure, overlapping the work and inseparable from it. The dancer's pain is used to transform the "inexpressible" into the "inexprimable," the socially significant body into art; the body is not only a means of expression, but the subject of expression itself. If an audience can see only the pleasure of dance, failing to acknowledge pain as part of the process, it is because the production of dance merges pain and pleasure in its visual images, playing out a doubleness the audience cannot see.

Twenty years after *Giselle*, Gautier's response to *Olympia* makes explicit the criticism of the dancer implicit in his ballet; compared to *Giselle*, Gautier's critique of *Olympia* reads like a slip of the tongue. The point of view of the text of *Giselle* is complicitous with an objectifying public gaze, with behind-the-scenes socioeconomic factors that make the dancer into an object. The dance served Gautier not simply as a way to bring poetry to life, as a visual image of resurrection or incarnation, but as a way to present the female form, and thus femininity, as visually constructed and visibly readable.

In this sense, the dance performance, making Gautier's thought visible, brings to light what was suppressed or repressed in his dance text. He used the medium to stage what he could not say about feminine sexuality. But his belief in the ability to say everything by showing, to verbalize by visualizing, outstripped his own ability to show or tell all, as well as that of the romantic ballet or ballerina. The ballet's enigmatic doubleness offered Gautier visual images for poetry, and an image for these images, but the significance of this ballet eclipses its literary ambition just as it eclipses purely visual definition. Everything cannot be seen in the dance because, in Gautier's own words, seeing takes long study, and it is only half the picture: "Il faut une longue étude pour apprendre à voir. Voir, c'est la moitié du génie."[101] And finally, though dancing hides nothing, what can be seen is at most only half of dancing.

Gautier's insistence that there is nothing the writer cannot express depends on his recourse to the dancer to express with her body what the libretto encodes. What cannot be said, Gautier believes, can be seen in the dance—as if everything can be seen in the dance. The ballet *does* what the libretto of *Giselle* can only say; but does it do what the libretto cannot say? In these pages, the ballet's tension between psychic freedom of expression and material subjection has been studied within the confines of the Opéra and the gaze of the Opéra public. What cannot be seen, in the romantic ballet, is the working of its illusion:[102] the tights that make the dancer's flesh more visible while hiding it; the skirts that seductively conceal the dancer's sex while drawing attention to it; the pleasure of performance which eclipses the work yet is produced by it. Nor does the public see, as such, the creative discipline that separates the dancer's work from hysteria and prostitution. What is not seen is what the dancer is repressing, the very fact that she *is* repressing; that the tremendous freedom of the dance is produced by a disciplined body.[103] In its overlapping of visible and invisible elements, pleasure and pain, discipline and freedom, the ballet represents repression. In nineteenth-century Paris's intensely visual culture of display in the social, economic, and artistic domains—a culture with complex codes of appearance actively informing everything from prostitution to shopping—dance functions as a locus of censure and discipline, symptomatic of that culture's urges and shortfalls.

Gautier the author of ballets is considered to be one of the fathers of the ballet without words; he is said to have announced "the age of purely ocular entertainments."[104] Yet the gaze turned toward the *femme-spectacle* is not purely ocular. The idealization of the dancer is always an image created by the eye of the beholder, an eye that sees more than it admits, and yet sees only half of what the dancer is doing, missing the dancer's subjective experience.

   Giselle does show and tell about feminine sexuality, even to a public reluctant to see, or pretending not to see. But the aspect of feminine sexuality it presents is all show, visually constructed, seen in the ballerina's movements as if she were the *femme-spectacle*, hysteric or prostitute. The romantic ballet, in Gautier's written version, goes only so far, and no further. The text does not critique the idea of feminine sexuality, deviance, or madness as readable on the body. It stops short at his notion of seeing and saying, suppressing its ultimate failure to do so. With critical perspective, in retrospect, we can see that the romantic ballet can and does take its audience further, beyond the power relations implicated in the visual realm.[105]

   The dancer moves back and forth between labor and illusion. She plays a role in a dramatic representation, a staged allegory, while presenting her body in a direct and literal way.[106] Dividing these qualities between two separate bodies, Baudelaire calls "almost nothing" the artifice that separates the courtesan from the honest woman, the illusion of being what she is not.[107] It is the same "almost nothing" which allows critics, poets, and public alike not to acknowledge a difference between what the dancer is and what she appears to be, between the materiality of her labor and the psychic component of her illusion: the distinction that creates illusion itself.

   The configuration of visual experience at the Paris Opéra in 1841 lends itself to multiple critical approaches and absorbs different kinds of explanations: from what we know, dance performances there seemed to merge the elements of pleasure, power, and pain that critical approaches separate out in their analyses. In one reading developed here, the difference between the dancer's physical reality and the illusion created by her performance can be located within the social and economic operations of her commodification: the dancer creates an image of femininity effected for and by the public gaze. In another, the dancer manages to shape a subjectivity in the public eye that escapes, in some crucial ways, the confines of the contemporary social order and social determination of gender. But it becomes impossible to separate the materiality of the performance and its means of production from the unconscious elements of its creation and reception. If the romantic ballerina represents some freedom of expression, it is a victory over economic and social forces. Social and economic history suggest that she is not free; yet whatever freedom she attains comes both in and through the public's gaze, in the field of the very forces that contain her.

The tension between physical and psychological aspects of dance, as well as their role in its interpretation, makes it an important terrain for debates that oppose materialist and psychoanalytic feminisms. Jacqueline Rose has described these as debates in which Marxist feminisms critique a psychoanalysis defined by its exclusively theoretical concerns and application; and psychoanalytic feminisms critique a Marxist feminist conception of a socially constructed sexual identity, defined as lacking a concept of the unconscious.[108] The dance's interest for this debate lies not only in the fact that it seems to welcome and withstand both kinds of readings, but in the unique way in which empirical and psychic elements are merged in dance performance.

Rose has argued, on the psychoanalytic side, that questions of sexual identity can only be addressed via the unconscious, and that Marxist explanations founder by considering feminine sexuality "a fully social classification relying on empirical evidence for its rationale."[109] The role of psychoanalysis, writes Rose, has been from its inception by Freud a rejection of Charcot's conclusion that woman's psychic condition can be read on her body, that the visible, empirical evidence tells the whole truth of what goes on inside. The concept of the unconscious is "Freud's challenge to the visible, to the empirically self-evident, to the 'blindness of the seeing eye.'"[110] In the same way, "feminism has always challenged the observable givens of women's qualities and social position."[111]

In the case of the romantic ballet, this challenge to the "observable givens" works both ways. On one hand, it can counter the criticism of the period which reduced the dance to mere exhibitionism, a calculated and superficial seduction, by pointing out that the ballet had an unseen artistic intent or content beyond the visible parameters to which its audience often reduced it. On the other hand, discounting the "observable givens" of the performance means discounting the artistry of its visual illusion and reducing it to physical labor. The visual aspect of the dance tells only half the story; a dichotomy between the visible and invisible elements of the dance cannot be neatly fitted onto a dichotomy between physical and psychic factors, as both are always at work in what the audience sees and does not see. Both a materialist and a psychoanalytic reading of the romantic ballet would challenge the idea that the dance event can be analyzed purely in terms of its visible elements; each reading is interested in what cannot be seen in it—the physical, social, or psychic structures that lie behind the illusion.

It is clear from this formulation that the dance event is complicated by the dancer's movement in a visual field shaped both by empirical and by psychoanalytic factors, and that the visual aspect of the dance is both a physical reality and an illusion which is no less physical, and no less real. The illusion of the romantic ballet rests on the grinding wheels of its reality, an illusion and a reality perhaps best illustrated by the dancer's legs: the illusion of the long, elegant lines of their turn-out achieved by daily, grueling, submission to the turn-out box, which forced feet and knees into the required baroque positions.[112] And yet at its best the machinery of dance is divine; the way in which that reality contradicts and creates the dance illusion is what makes the theoretical or ideological implications of that illusion so powerful. Blinded and looking back, victimized and championed, signaling from the "binocle" like the mute in the melodrama, and moving beyond language onstage, it is precisely the dancer's doubleness that makes her so historically powerful and her performance so theoretically complex.

Expressing both the submission to the institution and the ability—however briefly—to forge a subjectivity out of it, the dance demonstrates how repression works through what Freud calls, early on, "splitting of the mind" or "double conscience."[113] The nineteenth-century romantic ballet asks, and enacts, important theoretical questions: about the subject of creation, the body's meanings and its somatic metaphors, the theatricality of gender, the relation between madness and art, repression and expression. Closely examined, the romantic ballet renders two very different readings; their coexistence suggests not only the theoretical richness of the dance but an alternative to the model of unity that has been projected onto it. By presenting and representing simultaneously, this dance performance demonstrates the simultaneity—and not the unity—of oppositions. It goes beyond the romantic unity from opposites to show the very divisive splitting that makes both art and artists, that makes subjectivity itself. In this way the nineteenth-century dancer gives expression to the very inexpressible splitting that repression creates.

Unraveling the dancer's constructed unity reveals a doubleness at the core of the dance that is responsible for the genre's fascination. The duplicity of transformation or disguise that is standard in romantic ballet plots is a metaphor for performance itself. *Giselle*'s simple story of duplicity, ultimately the story of the dancer's own doubled existence, also relates a tale of madness—metaphorized as a passion for dancing. Telling a story while refusing to tell, hiding nothing and yet enigmatically never revealing everything, dance's doubleness depends on the complex visuality of its silent language. Though the romantic ballet's illusions are metaphoric or literary—with dancers playing roles, pretending to be something or someone they are not—later nineteenth-century dance in Paris will focus more on the nature of that illusion without metaphors or role-playing, and will emphasize its closeness to some forms of madness.

The overlapping or doubling of two very different kinds of things in romantic ballet—what might be described as the simultaneity or imbrication of "empirical" factors and the "psychic" experience of performance—complicate its visuality. An important part of the dance remains unseen, allowing the dancer some freedom of expression and the ability to shape a subjectivity, however briefly or tenuously, as an artist in the public eye. The crucial element of the dance that escapes visibility is precisely its doubleness: the romantic dancer has been misunderstood as an image of poetic or "primordial" unity.[114] Beyond this imposed or constructed unity, the dancer represents something more than a two-sided male fantasy, some freedom within a constrained institutional framework and the visual market of desire. Coexisting with the empirical facts of her disciplining at the Opéra, there is something more, the illustration of the strange process of self-expression.

This elusive something more can be found perhaps most tellingly in *Giselle*'s mad scene, the moment in the choreography when the prima ballerina has more freedom of expression, when she escapes complete choreographic control and thus mimes a transcendence of the institution and the controlled production of the ballet's images of beauty. Even when closely choreographed, the scene leaves the dancer room for a unique development of her character. By dancing the madness that comes from "dancing too much," the performer self-referentially comments on her own discipline and its link with hysteria. The mad scene dramatizes the link between madness and theatricality, suggested both by the traditional dances of possession, like the St. Vitus dance, and by the contemporary medical description of certain hysterias as "dancelike" *chorées* (choreas), a medical term in use since Sydenham. Yet while dramatizing the visual resemblance between some forms of dance and some forms of madness, what the mad scene makes clear is the repression that the dancer herself must employ in order to perform it. The mad scene gives expression to that repression itself, simultaneously showing how visually close madness is to dance and how far the dancer is from madness in her representation, how far her spectacle is from deviance.

Giselle's mad scene represents the violent eruption of the repressed: the character of Giselle is shattered, the ballet's romantic unity is unraveled into its component parts, and this unraveling of character and genre is staged as the breakdown of dance itself. In its history, *Giselle's* mad scene has been both danced and mimed, played with great violence and with fragile subtlety. What kills Giselle remains a mystery, as does the nature of her madness. Two different versions of Giselle's death were generated by Gautier in 1841: although the libretto has her die of "a broken heart" following on the heels of her fit of madness, Gautier's letter to Heine dated a few days after the opening describes Giselle toying with Albrecht's sword and dying on its point.[115] Despite the obvious eroticism of a death by her lover's sword, and its usefulness as an explanation, the libretto version offers a greater breadth of interpretation in performance, and it is the version that has entered the repertory, enriched by its many performers throughout the decades. Giselle's moment of madness is the crucial pivot necessary to make sense of the second act's "dead bacchantes": the passion of revenge is kindled in the folly that follows betrayal; the mad scene—representing women's weak hearts—is about the transition from woman to Wili. By leaving Giselle's death a mystery, the libretto builds a freedom of interpretation into the scene.[116]

This freedom of interpretation reflects medicine's own shifting interpretations of mental illness contemporary with *Giselle*. The inexplicability of Giselle's madness serves as timely commentary on hysteria's elusiveness to the medical profession. The uncertainty over what kills Giselle reflects contemporary debates over the locus and etiology of hysteria that took place in the French Académie de Médecine in the decades preceding and following *Giselle's* premiere. Mark Micale has discussed Baudelaire's "*Madame Bovary* par Gustave Flaubert" in *L'art romantique*, which refers to

a controversy that raged within the Parisian medical community during the 1830s and 1840s over the exact anatomical site of hysteria, a battle in which gynecological, neurological and cerebral interpretations clashed. In 1845, the Academy posed the question of the nature and origins of hysteria in a formal academic *concours*. . . . Baudelaire's citation of the *boule* as "the chief symptom" of female hysteria probably refers to Brachet's winning essay, later expanded into *Traité de l'hystérie* (1847) in which the sensation of the esophagean ball appears as the defining mark of the disorder.

Landouzy's uterine theory also shared the prize that year. For Baudelaire, Micale notes, this symptom occurring in women would express itself in "excitable" men by every kind of impotence as well as by a tendency toward every type of excess.[117]

Because it can be identified with prostitution and venereal disease, the Wilis' madness falls into the category in which hysteria's symptoms and causes were confused with those of syphilis: by the end of the century, both diseases were considered neurodegenerative, perhaps with etiological links. Syphilis is cited as provoking hysterical attacks; hysteria as incipient venereal disease; and syphilis the result of hysterically promiscuous behavior. Reflecting this confusion, a new term "hystero-syphilis" was coined by M. Hudeyo in 1892.[118]

But Giselle's madness is of a different stripe. *Giselle's* theme of love as a kind of madness, a form of possession, can find an analogue in one medical tradition of hysteria as connected to sexual desire in widows and young girls in search of husbands. Her vague and abstract nervous condition also makes reference to a tradition in which the ardent passion that typifies hysteria is thought to be linked to the phenomenon of excess internal heat causing convulsions throughout the body.[119]

The ballet describes Giselle's dancing as a kind of folly, and represents madness as dancing gone haywire; but significantly, madness functions not only as illness but also as a kind of expression beyond limit. *Giselle* has endured because it tells a story of troubling psychological depth that reflects both of these cultural stereotypes. Giselle's mad scene is danced on the shaky ground of idiopathic illness, the terrain that the medical science of the nineteenth century came to survey.

Penned by a prolific and influential author, a tremendous success in its time, and a cornerstone of the classical ballet repertory, *Giselle* serves as a good case study because it is particularly well documented. *Giselle* is, above all, a ballet about ballet: the leading character has become a signature role for the romantic ballerina in the way that Hamlet is the archetypal role for modern actors, and her destructive passion for dancing, like Hamlet's "antic disposition," stages the timeless confusion of madness and performance. In order to get at the kind of freedom of expression that performing madness can produce, it is necessary to interrogate the performer's experience of the role. Yet the wealth of textual, biographical, and archival materials surrounding the ballet and the role tell us very little about the subjectivity established by a dancer dancing it. To understand what the role of Giselle might have felt like from the inside out, to draw a psychological profile of the role and the subjective experience of its performers, we have to rely on more recent accounts.

Reflecting on Giselle, ballerina Violet Verdy describes it as an all-consuming role that can take a lifetime to work through:

I never prepared anything in my whole life as much as I did Giselle. It's a role that grows with you, opening up new aspects at every stage of your career and your own personal development. It's also a role that poses enormous technical and dramatic challenges; how you rise to these challenges at different stages of your life adds of course to the fascination of Giselle, both for the dancer and for the audience.

I have danced most of the classic heroines, including the Swan Queen and the Sleeping Beauty. But Giselle is special: it gives you the chance literally to give all of yourself and by the same token to discover how much you have to offer—in terms of the disappointments as well as the successes. Giselle gives you a chance to explore all your capacities; you have to be a complete dancer and a complete person.[120]

For Verdy, Giselle requires a complete erasure of self and a total psychological identification with the character that takes the form of self-discovery: "I cannot work on Giselle without going right back to the very beginning each time I dance it. I have to start out again—completely. To try to recapture her youth, her spirit, her freshness, her innocence, her belief, her aspiration, her joy; I am *forced*, with the character that I represent, to begin anew."[121]

Within the ballet's long tradition, each performer has had to work to interpret the role. Although dancers learn from other dancers as examples, and from great teachers,

when the moment of truth comes for yourself [as a performer] you can no more imitate those examples outright than you could slip into someone else's skin. You must go back to the *why* as well as the *how*. What did they go through, those performers, in order to do what you saw there on the stage? That gesture—what did they do to find it? That's where you go right back to the beginning and analyze—as I have said, start from scratch. . . . For content cannot be imitated; it must be understood. In spite of those moments of adoration, therefore, or even the occasional discouragement (well, it's been done, why should anyone bother?), the dancer must always come back to herself and the process of self-discovery; only in this way is it possible to build a role.[122]

In order to accomplish this rediscovery of self as the character of Giselle, the dancer must interpret Giselle's motivation. Verdy argues that the motivating force is Giselle's great love:

Then there is the essential quality, which so many dancers forget in Giselle, and which is love: such a powerful determinant in the first act—for if Giselle is not truly mad with love, how can one be transported and interested, above all, moved? Moreover, if a dancer forgets, in the realistic first act, that Giselle has found a great love, how can she successfully convey that feeling with clarity (and with even greater strength and profundity) amid the paradoxical abstractions of the second act?

Although Verdy sees this love tying together *Giselle*'s two acts, she insists on a schism between them, and remarks on the difficulty this poses for performance:

For those undertaking the role of Giselle, perhaps the most important aspect to be developed is the contrast between the two acts—between the directness, the wonderful joyousness of the first act, and the Romantic lithograph effects of the second act. In Act I, you dance with your whole body, with all the blood going. There are no inhibitions; the action is open, direct, and explicit. . . . Only [the inhibitions] of a "nun" offering herself to God, the inhibitions you expect in a Romantic heroine. . . . How then does the dancer reconcile these two acts which are almost separate ballets? Here both poet and choreographer provide a thread of continuity; it is the love of Giselle for Albrecht.[123]

Although Verdy understands Giselle's transformation as motivated by her love for a man, she describes a different tradition of Giselle interpretation revived by Yvette Chauviré: "one of the first French ballerinas to re-vive another tradition—that of the dedicated dancer who is almost a nun, wedded to her vocation."[124] The passion that motivates the dancing of Act I becomes the religious self-sacrificing love of Act II, in which dance and "love" merge in saintly "vocation." This is the Taglioni tradition of the dancer-as-nun, the kind of dancing Gautier described as "Christian."

Pierre Legendre has distinguished the love that the ballet stages from the simple love story within it: "What is important in *Giselle*, for example, is not the story of a crazy love and a dead fiancée, even less the way the plot conforms to the infallible recipe for romantic ballets; it is the way it undertakes to bring to the stage and to enshrine the word of love in the purest manner."[125] Although the disembodied love represented by Giselle in Act II certainly played to the audience on the level of eros ("These dead bacchantes are irresistible," as Gautier wrote to Heine), the second act has, over time, done more than market sex as otherworldliness.

Act II might be read as dramatizing that satisfaction of performance that leads ballerinas to describe their work as a "vocation." This notion of the dance as a calling reconnects the dancing "madness" to the religious possession of earlier ages. The dancer's fulfillment in dance's strange blend of pain and pleasure, discipline and freedom, depends upon that "inner eye" described by the coaching of ballet masters in the period of *Giselle*. This transcendence of the intersubjective looking at the Opéra, and the dancer's satisfaction in the "gaze," can be analogized to what Jacques Lacan calls *jouissance*; a pleasure "beyond the phallus" or "a different satisfaction" which approaches a Christian notion of God or of a divine love that Lacan calls *l'âmour*, or soul-love.[126] This is a love without object, or beyond the realm of the object: "this desire for good in the second degree, a good that is not brought about by a small *a* [object] [ce désir d'un bien au second degré, un bien qui n'est pas causé par un petit *a*]."[127] This *jouissance* is best represented, Lacan believes, by mystics like Teresa of Avila. Though it may look like passion, for example, in the statue of Teresa by Bernini, this *âmour* without object cannot explain itself. Mystics who experience this love can say nothing about it.[128]

The religious terms in which Gautier and Verdy describe one tradition of Giselle interpretation suggest that the "other satisfaction" Lacan ascribes to mystical possession is also a way to describe the dancer's experience. If hysterics become more frequently described as performers in medical writing of the second half of the nineteenth century, it is undoubtedly also because of this link between dancing and possession, a topic that Charcot and Richer will pursue in their *Les Démoniaques dans l'art*. Lacan sees Charcot and Freud misreading nineteenth-century mysticism as sexual perversion, attempting to "reduce mysticism to a matter of sex [ramener la mystique à des affaires de foutre]."[129]

In Lacan's view, then, mystics become hysterics in a culture in which the alienist becomes more and more powerful. Charcot's understanding of hysteria was a complex mix of social, religious, medical, and scientific thinking. Against the background of the professionalization of medicine, its adoption of laboratory science, medicine's reevaluation of madness affects the production and reception of dance forms as it recombines social and scientific approaches to the body and the mind.

If the mad scene of *Giselle* opened the door a tiny crack to let the romantic ballerina out of her institutional double-bind, it aptly dramatized the dancer's precarious position in the romantic ballet. Called upon to dance the deviant, the hysteric, the prostitute that the public imagined her to be, the dancer's only escape was precisely through acting out this role. Her dancing acknowledges the audience's repression projected onto her, and it dramatizes the cultural conception of the visual resemblance between dance and some forms of madness. *Giselle*'s mad scene opened the door as well onto an idiopathic understanding of madness: still performative, still resembling dance, but with no visible cause.

The modern dance considered in the next chapter takes a tremendous stride out the door that I have described as just barely opening in *Giselle*'s mad scene; a step away from institutionalized choreography to greater individuality of interpretation, with a broader scope of imagery coming from and defining the female body. With this step, dance performance moves toward addressing more openly and more precisely the link between dancing and some forms of madness. Though many other modern dance innovations of the late nineteenth and early twentieth century—many, but not all, developed by women[130]—deserve attention, the dance of one choreographer, theorized by one writer, will respond directly to the issues of repression and hysteria raised in *Giselle*. These issues acquire greater social and medical interest in the last two decades of the century, as another form of medicine takes center stage in the interpretation of bodily behaviors.

CHAPTER 3

The "Symptomatic Act": Mallarmé, Charcot, and Loie Fuller

In *Crayonné au théâtre*, a collection of theater reviews and reflections written mostly during the 1880s and 1890s, Stéphane Mallarmé describes Gautier at the vaudeville as a displeased spectator who is blinded by his opera glasses but unwilling to put them down:

> Facing the immediate and frantic triumph of the monster Mediocrity who paraded in the divine site, I love Gautier applying to his weary gaze the black opera glass as if in a kind of willful blindness and saying "*it is such an uncouth art . . . so abject*" before the curtain; but since he never would annul his viewing prerogatives because of disgust, his verdict was more ironic: "*there should be only one vaudeville—they could make a few changes from time to time.*"

> Mis devant le triomphe immédiat et forcené du monstre ou Médiocrité qui parada au lieu divin, j'aime Gautier appliquant à son regard las la noire jumelle comme une volontaire cécité et "*C'est un art si grossier ... si abject*," exprimait-il, devant le rideau; mais comme il ne lui appartenait point, à cause d'un dégoût, d'annuler chez soi des prérogatives du voyant, ce fut encore, ironique, la sentence: "*Il ne devrait y avoir qu'un vaudeville—on ferait quelques changements de temps en temps.*"[1]

Gautier's jaded view that all vaudevilles are alike in their banality is held by Mallarmé to be true for almost all theater. With notable exceptions, Mallarmé finds the theater unbearable, and yet he continued to go. For Mallarmé, the problem with the contemporary theater is not only one of monstrous mediocrity invading the "lieu divin," but a larger problem of spectatorship. A first reading of the texts collected in *Crayonné au Théâtre* suggests that Mallarmé wishes to locate himself in the tradition of writer-spectators like Gautier; for Mallarmé, going to the theater and writing about it would be a way to join the ranks of "grands lettrés" whom he admires. But the current state of the theater makes it impossible:

—I went to the theatre only rarely: hence perhaps the chimerical punctiliousness of such perceptions, and when I indicated some aversion to the newspaper articles or reviews after those—professional and marvellous—of Gautier, Janin, St. Victor, Banville, no—not at all, did I dream that the genre, honored by these great men of letters, would today resuscitate and lavish a brilliance belonging to theirs on everyone, clear, superior, impressive, with Catulle Mendes capable of writing magnificently, every day, about average events: I try, before such curtains of reason, prestige, loyalty and charm on that, that continues for me, a lack of interest or real familiarity with the theatre, with magic and fury draped, not to see the contemporary void behind it.

—je n'allais que rarement au théâtre: d'où peut-être la chimérique exactitude de tels aperçus, et quand j'y indiquais quelque éloignement pour les feuilletons ou comptes rendus après ceux, professionels et merveilleux, d'un Gautier, de Janin, de Saint-Victor, d'un Banville, non, du tout, je ne songeais pas, sérieusement, que le genre, honoré par ces grands lettrés, ressusciterait aujourd'hui et prodiguerait un éclat qui s'apparente au leur à tous, net, suprême, imposant, avec Catulle Mendès capable de se produire quotidiennement magnifique envers des occasions moyennes: j'essaie, devant de tels rideaux de raison, de prestige, de loyauté et de charme sur cela, qui continue, pour moi, un manque d'intérêt ou l'usage actuel du théâtre, avec furie et magie drapés, de ne percevoir pas le vide contemporain derrière. (1562)

Mallarmé's modest explanation of why he cannot write for the theater is also a critique of contemporary theater; he is not capable of the great theatrical criticism of Gautier's generation because the theater is so bad. It is so bad, in fact, that Mallarmé has to try not to notice it. If Gautier and the rest went to the theater to see something and write about it, Mallarmé here describes trying *not* to see. Rather, Mallarmé goes to the theater to see if there is anything to see, to study the problem of seeing. Reluctantly, he goes; despite a lot of looking, there seems to be very little of what he would define as seeing, doing something more than the incomplete looking that bad theater demands. Offering a lot to look at— overly decorated sets, overly emphatic gesture, costumes, characters, plots—bad theater makes "seeing" impossible. Implicit in his critique of what theater offers is a critique of the voracious spectatorship of Gautier's generation and what it has produced.

Crayonné au théâtre begins with the author in despair—"Despair uppermost in my mind [Le désespoir en dernier lieu de mon idée]"—finding himself at the theater with "lost looks [regards perdus]" and "features already tired out by nothingness [traits à l'avance fatigués du néant]" (293). He has brought along a friend, a woman who thinks the performance is fine: "But it's very good, it's perfect—what more do you hope for, my friend? [Mais c'est très bien, c'est parfait—à quoi semblez-vous prétendre encore, mon ami?]" (293). What has brought him to the theater, and what makes him displeased with what he finds there? His response: "my habitual unconsidered lack of foresight [un habituel manque inconsidéré chez moi de prévoyance]" (293).

He has come to the theater hoping to find in the performance the elusive "idée," which he defines as a collective coming together, the production or presence of divinity in the "lieu divin" of the theater: "if we must see a soul there, or else our idea (that is divinity present to man's mind) [s'il y faut voir une âme ou bien notre idée (à savoir la divinité présente à l'esprit de l'homme)]" (293). He wants to see something that is not visible: a divine presence manifested in the audience but not represented onstage.[2] While the horizon glows each evening, he notes, society goes to the theater, as if hungry, to be fed by the "social organization [l'arrangement social]" (294) of stage and spectators. This "idea" Mallarmé is looking for is theater itself; the two are equated in his notes for the project of Le Livre: "from whence Theater = idea [d'où Théâtre = idée]" (429). Theater brings the "idea" to light, not by presenting it onstage but by causing it to be present in this "social organization"; the stage creates "pleasures enjoyed in common [plaisirs pris en commun]" (314) and is "the majestic opening out onto the mystery that we are in the world to contemplate [la majestueuse ouverture sur le mystère dont on est au monde pour envisager]" (314). The theater is not a place for watching a representation but for envisioning a mystery.

This making-present-without-representing is what the ideal theater could do but what the contemporary theater almost invariably fails to do for Mallarmé. There is nothing in it to feed the soul: "the initial mistake remained going to the show with one's Soul [le tort initial demeura se rendre au spectacle avec son Ame *with Psyche my soul*]" (294). This theater "only displays a representation, for those not having to see the things themselves at all [montre seulement une représentation, pour ceux n'ayant point à voir les choses à même!]" (294). Representation is a shadow or screen obscuring "les choses à même," preventing the viewer from "seeing" things themselves. If Mallarmé goes to the theater it is because it offers "the charm perhaps unknown, in literature, of severely extinguishing, one by one, every view that would burst forth with purity [le charme peut-être inconnu, en littérature, d'éteindre strictement une à une toute vue qui éclaterait avec pureté]" (298). That is, the theater can both bring images to light and snuff them out, make them visible and then invisible.

In the prose poem "Un Spectacle Interrompu," Mallarmé describes his way of seeing—what he calls his "poet's gaze" (276)—and how it differs from that of the average spectator. The poet scorns the spectators at this show—a circuslike spectacle—who are listening as well as watching, clouding their view with thunderous applause: "All ears, they should have been all eyes [Tout oreilles, il fallut être tout yeux]" (277). The image of the spectator who is "all eyes" brings to mind the dandy at the Opéra, Gautier with his opera glasses; but it suggests a reversal of what Mallarmé described in that case as a "willful blindness." If, for Gautier, the dance makes the writer's words visible, allowing everything to be seen, and thus said, it demands a scrutiny of the female body onstage which Mallarmé is the first to describe as blindness. For Mallarmé, looking with a poet's eyes means seeing more than what is visible. Rather than being nothing but eyes, like the dandy armed with opera glasses, reducing all perception to the metaphor of sight, it means widening the metaphor of sight to describe all forms of perception; that is, using one's mind as if it were eyes, making the organs of sense perception and the mind into eyes. In contrast to Gautier's belief in the ultimate visibility of the writer's idea in the dancing body, Mallarméan vision depends upon a belief in the poet's ability to "see" more than the visible; widening the notion of the visual in theater to include what he calls the "intellectual" or "imaginative" component. After the interrupted show, the poet leaves with a strange sensation: "I got up like everyone else, to go outside and get some air, surprised once again not to have felt the same kind of impression as my fellow creatures, but serene: because my way of seeing, after all, was superior and even the true one [Je me levai comme tout le monde pour aller respirer au dehors, étonné de n'avoir pas senti, cette fois encore, le même genre d'impression que mes semblables, mais serein: car ma façon de voir, après tout, avait été supérieure, et même la vraie]" (278).

Mallarmé deems his way of seeing not only superior but true because it depends on insight rather than sight. He goes to the theater to see what is not there; that is, to "see" both what is missing ("le vide contemporain derrière") and what cannot be seen in the first place, an emptiness that is the full potential of ideal theater. Theater's ultimate capacity, Mallarmé suggests, would be to represent nothing at all, or rather to represent *the* "nothing." For Gautier and other "grands lettrés," the theater was an occasion not only to see, but also to say, something—everything. For Mallarmé, theater provides what he calls "l'occasion de rien dire" (297) which could be translated not only as "the opportunity to say nothing" but also as "the opportunity to tell of Nothing"; it provides the opportunity not only to see, but also to write, this "nothing." Mallarmé defines this "nothing" as what the purest poetry can express, in opposition to the nothingness of the empty production of words: "the idiot blabbers on saying nothing . . . in order not to express anything [le sot bavarde sans rien dire . . . afin de ne pas exprimer quelque chose]" (298).

If Mallarmé attempts to write this "nothing," his theater texts attempt both to stage it and to record its staging, most powerfully, in the dance. Dance is for Mallarmé the one form of theater that lets the spectator see what he alternately calls "things themselves [les choses à mêmes]" and "rien," because in ballet, mime, and, more often, modern dance, the performer gives the viewer less to see rather than more, stripping the stage of the trappings of historical costume, sets, and words. Loie Fuller, the dancer who most moves Mallarmé, is said to bring that nothingness to the stage: "here brought to Ballet is the atmosphere, or nothing [voici rendue au Ballet l'atmosphère ou rien]" (309).

This "nothing" which is represented by not being represented is "la divinité présente à l'esprit de l'homme": the divinity present in the human mind, the community of "culte" or worship disconnected from representation and yet for Mallarmé closely connected with the theater. Mallarmé's fascination with Loie Fuller sparks his critique of the contemporary theater; her work draws the line between empty theater and the theater of ideal emptiness. Loie Fuller's dances, swirling wide panels of silk into huge shapes under vividly colored electric light, come closer than any other performance to the ideal theater that he conceives of Literature as being. In the enigmatic paragraph "On Theater," Mallarmé writes:

I believe that Literature, traced to its source which is Art and Science, will give us a Theater, whose representations will be the true modern worship; a Book, explanation of man, matching our most beautiful dreams. I believe all this written in nature in such a way as to not allow the closing of one's eyes except for those interested in seeing nothing. This oeuvre exists, everybody has tried their hand at it without knowing it; there isn't a genius or a clown who hasn't found some feature of it without knowing it. To show that and to raise a corner of the veil of what such a poem can be, my pleasure and my torture in isolation.

Je crois que la Littérature, reprise à sa source qui est l'Art et la Science, nous fournira un Théâtre, dont les représentations seront le vrai culte moderne; un Livre, explication de l'homme, suffisante à nos plus beaux rêves. Je crois tout cela écrit dans la nature de façon à ne laisser fermer les yeux qu'aux intéressés à ne rien voir. Cette oeuvre existe, tout le monde l'a tentée sans le savoir; il n'est pas un génie ou un pitre, qui n'en ait retrouvé un trait sans le savoir. Montrer cela et soulever un coin du voile de ce que peut être pareil poëme, dans un isolement mon plaisir et ma torture. (875)

This chapter considers what Mallarmé means by a literary theater reconnected with its source in "art" and "science." It asks how such a literature produces a theater of imagination rather than purely visual spectacle, and why dance comes closer than other theater practice to this ideal theater. It wonders how such a theater's "representations" could create a sense of "culte"—a presence beyond the audience, a gaze greater than their own. It explores why this theater of the imagination can only be seen by those who do not use opera glasses when looking. It attempts to decipher what Mallarmé means by comparing the literary genius and the performing clown—both striving for such a theater work and hitting upon it without knowing it. This chapter considers how Mallarmé's pleasure, and torture, consist—like Loie Fuller's dance—in raising a corner of the veil of this literary mystery, only to leave it in place.[3]

Mallarmé's dance reviews and two "scènes"—poems meant for the stage—suggest that his interest in dance, despite his general distaste for theater, is a response to the "maître" Gautier and the belief that dance can stage the literary "idea." But if Gautier's interest in ballet was based on dance's ability to make "idea" visible, Mallarmé's interest in dance is precisely the reverse: dance can stage "idea" because, like *eidos* itself, it is visual without being entirely visible. In Mallarmé's famous semiotics of dance, dance is a coded, summary writing, and the dancer is Sign itself—"hieroglyph," or ideogram.

The visuality of the dance is more complex for Mallarmé than for Gautier; he considers it as a text that is not simply looked at but read, and he is interested not only in what it means, but in how it means:

The unique training of the imagination consists, in the regular hours of frequenting the sites of Dance without any preliminary aim, patiently and passively to wonder at each step, each strange attitude, on pointes or flat, allongé or jumping, "what can this mean" or better, with inspiration, to read it.

L'unique entraînement imaginatif consiste, aux heures ordinaires de fréquentation dans les lieux de Danse sans visée quelconque préalable, patiemment et passivement à se demander devant tout pas, chaque attitude si étranges, ces pointes et taquetés, allongés ou ballons. "Que peut signifier ceci" ou mieux, d'inspiration, le lire. (307)

Because the dance signifies like language, the spectator watching it is drawn to ask what it means, and then in a kind of suspension of disbelief, to simply read it on faith. As a special kind of writing—coded, fast-moving, free from the apparatus that writing needs—dance is the only art capable of presenting the Idea—"Dance alone capable, in its summary writing, of translating the fleeting and the sudden all the way to Idea [la Danse seule capable, par son écriture sommaire, de traduire le fugace et le soudain jusqu'à l'Idée]" (541). Like poetry, dance is so concentrated a form "that it would take paragraphs of prose in dialogue as well as description, to express, in the rewriting: poem disengaged from all writing apparatus [qu'il faudrait des paragraphes en prose dialoguée autant que descriptive pour exprimer, dans la rédaction: poëme dégagé de tout appareil du scribe]" (304).

Unlike drama, which Mallarmé calls "historique" (306), the dance is "allégorique" (296) or "emblématique" (306); it works through a practice that resembles allegory: "There is (one stirs the fire) an art, the only or pure that to enunciate means to produce: it roars its proofs by its practice. The instant that the miracle bursts forth, to add that it was this and nothing else, even will invalidate it: so much it admits no luminous evidence except by existing [Il est (tisonne-t-on) un art, l'unique ou pur qu'énoncer signifie produire: il hurle ses démonstrations par la pratique. L'instant qu'éclatera le miracle, ajouter que ce fut cela et pas autre chose, même l'infirmera: tant il n'admet de lumineuse évidence sinon d'exister]" (295). The practice of the production of meaning in the dance, the literal meaning embodied in the presentation of the dancing body, merges in performance with the allegorical art of saying "something else." The dance is "unique" and "pure" in its ability to enunciate "cela" while saying "autre chose"—presenting while representing, being simultaneously literal and allegorical. Mallarmé's concept of the dance's essentially poetic form, its allegorical way of saying something other than what it seems to be saying—or showing—entails a critique of the spectatorship of Gautier's generation, and Gautier's own belief in dance as show.

Nothingness itself is the subject of much of Mallarmé's poetry, from "Rien, cette écume, vierge vers [Nothing, this sea-foam, virgin verse]" of the opening "Salut [Toast]" of the collected poems, through the notes for

Fig. 12. Loie Fuller dancing. Photograph by Harry Ellis, reprinted by permission of the Musée Rodin, Paris [1318].

the never-completed "Livre." As studies of Mallarméan poetics have demonstrated, Mallarmé's verse seems to rise from the ashes of its self-consumption; the poet writes while erasing, and it is through this apparent consumption or erasure of verse, its denial or disappearance, that the poems are created.[4] Though Mallarmé's sketch of the ideal theater in "On Theater" describes it as Literature, and thus suggests such a theater only in the abstract, Loie Fuller's dance comes closest to making "nothing" visible in her serial imagery;[5] the "nothing" is indicated when "a dramatic work shows the sequence of the act's exteriorities such that no single moment keeps its reality, and such that, in the end, nothing happens [une oeuvre dramatique montre la succession des extériorites de l'acte sans qu'aucun moment garde de réalité et qu'il se passe, en fin de compte, rien]" (296).

Mallarméan poetics suggests that language works by veiling, through "evocation," "allusion," "suggestion," but denies that its effect is one of hiding: "Monuments, the sea, the human face, in their plenitude, native, conserving another kind of attractive virtue that no description will veil, no so-called evocation, allusion I know, suggestion [Les monuments, la mer, la face humaine, dans leur plénitude, natifs, conservant une vertu autrement attrayante que ne les voilera une description, évocation dite, allusion je sais, suggestion]" (645). In the Mallarméan poetics set out in "Crise de Vers," language can make present the object that is not there. Through evocation, poetry makes present what is absent: "I say: a flower! and, beyond the oblivion where my voice relegates no form, as anything other than known calyxes, musically arises, idea itself and suave, what is absent from all bouquets [Je dis: une fleur! et, hors de l'oubli où ma voix relègue aucun contour, en tant que quelque chose d'autre que les calices sus, musicalement se lève, idée même et suave, l'absente de tous bouquets]" (367). The subject of poetry, then, will not be the things themselves but their idea: "Abolished the pretension . . . to include in the volume's subtle paper anything for example other than the horror of the forest, or the silent thunder scattered in the leaves; not the intrinsic and dense wood of the trees [Abolie, la prétention . . . . d'inclure au papier subtil du volume autre chose que par exemple l'horreur de la forêt, ou le tonnerre muet épars au feuillage; non le bois intrinsèque et dense des arbres]" (365–66).

The dance comes closer to the Mallarméan poetics of an ideal theater because it provides the spectator with the opportunity to imagine, rather than simply to see "things": "ballet gives only a little: it is the genre of the imagination [le ballet ne donne que peu: c'est le genre imaginatif]." In the opening pages of *Crayonné au théâtre*, seeing the dance becomes for Mallarmé an act of the imagination, an act of imagining—or imaging—the dancer:

When a sign of the scattered general beauty is isolated for the gaze, flower, wave, cloud and jewel, etc., if, in us, the exclusive means to know it consists in juxtaposing its aspect to our spiritual nudity so that it feels analogous and adapts itself to it in some exquisite confusion of itself with this flying form—nothing but through the rite, there, the enunciation of Idea, does not the dancer seem to be half the causal element, half humanity apt to be confused with it, in the floating of the dream? The operation, or poetry, par excellence, and the theatre. Immediately the ballet turns out allegorical.

Quand s'isole pour le regard un signe de l'éparse beauté générale, fleur, onde, nuée et bijou, etc., si, chez nous, le moyen exclusif de le savoir consiste à en juxtaposer l'aspect à notre nudité spirituelle afin qu'elle le sente analogue et se l'adapte dans quelque confusion exquise d'elle avec cette forme envolée—rien qu'au travers du rite, là, énoncé de l'Idée, est-ce que ne paraît pas la danseuse à demi l'élément en cause, à demi humanité apte à s'y confondre, dans la flottaison de rêverie? L'opération, ou poésie, par excellence et le théâtre. Immédiatement le ballet résulte allégorique. (295–96)

The viewer projects or juxtaposes the dancer's series of signs against his own spiritual "nudity," his threadbare ideas. The dancer is only half responsible for these signs or for their inclusion in the viewer's imagination. She is the agent or catalyst, sending these images out in her "opération," which is the essence of poetry and theater. The ballet's allegory depends on her "half-humanity," the fact that she is, after all, the body incorporating and generating these signs. But the dancer is only half-human; in Mallarmé's view the body becomes detached from its "personal" meaning: "in some signification other than personal [sous quelque signification autre que personelle]," for example, legs become "an express instrument of idea [un instrument direct d'idée]" (312). The best dancer is one whose personality, sex, and humanity disappear during the performance; the dancer who becomes "l'*in*-individuel ... jamais qu'emblème point quelqu'un" (304).

Mallarmé's most direct formulation of the dancer's impersonality is located in this problematic passage from *Crayonné au théâtre*:

To understand that the dancer *is not a woman dancing*, for the juxtaposed causes that she *is not a woman*, but a metaphor summarizing one of the elementary aspects of our form, sword, cup, flower, etc., and *that she does not dance*, suggesting, by the marvel of ellipsis or elan, with a corporeal writing that would necessitate paragraphs of prose in dialogue as well as description to express, in the rewriting: poem disengaged from all writing apparatus.

A savoir que la danseuse n'est pas une femme qui danse, pour ces motifs juxtaposés qu'elle n'est pas une femme, mais une métaphore résumant un des aspects élémentaires de notre forme, glaive, coupe, fleur, etc., et qu'elle ne danse pas, suggérant, par le prodige de raccourcis ou d'élans, avec une écriture corporelle ce qu'il faudrait des paragraphes en prose dialoguée autant que descriptive, pour exprimer, dans la rédaction: poëme degagé de tout appareil du scribe. (304)

Having deprived the dancer of her humanity, the poet is all admiration of her ability to be poetry itself even though she is also

the unlettered ballerina delivering herself to the games of her profession. Yes, she (would you be lost in the audience, very foreign spectator, Friend) for little that you deposit with submission at the feet of this unconsious revealer, just as the roses that the play of her pale satin vertiginous slippers raises and flings into the visibility of higher realms, first the Flower of your poetic instinct, expecting from nothing else the making evident and in the real daylight of a thousand latent imaginations: then, through a commerce that her smile seems to spill the secret of, without hesitation she delivers to you across the final veil which always remains, the nudity of your concepts and will silently write your vision in the manner of a Sign, which she is.

la ballerine illettrée se livrant aux jeux de sa profession. Oui, celle-là, (serais-tu perdu en une salle, spectateur très étranger, Ami) pour peu que tu déposes avec soumission à ses pieds d'inconsciente révélatrice ainsi que les roses qu'enlève et jette en la visibilité de régions supérieures un jeu de ses chaussons de satin pâle vertigineux, la Fleur d'abord de ton poétique instinct, n'attendant de rien autre la mise en évidence et sous le vrai jour des mille imaginations latentes: alors, par un commerce dont paraît son sourire verser le secret, sans tarder elle te livre à travers le voile dernier qui toujours reste, la nudité de tes concepts et silencieusement écrira ta vision à la façon d'un Signe, qu'elle est. (307)[6]

A series of seeming contradictions, the dancer is an unlettered, and unconscious, "révélatrice" of poetry; in the state of "full revery" she is nonetheless capable of "adequation," the function of language. Yet she knows no eloquence other than her own vocabulary of movements: "The librettist does not usually know that the dancer, who expresses herself in steps, understands no other eloquence, even gesture [Le librettiste ignore d'ordinaire que la danseuse, qui s'exprime par des pas, ne comprend d'éloquence autre, même le geste]" (306). The dancer, unaware that she is a poem, is not here a model for the dandy-poet whose person is his own best creation, as she is in Baudelaire's *La Fanfarlo*; she is rather the image of the artist who has managed successfully to lose all identity in the work. She can write the poet's vision because onstage she becomes a pure sign, recreating the enigma Mallarmé believes literature must have: the mystery present in language itself. An artist whose body is a sign, who signifies signification itself, and knows no other form of expression, cannot be a woman, and cannot be simply dancing.

In fact, it is clear that if the dancer is Sign, a poem detached from its own writing, it is precisely because she is a woman, and because she dances: her sex, her body, her personality do not get in the way of her presentation of images. Loie Fuller's dances, examined through Mallarmé's texts, visual images, and her own writings, suggest to what extent the female body dancing is at the center, rather than the margins, of his formulation. Signifying across the veil that always remains, the female dancer's enigma, and that of her body, is inextricably linked to the enigma of language.

Fuller's dance of veils inspires more than looking and resembles Mallarmé's ideal theater because, principally, the veils moving across the body work like music: "However this transition from sonorities to fabric (is there anything, better, resembling gauze than Music!) is, uniquely, the sorcery that Loie Fuller effects ... [Or cette transition de sonorités aux tissus (y a-t-il, mieux, à une gaze ressemblant que la Musique!) est, uniquement, le sortilège qu'opère la Loïe Fuller ...]" (308–9). Like music, like poetry at its best, Fuller's veils work rhythmically, shifting rhythm from sound to silk. For Mallarmé, rhythm makes evocation, allusion, or suggestion possible because it functions in language like the veil, seeming to hide, while in fact it reveals. And, like the veil, rhythm works through condensation; it is an overlapping rather than an excision or deletion.

For Mallarmé, rhythm is a way to describe the form that structures both poetry and dance, language and the body: the form that structures but that cannot be seen. He cites Georges Rodenbach, the only writer he finds to have written with ease about dance, "this subject virgin as mousseline [ce sujet vierge comme les mousselines]" (311), in which "their body appears only as the rhythm on which everything depends, but which hides it [*leur corps n'apparaît que comme le rythme d'où tout dépend mais qui le cache*]" (311). In Mallarmé's reformulation of Rodenbach, the body in ballet appears to function just as rhythm does in music, as the structure that everything depends on, but also covers. The ballet costume hides the dancer just as programmatic orchestral music covers its structural underpinnings with melody. But the typically Mallarméan syntax also leaves open the reverse possibility, that it is the body, like rhythm, which hides "everything." Mallarmé plays with his usual perspicacity on this "everything" that the dancing body reveals or conceals in ballet, as opposed to the "Nothing" that dance can ideally stage (a "Rien" which is not nothing but something, Idea); and thus he responds to the tradition of voyeuristic or fetishistic scopophilia characterized by Gautier and others.

To describe how Loie Fuller manifests this structuring "rhythm" of the body, without simply showing it, Mallarmé uses the word "armature," playing on the resonance between the body and music:

An armature, which is of no particular woman, and thus instable, across the veil of generality, draws onto such a revealed fragment of the form and there drinks the flash that renders it divine; or exhales, in return, by the undulation of fabrics, floating, palpitating, scattered, this ecstasy.

Une armature, qui n'est d'aucune femme en particulier, d'où instable, à travers le voile de généralité, attire sur tel fragment révélé de la forme et y boit l'éclair

qui le divinise; ou exhale, de retour, par l'ondulation des tissus, flottante, palpitante, éparse cette extase. (311)

What is this "inner form" which structures both the body and the dance,
but cannot be seen, the form that allows the *idée* to be generated, fleshed
out with visible form, translated from "sonorités" to "tissus"? The form
structuring the body but hidden, itself, in the body?

Read in the context of Mallarmé's problematization of spectatorship
at the Opéra, his reaction to Gautier's passionate but blind gaze, the inner
rhythm that Mallarmé finds so crucial for the dance can be taken as a
metaphor for what the dandy armed with opera glasses hoped to see but
could not: the dancer's sex under her skirt. Against the voyeuristic or
fetishistic gaze of the dandy ballet-goer, defining feminine sexuality as
lack or deviance in the visual realm and substituting other, visible parts
of her body for that lack, Mallarmé defines the dancer's femininity in
rhythmic, rather than purely visual, terms.

In "La notion de 'rythme' dans son expression linguistique," Emile
Benveniste traces the origins of "rhythm" to the Greek *ruthmos*, and considers its shift in meaning from a term used to describe spatial form to a
term used to describe aural form. Benveniste attributes the modern
meaning of "rhythm" to Plato, who uses the word in its traditional meaning of spatial form, disposition, or proportion, but also gives it a new
meaning by applying it to dance. In Benveniste's reading, dance is the art
in which the form and the content are not simply inseparable, but indistinguishable, and both can be described by the word "form." Dance is inseparable from the human form dancing it; to some extent, the formal aspect of dance is itself the human form. The dancing body thus provides
the meeting ground for the overlap of "rhythm" in its concrete and abstract, human and extrahuman senses: the form or shape of the body
("attitudes corporelles") and the formal movement of that body in space
and time ("mesure" or "metre" of the movement).[7]

For Mallarmé, Loie Fuller's dance, like the word "rhythm" itself, describes a form neither exclusively visual nor exclusively metrical, neither
exclusively plastic nor poetic, but somewhere between the two; a form
defined by its movement between realms, and defined as movement.
Only glimpses of this form are possible; or rather, the form can only be
seen as a fragment. Fragmented glimpses or glimpses of fragments suggest
a rhythmic viewing, alternating between seeing too much and too little:
"Yes, the Dance's suspense, contradictory fear or desire to see too much
and not enough, demands a transparent prolongation [Oui, le suspens de

la Danse, crainte contradictoire ou souhait de voir trop et pas assez, exige un prolongement transparent]" (311).

What is this contradictory fear and wish to see both too much and not enough? And what is the transparent prolongation that the dance requires, or suspends? In Mallarmé's formulation, seeing too much and not seeing enough are not contradictory: "to see too much *and* not enough." The contradiction comes only in the alternation of fear and desire for this kind of seeing; it could be read as "crainte, ou souhait contradictoire," although here again there is a kind of equivalence being set up between two apparent opposites—fear is equal to a contradictory desire. This looking-at-what-is-there-or-not-there, like the gaze of Gautier voluntarily blinding himself with opera glasses, can only construct a female body which, in its anatomical difference from the male, can only be seen as lacking. But here Mallarmé offers an alternative way of looking, focusing on the structure of the body ("armature") that we cannot see, though we know it is there. Hidden by the "veil of generality," unseen because of the obscuring gaze of an avid public, the body's inner form eludes the gaze. Requiring insight rather than sight, allowing the "transparent prolongation" of the gaze, dance allows to be seen, not emptiness or lack, but the "nothing" that Mallarmé locates at the heart of theater.

If Loie Fuller's dance can represent "nothing" it is because of the nature of her dance and of the body dancing it. Beyond its familiar nineteenth-century idealization of dance, with its dehumanizing underside, *Crayonné au théâtre* provides a richer view of the dancer; Mallarmé is fascinated by how the dancer's sex, and subjectivity—so crucial to the romantic ballet—disappear in dance. The dancer's nature as both female body and pure idea is resolved by Mallarmé into a philosophical puzzle here inspired by the ballet: "To deduce the philosophical point at which is situated the dancer's impersonality, between her feminine appearance and a mimed object, for what hymen: she pricks it [pique] with a sure point, puts it down [A déduire le point philosophique auquel est située l'impersonnalité de la danseuse, entre sa féminine apparence et un objet mimé, pour quel hymen: elle le pique d'une sûre pointe, le pose]" (296). The dancer's ability to signify from behind the veil depends on the relationship between her sex and the material of her dance. The dancer's femaleness, "sa féminine apparence"—that is, her body—and the mimetic material of her dance ("un objet mimé") appear to be at opposite poles; the literal body presents itself onstage, and the "mimed object" is represented by it. Yet sex and matter come together, and become indistinguishable, in the work of Loie Fuller.

Mallarmé is referring to the ballet and not to Fuller in this passage, which describes both the dancer's sex and her art through the use of the word "hymen." This "hymen" is the means by which she signifies: "elle le pique d'une sûre pointe, le pose." In the ballet, the dancer's feet seem both to poke through the veil of the stage space and to hold it in place. The image recalls the romantic ballet as shaped by Gautier, the simultaneous covering and revealing of the female body; the dandy bored with what he sees but unwilling to put down his opera glasses, the voyeur or fetishist frustrated by what he cannot see, and yet determined to look.

What is this veil through which, or by which, the dancer's signification is projected? It is this veiling that allows "idea" to be seen in the dance, not unlike the way in which the ballerina's veiling—her transparent costume—covers her body without hiding its form, as Baudelaire noted in *La Fanfarlo*. In Loie Fuller's dance, under the electric light the veil-like panels of silk increase the apparent speed of her movement and allow its imagery to be writ large on the performance space:

In the terrible bath of fabrics swoons, radiant, cold, the performer who illustrates many spinning themes from which extends a distant fading warp, giant petal and butterfly, unfurling, all in a clear and elemental way. Her fusion with the nuances of speed shedding their lime-light phantasmagoria of dusk and grotto, such rapidity of passions, delight, mourning, anger: to move them, prismatic, with violence or diluted, it takes the vertigo of a soul as if airborne by artifice.

Au bain terrible des étoffes se pâme, radieuse, froide la figurante qui illustre maint thème giratoire où tend une trame loin épanouie, pétale et papillon géants, déferlement, tout d'ordre net et élémentaire. Sa fusion aux nuances véloces muant leur fantasmagorie oxyhydrique de crépuscule et de grotte, telles rapidités de passions, délice, deuil, colère: il faut pour les mouvoir, prismatiques, avec violence ou diluées, le vertige d'une âme comme mise à l'air par un artifice. (308)

With the excitement of fireworks, the fantasy of dusk and dark, Loie Fuller's performance creates in the viewer a rapid series of passionate reactions to the performer's abstract actions. Or is Mallarmé attributing these passions to the dancer herself? For at the center of these seemingly self-generating images there is a woman dancing: "That a woman associates the flight of clothing with the powerful or vast dance at the point of supporting them, infinitely, as her own expansion [Qu'une femme associe l'envolée de vêtements à la danse puissante ou vaste au point de les soutenir, à l'infini, comme son expansion]" (308). It is a woman who is controlling these tremendous wings or petals, a woman fusing abstract images and the real emotions they create.

Mallarmé closely links the theatrical space—ideally full of nothing—to the woman in it. The fabrics Fuller swirls around her constitute both the woman and the dance; they are the visible expansion and representation of feminine "matter." Fuller's manipulation of her costume creates the theater space itself: "the magic that this Loie Fuller creates, with instinct, with exaggeration, the contraction of skirt or wing, instituting a place. The enchantress creates the ambience, draws it out of herself and goes into it, in the palpitating silence of crêpe de Chine [le sortilège qu'opère la Loie Fuller, par instinct, avec l'exagération, les retraits de jupe ou d'aile, instituant un lieu. L'enchanteresse fait l'ambiance, la tire de soi et l'y rentre, par un silence palpité de crêpes de Chine]" (309). Playing on the homophony of "soi" and "soie," Mallarmé explains that Fuller draws a theater space out from inside her body, but then enters into that space with her body; merging inside and outside, the empty, idealized theatrical space with the female body. This dancer does not pierce any imagined veil or "hymen," but like the ballerina on pointe she also reinforces the space's "virginity": "When, at the rising of the curtain in a gala audience, entirely local, thus appears like a (snow)flake blown from where? furious, the dancer: the floorboards avoided by bounds or hard to the pointes, acquires a virginity of site undreamt of, that the figure isolates, will build, will flower [Quand, au lever du rideau dans une salle de gala et tout local, apparaît ainsi qu'un flocon d'où soufflé? furieux, la danseuse: le plancher évité par bond ou dur aux pointes, acquiert une virginité de site pas songé, qu'isole, bâtira, fleurira la figure]" (308). In the same way, the space's virginity allows Fuller's images to flower. Here "hymen" is both the "nothing" represented by this ideal form of theater, and the means by which it is presented: "here, rendered unto Ballet is atmosphere or nothing, visions scattered as soon as they are known, their limpid evocation [voici rendue au Ballet l'atmosphère ou rien, visions sitôt éparses que sues, leur évocation limpide]" (309).

More than a simple alternation of a dilating body and a reified, statuesque frame, the changes of this body—and the poet's changing views of it—suggest the intimate, indissoluble connection within the body between hard and soft, expansion and control, liberating flights and centering structure. Just as the fantastic images created by huge wings of silk are made possible by the artist manipulating them, so the dance itself—

the dilation of the body into images—is impossible without the anchoring structure of bone and muscle.

As Mallarmé sits at Loie Fuller's spectacle, he attempts an explanation of the contradictions of an art generated by and ultimately detached from the body, an art of rapidly changing images in rapidly changing relation to the body generating them. Loie Fuller produces, in the electric light, a series of moving images: she is flower, butterfly, bird, fountain, and more abstract things—not because she pretends to be them, allegorically or metaphorically incarnating a role, but because her stage image makes it possible for the viewer to imagine he sees them. Mallarmé describes her image-making as an inextinguishable fountain of self-transformations: "la Loie Fuller, fontaine intarissable d'elle-même" (311). In the dancing body, there can be no clear demarcation of inside and outside; the dancer seems to contain the space in which she is contained. She is a box full of images filling the space, and also simply another image in that box of space. She is both the generator and the product, or artist and artwork; she is both mother and child of her dance, inexhaustibly re-creating herself; her dance is a hatching or birth, an "éclosion contemporaine" (309).

More significant than the way in which Loie's dances might seem to represent the female body in their imagery is the way in which they redefine that body by redefining the way in which dance represents, and the role of the body in that representation. Her dance represents a different theatrical possibility for hymen or *hystera*, a different theater of femaleness. Fuller's work stages the body as the producer of serial images in movement, and the movement from image to image—a metonymic movement rather than a production of bodily metaphors. Rather than the simple embodiment of images, what Fuller stages is a simultaneous representation and presentation of the female body. Her dancing redefines the female body as a producer of images, and redefines femininity as a series of roles or images, as the rapid movement from role to role or image to image.

Fuller's "éclosion," then, her rhythmic production of images, makes the theater into a feminine space, transforming its womblike emptiness from a space of potential hysteria into a space of poetic expression. Her dance presents, and represents, a different theatrical possibility for *hystera*, traditionally the locus of hysteria,[8] an interior theater that Mallarmé theorizes in his writings on her in *Crayonné au théâtre*. Beyond the mediocre theater of the nineteenth century, and the century's theatrical hysterics, beyond the theater tradition in which it is hymen that traditionally closes comedy or opens tragedy, it is the woman dancing who moves Mallarmé to figure a different theatrical "hymen," from the inside out.

Mallarmé's description of Fuller's serial production of images strikingly parallels his description twenty years earlier of himself. Before the elegant formulation of the famous "elocutionary disappearance of the poet [disparition élocutoire du poëte]" (366), in "Crise de Vers" ("Crisis in Verse"), the young Mallarmé struggles to conceive of himself writing. In the letters describing his state during his struggle with the Salome poem "Hérodiade," in 1864–65, Mallarmé moves through a series of roles, rhythmically taking them on and casting them off. The dancer's theatrical subjectivity—multiple and "emblematic"—is theorized by Mallarmé as the role of the poet himself, the poet who disappears in his enunciation, but also casts himself in a series of roles of which absence is only one.[9] In the mid-1860s Mallarmé declares himself dead, insensible, hysterical when trying to write at the beginning of his poetic career.

It is around the time that Mallarmé announces his own "death" in a letter of 1866 to Théodore Aubanel ("Je suis mort"), and again a year later ("je suis parfaitement mort"),[10] that he first generates a poem originally conceived for the stage, and then as part of the master project for the Livre.[11] He will rewrite this poem significantly throughout his life, and return to it just before his death. At the same time, he speaks of making poems that are about emotion, sensations rather than things.[12] Mallarmé closely links "Hérodiade" to his identity as a poet and his attempt to create a new kind of poetry. The early and late versions of "Hérodiade" can be read as leading up to, and later reacting to, Mallarmé's reflections on the dancer and the ideal theater in Crayonné au théâtre. The poem's writing and rewriting trace Mallarmé's identification with the dancer—even or especially one who is not dancing—and the relation of dance to writing. In his notes and letters on "Hérodiade," Mallarmé connects the new poetics of this poem to its problematic dancer. Like the prose essays on the dance, the texts surrounding "Hérodiade"—including letters, unpublished revisions, and notes—all suggest that the dance is of particular poetic interest to him, and, located in the female body, a model for poesis.

It is telling that what provokes this early crisis of writerly identity is the writing of "Hérodiade"—a text in which the dancer, instead of dancing, philosophizes, and a text surrounded by problems of hysteria, hymen, and hystera. In December 1865 he writes that for a week he has

suffered a horrible "névralgie": "I live in unviolated solitude and silence."
In 1869, his letters again describe writing as a mental torture which he
must stop: "the simple act of writing lodges hysteria in my head [le simple acte d'écrire installe l'hystérie dans ma tête]."[13]

Hérodiade herself fits one profile of female hysteria. From its inception, "Hérodiade" is described by Mallarmé in gendered terms. In two
separate but related gestures during the creation of "Hérodiade," Mallarmé constitutes its central figure as a real woman—his child, his mistress—and ultimately identifies with her, using the writing and rewriting of the poem to address his own artistic and psychological problems.
Born the same year as his daughter Geneviève, "Hérodiade" is for Mallarmé first the poetic progeny who suffers from the birth of his real child:
"this bad baby made Hérodiade run away, with locks cold as gold, with
heavy robes, sterile [ce méchant bébé a fait s'enfuir Hérodiade, aux
cheveux froids comme l'or, aux lourdes robes, stérile]."[14] His friend
Lefébure refers to Geneviève and Hérodiade as the poet's "two daughters."[15] In January 1865, Mallarmé finds time to begin work again, and
writes "unfortunately, I get no pleasure from this charm circulating
around a cradle . . . I took up my tragedy of Hérodiade seriously . . . me,
sterile and crepuscular, I chose a terrifying subject [Malheureusement, je
ne jouis pas de tout ce charme qui voltige autour d'un berceau ... Je me
suis mis sérieusement à ma tragédie d'Hérodiade ... moi, sterile et cré-
pusculaire, j'ai pris un sujet effrayant]."[16] Identifying his own sterility
with Hérodiade's, he sees the poem as a serious challenge to his powers
of creation, a power unfulfilled by paternity. "Hérodiade" becomes a project that will be as artistically and psychologically taxing for him as the
project of the Livre.

His description of the project is loaded with religious and spiritual
significance. In 1866, he writes that he has created "a world I'm the God
of" and "a work that will come from it" ("un monde dont je suis le
Dieu"; "un Oeuvre qui en résultera"). "Hérodiade" is destined to be one
of the "splendid and salomonesque twisted columns of this Temple
[colonnes torses, splendides et salomoniques, de ce Temple]."[17] Mallarmé
writes in 1865: "the most beautiful page of my oeuvre will be that one
that will contain only this divine name Hérodiade [la plus belle page de
mon oeuvre sera celle qui ne contiendra que ce nom divin Hérodiade]."[18]
Mallarmé's conception of the poem in May 1867 is immaculate: "I have
just spent a terrifying year: my thought was thought and arrived at a pure
Conception. ... I am perfectly dead [Je viens de passer une année ef-

frayante: ma Pensée s'est pensée, et est arrivée à une Conception Pure. ...
Je suis parfaitement mort]."[19] Mallarmé treats the poem now as if it were
a woman, no longer his child. But the failure to achieve what he wants
with the poem discourages him, and he describes himself as a rejected
lover:"to come to Paris without my Hérodiade . . . is a great sorrow and
humiliation [venir à Paris sans mon Hérodiade ... est une grande douleur
et une humiliation]."[20] Like an expensive and idealized mistress, he fears
she will prove to be beyond his reach: "she will have been beyond my
poor means [elle aura été bien au-delà de mes pauvres moyens]."[21] But
the poem simultaneously serves as a model of spiritual or aesthetic purity
identified with femininity, "a purity that man has not attained [d'une
pureté que l'homme n'a pas atteinte],"[22] and he wants to keep it pure—
"let's not vulgarize her/it [ne la vulgarisons pas trop]" (1444)—by carefully controlling its appearance in print.

Mallarmé is thus consecutively the father and lover of Hérodiade:
"For me, poetry holds the place of love, because she is taken with herself
and her voluptuousness falls deliciously back into my soul [Pour moi, la
Poésie me tient lieu de l'amour, parce qu'elle est éprise d'elle-même et
que sa volupté d'elle retombe délicieusement en mon âme]."[23] If the
poem expresses and reveals Mallarmé's sterility it is because paternity and
human love must give way to Poetry, and Poetry is created by sterility.
Mallarmé describes himself in a letter of this period as thinking not only
with his mind, but with all of himself: "I was trying not to think any
longer from my head [j'essayai de ne plus penser de la tête],"[24] manifesting a physical engagement with his writing. As Leo Bersani has summed
up, the history of the writing of "Hérodiade" is not only a story of gendering the poem as female and identifying with it, but a story of frustrated and repressed desire. For Bersani, this "thinking with his body"
can also be formulated as a "masturbatory atttention to certain images":

an attention which, inevitably, cannot stop producing other images in its annihilating replication of mental objects of *jouissance*. . . . The compositional procedures of "Hérodiade" record the moves of a sexualized mental text. Mallarmé's
specularizing strategies are attempts to reduce, even to abolish all the inexplicable, anguishing distances created by excited thought, just as Hérodiade's narcissism is the princess's wished-for solution to the unending self-remoteness which
is the price of her secret wish to be shattered by the desiring look of another.[25]

"Hérodiade" thus blurs conceptions of masculine and feminine sexuality; and both figure into the development of Mallarmé's sexual sensibility in the personal and poetic spheres. Hérodiade's sterility, and Mal-

larmé's identification with it, can be read as his attempt to rewrite what he called the "priapism" of his youth. But in response to the sterility of this poem, in June 1865 Mallarmé significantly interrupts his work on "Hérodiade" to write "L'Après-midi d'un Faune," also intended for the theater: "I've left Hérodiade for the cruel winters: this solitary work had me sterilized, and in the interval, I'm rhyming a heroic interlude, whose hero is a faun [J'ai laissé Hérodiade pour les cruels hivers: cette oeuvre solitaire m'avait sterilisé, et dans l'intervalle, je rime un intermède héroique, dont le héros est un faune]."[26]

"L'Après-midi d'un Faune" can be read as the perfect complement to "Hérodiade," the place Mallarmé put all of the material he wished to write out of the "solitary" work. The erotic adventures of its hero counter her cold isolation, and though they, too, are set in a tone of dreamlike doubt, an unmistakable sense of pleasure fills the poem, aptly recreated as a "masturbatory attention to certain images" in the ballet Nijinsky created in 1912 to Debussy's musical version of the poem.[27] The active pleasure of "rhyming" a summer poem appears to break the writing block of the winter poem. Like Hérodiade, the Faune narcissistically muses over the nature of dream and reality, the flux of identity, and sexual and power relations. After rhyming "L'Après-midi d'un Faune," Mallarmé is better able to "dream" "Hérodiade": "I dreamed my entire poem of Hérodiade admirably [je rêvais admirablement mon poème entier d'Hérodiade]"; "I'm returning to Hérodiade, I dream her so perfectly that I just don't know if she will ever exist [Je reviens à Hérodiade, je la rêve si parfaite que je ne sais seulement si elle existera jamais]."[28] Like the Faune himself, Mallarmé is now dreaming Hérodiade as if she were one of the nymphs. The writing of the poem becomes at this stage an attempt to make the dream real.

The writing and rewriting of "Hérodiade" repeat to some extent the creative and sexual development of Mallarmé, but realizing its dream is a process that he cannot control or enjoy. A first draft is presented to a friend as "Hérodiade, the work of my ravished nights" ("L'Hérodiade, oeuvre de mes nuits ravies").[29] As early as 1864, Catulle Mendès asks him, "Do you really need to shut yourself up in your spleen? . . . shouldn't one profit from one's talent and sing a little bit in its joy? [Avez-vous besoin de vous confiner dans le spleen? ... ne doit-on pas profiter de son talent et chanter un peu dans la joie?]"[30] The writing of "Hérodiade" makes Mallarmé himself into a victim; in his letter to Cazalis in December 1865, about his horrible "névralgie," he comments:

I threw myself like a despairing maniac into an unfathomable opening to my poem that sings in me but that I cannot note down . . . isolating myself in the unknown regions of Dreaming for this work that captivates me, I cannot be distracted and let myself have nice friendly conversations. I live in unviolated silence and solitude.

Je me jetais en maniaque désespéré sur une insaisissable ouverture de mon poème qui chante en moi mais que je ne puis noter ... m'isolant dans les régions inconnues de la Rêverie pour cette oeuvre qui me captive, je ne puis me distraire et me laisser aller aux douces conversations amicales. Je vis dans une solitude et dans un silence inviolés.[31]

Both "L'Après-midi d'un Faune" and "Hérodiade" indicate Mallarmé's willingness to give himself up to his poems, his ability to enter into their writing and identify with their central figures. They are two in a series of roles he imagines himself playing. In his changing conceptions of himself as a poet, Mallarmé moves from father to lover to woman, constantly recreating himself as a creator in another guise. There is the famous letter in which he writes before a mirror which alone guarantees his existence. In other letters there are fantasies in which he plays different roles—in one incarnation, he is a "sacred spider" weaving a lacework web of Beauty.[32] More than theatrical role-playing, this seems to be a rhythmic subjectivity, casting itself as hysterical, closely connected to what he will later admire in Loie Fuller—a subjectivity Mallarmé will later theorize as that of the poet himself.

Mallarmé originally conceived "Hérodiade" for the stage, but from the beginning it was unperformable by current standards of theatrical practice. In 1865, Théodore de Banville encouraged Mallarmé to think of staging "Hérodiade" at the Théâtre Français and to make sure it had sufficient "intérêt dramatique" in addition to poetry, stressing that Mallarmé should avoid making it "more poetic and less playable [plus poétique et moins jouable]."[33] Banville had perfectly predicted Mallarmé's intent: "Hérodiade"'s central figure is a Salome without the usual dramatic interest, who sits in her room at her mirror; and its central section dramatizes not the deadly dance, but a dialogue between the girl and her nurse. The character in this "Scène," as it was originally titled, is barely identifiable as Salome at all; she is certainly not a woman dancing, and is difficult to imagine onstage.

This is not to say that, in its earliest form, the poem is not theatrical.

In the "Scène," we find Mallarmé's first meditations on the idea of theater as a place in which it is possible for Nothing to happen. It is a place
in which Nothing can be seen, when "seeing" is understood to involve
more than looking. In "Hérodiade," the infamous dancer, while indulging
in narcissistic self-absorption, questions the conventional visual definitions
of feminity and spectacle. If Banville found the subject ripe for the stage,
it is not only because of the traditional showiness of the story, but because
of the woman at its center: he claims, "I have in mind not to compliment
you, but to help, if I can, your living and penetrating poetry to arrive all
palpitating before a crowd [j'ai à coeur non de vous complimenter, mais
d'aider si je le puis votre vive et penetrante poésie à arriver toute palpitante devant une foule]."[34] Banville makes clear, by confusing the poem
"Hérodiade" with the woman it presents, that what the crowd wants is
not poetry, but palpitation—the *"femme-spectacle."*

The Salome story traditionally provides the potential both for the excitement of visual spectacle and the power of legend; but Mallarmé's Salome is identified with poetry rather than with action, turning inward in
specular self-reflection.[35] "Hérodiade" has been read as the story of a future violation which will simultaneously end the girl's virginity and the
prophet's life—a "viol oculaire"[36]—thus opening the poem to a study of
the phenomenology of the gaze. The poem has been read as illustrating,
in Hérodiade herself, the "see-sawing"[37] or "rhythmic suspension" or "alternation" between abstract concepts such as the positive and the negative, opening up the poem to a study of the dialectic enacted in Mallarmé's ambiguous grammatical constructions and to deconstructive
study of the writing and its philosophical sources or implications.[38] The
poem has been read as a study of narcissism in which the central female
figure stands for poetry itself, opening the work up to feminist and psychoanalytic studies of the subject and subjectivity.[39] The poem easily
lends itself to other readings, focusing on the Salome legend's relationship
to questions of the sacred and the profane, sex and death, art and religion,
and the metaphor of the split between mind and body, all in the context
of nineteenth-century literature, art, and orientalism.[40]

Leo Bersani has charted how Hérodiade's refusal to dance serves to
turn the poem away from the idea of show, from visual imagery to abstraction, from objects or even objectivity to narcissistic subjectivity:

At this level of abstraction, the notion of vision itself becomes unintelligible, and
in "Hérodiade" Mallarmé brilliantly uses narcissism as a psychological metaphor

for the replicating and annihilating operations of thought. The attempt to achieve self-possession through specular self-immobilization is, in the poem, a dramatic figure for the inevitably abortive adherence of thought to its object.[41]

Mallarmé describes the work as producing a new kind of poetry: "At any rate, I have found there a private and singular way to paint and note very fleeting impressions [J'ai, du reste, là trouver une façon intime et singulière de peindre et de noter les impressions très fugitives]."[42] This poetry describes effect, sensation, relations between things rather than things themselves: "To paint, not the thing, but the effect it produces [Peindre, non la chose, mais l'effet qu'elle produit]."[43] "Hérodiade" links this effect to the female figure at its center. To paint internal effect rather than external image, to turn away from superficial ornament, poetry must turn inward, as its main character does, "taken with herself." In "Crise de Vers," Mallarmé will explain, in the 1890s, how this poetry works. The disappearing poet leaves the initiative to the words themselves: they are set in motion by their different weights, their "inégalité mobilisés" (366). The tradition of lyric poetry in which the poet's own voice marks the verse is replaced by the light of words playing off each other like gemstones:

The pure work implies the elocutionary disappearance of the poet who cedes the initiative to words, mobilized through their colliding inequality; they light up with reciprocal reflections like a virtual train of fire on gemstones, replacing perceptible respiration in the old lyric breath or the personal enthusiastic direction of the sentence.

L'oeuvre pur implique la disparition élocutoire du poëte, qui cède l'initiative aux mots, par le heurt de leur inégalité mobilisés; ils s'allument de reflets réciproques comme une virtuelle traînée de feux sur des pierreries, remplaçant la respiration perceptible en l'ancien souffle lyrique ou la direction personnelle enthousiaste de la phrase. (366)

This formula has been read as a formalism that takes all the humanity or personality out of poetry, creating poems like the so-called "Sonnet en -yx." But if Mallarmé here praises words' self-reflecting, jewel-like qualities, elsewhere he argues that bad poets, like women without taste, value jewelry rather than its poetic equivalent. The words of poetry are not themselves jewels, carefully arranged to adorn verse, but states of the soul set out to gleam like jewels. He criticizes this precious style of poetry:

The childishness of literature up to now has been to think, for example, that to choose a certain number of precious stones and to put their names down on paper, even superbly well, was to *make* precious stones. Not at all! Since poetry consists of creating, one must take from the human soul certain states, certain glimmerings of such absolute purity that, skillfully sung and brought to light, they indeed constitute the jewels of man: there, there is symbol, there is creation, and the word poetry takes on its meaning: that, in sum, is the only human creation possible. And if, truly, the precious stones one dresses in do not manifest a state of mind or mood, then one has no right to wear them ... Woman, for example, that eternal thief.

L'enfantillage de la littérature jusqu'ici a été de croire, par example, que de choisir un certain nombre de pierres précieuses et en mettre les noms sur le papier, même très bien, c'est *faire* des pierres precieuses. Eh bien! non! La poésie consistant à creer, il faut prendre dans l'âme humaine des états, des lueurs d'une pureté si absolue que, bien chantés et bien mis en lumière, cela constitue en effet les joyaux de l'homme: là, il y a symbole, il y a creation, et le mot poésie a ici son sens: c'est, en somme, la seule creation humaine possible. Et si, véritablement, les pierres precieuses dont on se pare ne manifestent pas un etat d'âme, c'est indûment qu'on s'en pare ... La femme, par example, cette éternelle voleuse. (870)

Mallarmé interrupts himself to make a comparison between such poets and the women who prize jewelry rather than the jewels of the human soul:

And think, *adds my interlocutor half-laughing*: what is admirable about those high-fashion stores is that they have sometimes revealed to us, through the chief of police, that women have been illegitimately wearing what they didn't know the hidden meaning of, and which consequently does not belong to them.

Tenez, *ajoute mon interlocuteur en riant à moitié*, ce qu'il y a d'admirable dans les magasins de nouveautés, c'est, quelquefois, de nous avoir révélé, par le commissaire de police, que la femme se parait indûment de ce dont elle ne savait pas le sens caché, et qui ne lui appartient par conséquent pas. (870–71)[44]

In this complex formulation, Mallarmé describes the understanding of words' "hidden meaning" as true ownership of valuable goods. Lacking the understanding of jewels' real value, women do not deserve to wear them. But the reference to department stores selling "novelties" and to police commissioners, who protect "hidden" value, gives the story a different spin: "kleptomaniac" women spurred into petty crime by the hysteria of shopping at the new department stores do not realize that the real value of jewels is their pure representation of light and soul.[45] Like bad poets, they want to display their gems—even fake—for the wrong reason.

The word "pierreries" figures prominently as the last word of "Hérodiade"'s "Scène," its referent shifting from the elements of poetic form to the elements of the female form in whom the poetry resides. If Mallarmé tends to trivialize the very objects—jewels, baubles, "parure"—which serve as seemingly inconsequential touchstones for his poetry, they are, Philippe Lacoue-Labarthe has noted, the crucial starting points for meditations on Nothingness ("le Néant"). Here, following in the tradition that links virginity to treasure, Hérodiade's jewels are her body: "a childhood sensing among its dreamings / finally the separation of its cold gemstones [une enfance sentant parmi les rêveries / Se séparer enfin ses froides pierreries]."[46] The pure poetry that "Hérodaide" represents is thus identified with Hérodiade's sex.

Not only does the poem present the young woman thinking, and equate her thinking and her body with poetry, it also represents her thinking about herself as the same as the poet's thinking about poetry. This reflexivity, Barbara Johnson has argued, is part of how Mallarmé's poetics create a feminine voice critiquing "pretensions to representationalism and realism in the literary text":

By thus opposing naive referentiality and privileging blankness and silence, Mallarmé . . . implicitly shifts the gender values traditionally assigned to such questions. If the figure of woman has been repressed and objectified by being equated with the blank page, then Mallarmé, by *activating* those blanks, comes close to writing from the place of the silenced female voice. In his ways of throwing his voice as a woman, of figuring textuality as a dancing ballerina, and of questioning simplistic pretensions to expressivity, potency, and (masculine) authority, Mallarmé's critique of logocentrism opens up a space for a critique of phallocentrism as well.[47]

Part of this critique is a revalorization of the difficulty—even inability—to write associated with "Hérodiade." For Johnson this "state of castration," the writer's block Mallarmé experiences in "Hérodiade," is invoked by him as a Muse: "the lack of inspiration has become the source of inspiration. Mallarmé, as has often been noted, has transformed the incapacity to write into the very subject of his writing."[48]

Thus the body of the woman is associated with expression, writing, text, poetry, and also with its impossibility. The "castration" of Mallarmé's writing—for Johnson, the very condition by which it is produced—is identified with "the feminine" in "Hérodiade," in which the female body represents that "castration." But rather than simply figuring castration, Hérodiade problematizes it, manifesting what Michèle Montrelay has called a "fear of femininity": "fear of the feminine body as a non-repressed and unrepresentable object." Such "femininity" experiences as real and immediate the blind spot of the symbolic processes analysed by Freud. Thus although, in Freudian terms, the female body represents castration when castration is figured simply as the lack of male genitalia, this "lack" is camouflaged defensively, by female narcissism or by silence—strategies used by Hérodiade. In this way the female body presents or represents a castration that is not only anatomical but also psychological:

It is a question of the organization not of a symbolic, but an imaginary representation of castration: a lack is simulated and thereby the loss of some stake—an enterprise easily accomplished in that feminine anatomy, in fact, reveals to the eye a lack, that of the penis. While remaining her own phallus, then, the woman will disguise herself with this lack, making the dimension of castration arise in *trompe-l'oeil*. The shapes this can take are multiple. One can play out the absence of penis as silence as well as in a noisy vanity.

Il s'agit d'organiser une représentation non plus symbolique, mais imaginaire de la castration: on simulera un manque, et, par là, la perte de quelque enjeu. Entreprise d'autant plus aisée que l'anatomie féminine, justement, donne à voir un manque, celui du pénis. Tout en restant son propre phallus, la femme se travestira donc de ce manque, faisant surgir en trompe-l'oeil la dimension de castration. Les modes de figuration sont multiples. On peut jouer de l'absence de pénis tout aussi bien par le silence que par une vanité bruyante.[49]

For Montrelay, the feminine masquerade thought to travesty the lack in the female body in fact signals the lack in every body by representing it; feminine adornment can be interpreted as blinding the viewer in such a way that no lack can be seen, and yet serves to point out the blindness in the thinking that cannot see any lack. In Johnson's view, Mallarmé does not simply opt for a feminine rather than masculine model of creation, or female reproduction as a model for male poetic production; but describes both masculine and feminine creative powers in similarly castrated terms. Johnson notes that Mallarmé's work is not another "typical example of the male pen expressing its womb envy"[50] because most often in his poems, in "Don du Poème" (Gift of a poem), for example, femininity and masculinity are both sexless. And yet that lack of identity, that sexlessness, is figured in Hérodiade as it will be later in Loie Fuller—as depending upon femininity, and the female body is described as poetry itself.

Mallarmé's theater ideal, and his interest in the intimate theater of the female body in dance, are announced in opposition to Wagnerian theater, the major French theater event of Mallarmé's theatergoing lifetime. In his development of Mallarméan texts on dance, theater, music, and rite in *Musica Ficta*, Philippe Lacoue-Labarthe argues that for Mallarmé, from the beginning of his "adult" writing, the question of poetry—a philosophical question—is a question of the relation between poetry and music as epitomized by Wagner and Baudelaire's response to him: an ultimate recognition of music as the real lyric poetry.

But the question of poetry for Mallarmé is also closely connected to the problem of dance. As an alternate form of what Lacoue-Labarthe names, from Adorno, "musica ficta"—as fictioned music or embodied, fleshed-out rhythm, dance raises many of the same philosophical issues as Wagnerism and anti-Wagnerism. Although dance was, significantly, never a part of the total work of art, many of the questions that Wagner's music and its reception raise about the lyric subject and the choral community are also raised by dance as it is treated in *Crayonné au théâtre*. The issues raised by Wagner and Wagnerism—lyricism, legend as opposed to myth, spectacle as opposed to chorus, hysteria—are all in play in Mallarmé's understanding of dance. His interest in how different forms of dance address these questions moves through his entire writing career, especially in the continuous rewriting of "Hérodiade."

Dance is for Mallarmé very much part of the argument about whether Poetry is the product of the poet or the musician, the question concerning Wagner. Lacoue-Labarthe notes that for Mallarmé, Wagner's work is neither theater nor music. This too could be thought true of dance: too concrete, too narrative to function like music; closer to what Mallarmé calls "legend" in Wagner; and not "myth"—not mythic enough, like Wagner, to be ritual or tragedy. But when describing theater and what Wagner has done to it, Mallarmé isolates dance from theater because it is closer to Idea and to writing: "Omission made of glances at the extraordinary but unfinished splendor today of plastic figuration, where, at least, in its perfected rendering, is isolated the Dance alone capable, in its summary writing, of translating the fleeting and the sudden up to the Idea—same vision constitutes all, absolutely all the future Spectacle— [Omission faite de coups d'oeil sur le faste extraordinaire mais inachevé aujourd'hui de la figuration plastique, d'où s'isole, du moins, en sa perfection de rendu, la Danse seule capable, par son écriture sommaire, de traduire le fugace et le soudain jusqu'à l'Idée—pareille vision comprend tout, absolument tout le Spectacle futur—]" (541). While Wagner hammers out a new relation between music and drama, dance has already outstripped him, moving like writing, through condensation, from theater (almost) all the way to Idea. Although the arguments Lacoue-Labarthe develops in *Musica Ficta* about the relation between music and Mallarméan "Littérature" generally hold for dance (with perhaps only one crucial difference, the problem of the "Type," to be considered here), dance becomes marginal to his point, which is to show how Mallarméan Literature depends upon an ontotypology, a "theater" of the Type that borrows elements of the Catholic mass or the Greek chorus in its manifestation—but not representation—of the presence of the crowd, the "being-there" of community in "communion."[51]

Although his ideal "theater" of Literature or Poetry is, as Lacoue-Labarthe says, anti-Aristotelian, anti-empathetic, and anti-hysterical, Mallarmé—throughout his writing life—conceives of poetry in the dancer's form, speaking through elocutionary disappearance. The dancer disappears from Lacoue-Labarthe's argument because in the nineteenth-century context, and in Mallarmé's text, the dancer is female, and the subject of her dance is femininity itself: *hystera* and hysteria, the female and the effeminate. For Lacoue-Labarthe, Mallarmé's theater, with its civic and religious tone, is the theater of "no one" or "any one"—the theater of the Type. And it is an anti-Aristotelian theater, a theater without mimesis or catharsis, in no way to be confused with the hysterical, empathetic theater of Wagner. The only femininity that can be figured into this civic/religious theater is that of a universal Mother,[52] whom the dancer can never reproduce. Inasmuch as nineteenth-century dance is about the female body, it cannot be the drama of any body. And though Mallarmé also identifies a mystery on the side of conception, associated with the Mother, the dance could never be this either. Though Mallarmé describes Loie Fuller's dance in uterine terms, as *éclosion* or birthing, she gives birth only to herself as images and through images; she is the "inextinguishable fountain" only of herself.

In the systematic equations of Mallarméan formulation in the notes to the Livre, poetry equals idea, and idea equals theater. Dance, like Wagnerian theater itself (and inasmuch as it resembles Wagnerian theater for Lacoue-Labarthe), drops out of the argument; and yet, despite dance's limitations, rooted as it is in the body, dance continues to be present, if invisible, in the Mallarméan formulation of Literature as theater. The etymology of "rhythm" as traced by Emil Benveniste and suggested by Mallarmé's use of the term partly explains what in dance interests Mallarmé. Watching Loie Fuller, Mallarmé sees rhythm as a way to reconceive the relation between inside and outside in the structure of the body and the relation of the artist to the artwork. Such rhythmic relation, manifest in the dance and the dancer, whose body is not fixed, and who does not really represent, are also at issue in the Type. Although the dancer is excluded from this ontotypology, inasmuch as she is rhythmic she remains very close to Mallarméan poesis. Dance does not include everything that Mallarmé means by "rhythm," but because rhythm is a way to describe what is significant in dance, it suggests how close to Poetry dance remains for him conceptually.

For Mallarmé, music, like Literature, is Mystery; it creates or manifests the presence of the crowd. The chorus is the locus of this presence, not the stage; and for Lacoue-Labarthe, dance does not create, in Mallarmé's mind, the communion or community that song can. Mallarmé is interested in dance for other reasons; but he tellingly names as his two favorite arts the unlikely pair of organ music and dance. Both must contain the Mystery he says Literature (or Poetry) contains, and which he locates as well in his ideal theater, the "theater" that idea (or poetry) is. Organ music is a very institutional kind of mystery: in it one hears the walls of the church that contain it—yet the music itself also often seems to render the church empty, the organist alone. Does Mallarmé like dance for the same reason—because it is at once an institutional and a solitary art, the secular counterpart to the organ? or its complement? This odd pairing suggests that dance is more important to Mallarméan mystery than has been thought. The dance that interests Mallarmé is not "choral" in the usual sense of the group that fills the orchestra; it is "choral" in the sense that it presents, or represents, that same walled, empty space.

In the case of Loie Fuller, that space will be simultaneously located within the body and without. Mallarmé's descriptions of this space Fuller creates and dances in more closely resemble what Julia Kristeva calls "chora,"[53] and in its association with the feminine, the nonverbal, the womb, such a theater also inevitably raises the issue of "chorea" or hysteria. Unlike the hysteria of Wagnerian music drama, dance chooses not to speak; Lacoue-Labarthe calls it écriture. But because it chooses, not-speaking, to speak with the body, it complicates the status of its nonspeaking subject. I have suggested in this chapter that by calling the dancer Sign, Mallarmé suggests a semiology of dance that includes what would later be thought of as the represssion that aligns her production of dance with that of the subject in language, and her signs with the production of symptom.

Rhythm is a way to describe that aspect of the female body dancing that makes it a useful concept for Mallarmé to conceive of writer and writing. The dance, for Benveniste's Plato, is the art in which the form and the content are not simply inseparable, but indistinguishable. Dance is inseparable from the human form dancing it; its form is ultimately the human form. But dance complicates this formal relationship by forever scrambling the two forms, body and movement, making it impossible to identify one as signifier and the other as signified.

Readings of Mallarmé usually situate rhythm in a sphere of poetry that has little to do with his interest in the theater of his time or the life and art of the body. His references to rhythm are often mystical or purely literary. In the texts of *Crayonné au théâtre* and in his prose texts on poetry, rhythm is the soul: "every soul is a rhythmic knot" (644). Rhythm is also what Poetry is all about—it is style, the personal mark of the writer on the writing: "rhythm as soon as style [rythme dès que style]" (361). Or it is the impersonal mark of the writing itself. For Mallarmé, "the poetic act consists of seeing, suddenly, an idea fractured into a number of motifs of equal value, and in grouping them; they rhyme." Serving as their external imprint or seal is their rhythm: "for external seal, their shared measure that the final stroke connects [pour sceau extérieur, leur commune mesure qu'apparente le coup final]" (365). For Mallarmé, rhythm—poetry—is produced in this fractioning of idea rather than in its presentation in uninterrupted flow. Lacoue-Labarthe reminds us that rhythm, *rythmos* in the archaic Greek (of Democritus, for example), could also signify "letter"; and that in Heidegger's etymology *rythmos* originally signifies the mark or the imprint (*empreinte*).[54]

Platonic *ekmageion*, the womb that gives the mark or stamp of form, is clearly referred to by the "éclosion contemporaine." But it is the infinite potential, not the real productivity of the female body that figures poetic typology, its capacity for art that mimes reproduction. Considering his early tension with reproduction, if Mother (with a capital M) makes it into the late typology of *Catholicisme*, it might be at least in part because of the dancer, via the reconception of the female body as *rythmos*—and its alternate theatrical potential for *hystera*.

While dance may translate Idea into its condensed writing (or translate writing into Idea), it does so via the body, with *hystera*, the female form—here I think understood as Platonic *ekmageion*, form-giving (translated in French as *porte-empreintes*) rather than as Aristotelian deviation from form. And thus it ultimately fails, in its incorporation, to translate *idée*. Although in earlier writing, Mallarmé finds in the dancer all the qualities that will later congeal in the "Type"—that she is no one, that she both represents and presents "idea"—with "Les Noces d'Hérodiade," at the end of his life, the romantic or Symbolist notion of the dancer as the ultimate incarnation of poetics, the embodiment of "idea," gives way.

The rewriting of "Hérodiade" throughout his lifetime traces Mallarmé's continuous interrogation of his theory that dance can represent "idée" by not-representing with the nonsexed, nondancing body. In "Hérodiade," the myth of pure poetry is closely connected with the purity of the female body in its virginity, its isolation, its stillness; the partial pages and notes of "Les Noces" bring in the blood, passion, and action drained out of the triptych. If Mallarmé's first "Hérodiade" represents the dance as unrepresentable, and turns away from hysteria, deflecting it onto its author at the mirror, the late version reinstates both in the missing dance.

This final version of "Hérodiade" is announced in a "Bibliographie" included with the manuscript as a continuation of the earlier project:

Only a fragment of this poem had been published—from—to—; it was preceded by an Overture that I am replacing with another, in the same vein—and as for the monologue—as to why the crisis indicated by the piece—I confess that I had stopped in my youth. I give here the motif as it has since appeared, attempting to treat it in the same spirit.

Un fragment seul de ce poème avait été publié—de—à—; il était précédé d'une ouverture que je remplace par une autre, en le même sens—et quant au monologue—au pourquoi de la crise indiquée par le morceau—j'avoue que je m'étais arrêté dans ma jeunesse. Je le donne, ce motif tel qu'apparu depuis, m'efforçant de traiter dans le mê me esprit.[55]

Despite his insistence on finding the "same spirit" after twenty years or more, the fragments of this manuscript suggest the outline of a poem very different from the earlier versions, and much closer to the Salomes of the "l'art pour l'art" movement. Yet in a brief preface to the poem, one section of a series of introductory remarks scattered on different sheets of paper, Mallarmé defines the project against the fin-de-siècle passion for Salome most notable in Wilde's 1891 play:

I left the name of Hérodiade in order to differentiate her clearly from the Salome I will call modern, exhumed with her ancient *fait divers*—the dance, etc. to isolate her as the solitary paintings have done, even in the terrible and mysterious act—and to make dazzling what probably haunted—appearing with her attribute—the saint's head—the young lady had to constitute a monster for the vulgar lovers of life—the ornament was bothersome.

J'ai laissé le nom d'Hérodiade pour bien la différencier de la Salomé je dirai moderne ou exhumée avec son fait divers archaï que—la danse etc. l'isoler comme l'ont fait des tableaux solitaires dans le fait même terrible, mystérieux— et faire miroiter ce qui probablement hanta—en apparue avec son attribut—le chef du saint—dût la demoiselle constituer un monstre aux amants vulgaires de la vie—parure gênait.[56]

Although Mallarmé here comes down against the art-for-art's sake Salomes with their severed heads and monstrous dances, the text of the poem problematically embraces the dance after this initial refusal.[57] To reintroduce the dance in the late version is to return to the myth of Salome so hidden in the earlier version. If the beginnings of Mallarmé's poem in the 1860s treated a Salome figure already familiar in the context of nineteenth-century French literature, the versions from the late 1880s and 1890s treat a figure who had become infamous.

What had been of interest to the other writers adopting the figure as a literary vehicle of "l'art pour l'art" seems to be of interest to Mallarmé in this late rewriting of the story: Salome's uncanny ability to incorporate the contradiction of a divided self, to represent a horrifying split between mind and body, not only in the decapitation her dance provokes, but in the way in which her dance illustrates a beautiful body at the service of an evil mind. Every version has to take a stand on whether Salome is the unwilling agent of her mother, unaware of the evil in which she is engaged, or whether her dance is a willful seduction.[58]

Although critics have noted in these lines Mallarmé's rejection of the "fait divers archaïque" and linked it to his alleged repugnance for Wilde's 1891 Salomé, Wilde's play, although it does call upon the actress to dance, says nothing about that dance. A black hole at the center of the play, the dance is never described by Wilde except in a personal note to the play's illustrator, Aubrey Beardsley.[59] Because Mallarmé's rewrite is unfinished, and because of Mallarmé's own hesitation, highlighted by red pencil marks crossing out entire pages of notes, the fragments do not lend themselves to textual analysis. Rather, what is significant is the reappearance of the dance as a spectacle, in contrast to "Hérodiade"'s meditation on it.

Reinserting the dance completely changes the tone of the earlier poem's themes of desire, spectacle, and victimization, and reinserts them into a mythic context. Mallarmé explains that he broke off the earlier "Hérodiade" project because he did not understand its "motif": "I realized the *motif* / the ignorance of which / had made me stop [je me / rendis compte du *motif* / dont l'ignorance / m'avait fait interrompre]." The "motif"—both motive and formal motif—that the unfinished "Les Noces" reintroduces is the dance, with its ritual violence. In two consecutive pages of notes for the preface to "Les Noces," Mallarmé writes:[60]

> Preface
> legend stripped
> of dance
> and even of the
> vulgarity—of the head
> on the platter

> Préface
> légende dépouillée
> de danse
> et même de la
> grossièreté—de la tête
> sur le plat.

And on the next page:

> Pref.
> before the cold wins—
> today
> I would find again
> the dance
> —displacement of
> the dance—here—and
> not anecdotal.

> Préf.
> avant que le froid ne gagne—
> _____
> aujourd'hui
> je retrouverais
> la danse
> —déplacement de
> la danse—ici—et
> pas anecdotique.

He does indeed recreate the "fait divers archaïque" in the pages of notes for "Les Noces." In passages reminiscent of Flaubert's *Hérodias*, this dancer is unveiled and acrobatic:

does she lean to one
side—to the other—
revealing one
breast*—the other—
and surprise
without veil
*like this breast, that one
identity

se penche-t-elle d'un
côté—de l'autre—montrant un
sein*—l'autre—
et surprise
sans gaze
*selon ce sein, celui-là
identité.[61]

And on another page, the notes read:

*in what she held the
head above bust
flowing dress*
breasts
—by myself
to withdraw—never her.

*dans ce qu'elle tenait la
tête au dessus buste
robe couler*
seins
—de moi-même
reculer—jamais elle.[62]

Gardner Davies has argued that Mallarmé intended to end "Les Noces" with a dance that would be "purely intellectual," a dance that would
"symbolize . . . in Mallarmé's eyes the reciprocal subjection of the genius
and of his dream of beauty, which is the condition for the pure work."[63]
Davies's argument rests on a comparison between the movement of the
boat in "Un Coup de Dés" ("penché de l'un ou l'autre bord"), and the
danse in which Hérodiade "se penche-t-elle d'un côté—de l'autre."[64]
Such a reading ignores the eroticism of "Les Noces" by ignoring—for
example—the line which follows: "montrant un sein—l'autre." This
dance of display and its detailing of the naked body, sketched out in the

passage Davies cites, can in no way be mistaken for a "danse purement intellectuelle."

In contrast to dances described in *Crayonné au théâtre*, this simple belly dance is only "a sort of dance":

> And that makes—on
> one foot the other,
> themselves
> on the feet
> breasts
> a sort of dance
> terrifying sketch
> —and in place, without
> moving
> —a null site.

> et cela fait—sur
> un pied l'autre,
> eux-mêmes
> sur les pieds
> seins
> une sorte de danse
> effrayante esquisse
> —et sur place, sans
> bouger
> —lieu nul.[65]

This "sort of dance" takes place in a "null site"[66] which recalls both the ideally empty space, and the "contemporary emptiness [vide contemporain]," of the modern theater. It seems far from the "poème dégagé de tout appareil du scribe" because it is quite explicit, "effrayante" rather than enigmatic, a sketch rather than a summary. Yet at some points, the poem hesitates in its presentation of the dance, seeming to reject external "show" for a dance that would reflect the interiority of the earlier triptych:

> imagined
> monologue—
> silence and dance—
> attitudes—
> only monologue
> internal brilliance

pensé
monologue—
silence et danse—
attitudes—
seul monologue
éclat intérieur.[67]

All three potential endings pair Hérodiade with the prophet, a pairing that is common in the nineteenth-century Salome stories, presenting her as an image of apparent unity of mind and body that are in fact terrifying in their disunity, in contrast to the saint, whose mind and body are one. The essence of this pairing, of the dance, and of the notes for the "Finale" is ambiguity:

the ambiguity of Hé-
rodiade and of her
dance.
she masters this
revolted head
that wanted
to think higher—
where is extinguished the idea
unheard of and [ ]

"l'ambiguité d'Hé-
rodiade et de sa
danse.
elle maîtrise cette
tête révoltée
qui a voulu
penser plus haut—
où s'éteint l'idée inouïe et [ ][68]

The ambiguity of Hérodiade and this dance moves beyond the ambiguity of Mallarméan syntax. This is an ambiguity of power relations, and the logic of ritual sacrifice. Writing about the Salome story as told in the Gospel of Mark, René Girard comments on the dancer's power to turn the crowd's desire from herself to the head of the prophet: "A successful dance puts the mimetic power in the hands of the dancer, who channels it in the direction of her choice, whereas an unsuccessful dance . . . turns the dancer herself into a victim."[69] The ambiguity of dance, and thus its closeness to ritual, depends upon its ability both to represent and present;

to work metaphorically or allegorically, while incorporating or making-present. This doubleness is precisely the ambiguity of the "Type," the "hero" of Mallarmé's ideal drama.

Mallarmé defines dance as an intermediary: "I am speaking here about Ballet that merges with the personal Drama to bring to it a more strictly allegorical element, thus brings it from history or legend closer to poetry or pure myth [je parle bien du Ballet qui mêle au Drame personnel pour y apporter un element plus strictement allégorique, le ramène ainsi de l'histoire ou même de la légende à la poésie ou au mythe pur]."[70] But it is not at all clear from the unfinished text how the dance of "Les Noces d'Hérodiade" succeeds in purification or mythification. The Mallarméan conception of dance as idea seems not to be operative in this text about the "idée inouie" or "unheard of idea." Perhaps the dance simply reestablishes the rhythmic, ritualistic rapport among things that is crucial both to Mallarméan poetics and to theater—not a theater of objects and subjects but a theater of rhythmic relations: "things exist, we don't have to create them, we only have to understand their relationships; and it is the threads of such relationships that form verse and orchestras [les choses existent, nous n'avons pas à les creer; nous n'avons qu'à en saisir les rapports; et ce sont les fils de ces rapports qui forment les vers et les orchestres]" (871). The "orchestra," differentiated from the stage or *skena*, is the heart of these "rapports." Mallarmé's ideal theater would discard the "scène" in favor of the orchestra, the chorus, in an attempt to eliminate audience identification with the stage hero.

The theater that Mallarmé envisions to replace the "scène" is a quasi-religious drama with a Christlike hero and a ritual form resembling in some of its nonpresentational aspects the Catholic mass;[71] but he does not accept the identification that such a hero seems to demand from an audience. Nor does he speak of the crowd that seems necessary for ritual in "Catholicisme" or "De Même," the two most explicit explorations of the idea. Such a theater is what "Les Noces d'Hérodiade" seems to sketch out; after the pure early poetry and the abstract dance of Loie Fuller, "Les Noces" seems to try, via its dance, to bring the legend and the allegory back into the more purely poetic myth. Ironically, it is the very reasons that made the first "Hérodiade" possible in Mallarmé's mind—the death of the poet, the poem's pivoting ambiguity (no longer metaphors but both now literal)—that here keep the dance from representing "idée." Mallarmé's theories of poetry locate themselves in a range of dancers: real or fictional, the dancer becomes the terrain for the problem of writing "nothing," a model both for pure poetry and for ritualistic myth, for translating "idea" and for its unrepresentability; for the shifting identity of the poet as image-maker. But Mallarmé's unfinished struggles with the versions of "Hérodiade" suggest dance's ultimate failure at the kind of nonrepresentation "idée" requires; or rather, the unrepresentability of "idée" itself.

Nineteenth-century French art's fascination with Salome is a fascination with the problems of representation and hysteria; with the impossibility of representing Salome's strange, simultaneous madness and beauty. The story of Salome raises the issues of feminine sexuality, perversion, evil, and agency; the various versions of the Salome tale all pass judgment on whether Salome is to blame for the beheading of the prophet or is only the agent of her evil mother, in what ways the dancer's beauty is at odds with the bloody result of the dance and whether the dancing body can lie.

Salome illustrates a problematic relation between mind and body typical of hysteria's myriad forms. The central image from the Salome story is that of a head divided from its body—the prophet's—figuring the dancer's own division, her beautiful body at the service of an evil mind. Mallarmé's versions of the myth, and Wilde's as well, insist on a doubling of the prophet and the princess which underlines their complementarity: on one hand, the prophet's beheading is, in Bersani's reading of the final poem of Mallarmé's triptych "Salut," a sign of the transcendant unity of body and spirit after death: "Decapitation provides an opportunity for an unprecedented harmony between mind and body."[72] On the other hand, the dance's apparent unity of mind and body, purpose and process, do not match with Hérodiade's introspective indecision; Salome dances like someone who has, metaphorically at least, lost her head.

The nineteenth-century fascination with Salome, often described as Decadence's romance with the evil and erotic excess embodied in her story, is not only a fascination with the drapery of the myth but with the character herself. Among the most famous French versions—Flaubert's *Herodias*, Huysman's *A Rebours*, Mallarmé's "Hérodiade," and Oscar Wilde's *Salome*—the latter three focus on and develop the character of the girl who remains a cipher in Flaubert's short story. In the Gospel of Mark, Salome is only the pawn of her mother's scheming to get the head of the prophet whose resounding warnings include direct attacks on her for sins which include a second marriage to her dead husband's brother. In *Herodias*, similarly, the daughter is nothing but the dominating mother's agent. But in the other texts, Salome becomes an image for the writer's aesthetic, the push toward the limits of expression, and the danger implicit in it.

In Wilde's version, widely read as an imitation of Mallarmé but for Wilde himself the masterpiece of his oeuvre, on which he staked his reputation, the dance remains a mystery. Salome is again a cold, narcissistic virgin, in love with herself until she forces the guard to let her see the prophet, and her dance—presumably here a dance of desire and revenge—is a blank in the text. The stage direction gives no instructions for movement or music. Wilde found it impossible to stage the play during his lifetime; a 1892 London production with Sarah Bernhardt was called off in rehearsals by Queen Victoria's chamberlain. After Wilde's death, a London production of the play with Maud Allen, coached by Loie Fuller, became the subject of a scandalous censorship trial, in which her homosexuality, almost as a stand-in for Wilde's, was put on trial.[73]

Huysman's esthete and antihero, des Esseintes, has a particular interest in Salome which bespeaks her fascination for the "l'art pour l'art" movement, which we find in one form earlier (in Mallarmé) and later in Wilde's play. Des Esseintes is the happy owner of one of Gustave Moreau's paintings of Salome, from which he derives a certain amount of scopophilic pleasure; the representation of Salome is both highly elegant and erotic. The woman herself is at once beautiful and depraved, an ideal image for the art of the Décadence, with its interest in destructive beauty. Des Esseintes points out that none of the Bible accounts had "enlarged on the maddening charm and potent depravity of the dancer."[74] In fact, she had always been unrepresentable, "had always passed the comprehension of the writing fraternity, who never succeeded in rendering the disquieting delirium of the dancer, the subtle grandeur of the murderess."

Salome's unrepresentability in writing signals several reasons why she is of such interest to Décadence: she cannot be written because her fascination rests in the visual rather than the verbal sphere, as a moving image rather than as a story; her crime is so great, her dance so terrible, that it defies representation. The unsayable is both the unspeakable and the sacred in this myth, both the horror of the dance and the holiness that the dance defiles. Moreau's painting, by representing her in the dance, does what Des Esseintes's or Symbolist art tries to do, to name the unnameable, to speak the unspeakable. It is important to note the two conditions that Des Esseintes attributes to Moreau, which make him capable of such expression: first, his essential originality—he is no one's pupil; and second, the fact that he has "crossed the frontiers of painting to borrow from the writer's art its most subtly evocative suggestions" as well as borrowing from the enameller and the etcher. The reference is to earlier Symbolist doctrines of evocation, particularly that of "the sorcery of certain of Baudelaire's poems." It is clear why Huysman's work was considered a kind of compendium of Symbolist-Décadent art, as he hits here its crucial issues: representation of the unrepresentable, utter originality, cross-fertilization of artistic media, evocation rather than direct representation, and perhaps most important, the contradictions or misrepresentations inherent in these assertions; for example, art that is original though it restages an old myth, art that represents what cannot be represented.

What is important to note is that the dancer herself is an image for this artistic doctrine. The dance of Salome is unrepresentable not simply for formal reasons. In the painting, she moves with "her eyes fixed in the concentrated gaze of a sleepwalker." She does not see, or seem to know, what she is doing. What is unrepresentable here is the dance itself; for all that the painting pretends to capture it, it misses, of course, the crucial movement and rhythm, which it can only freeze or "fix" in the way Salome's eyes are fixed. Des Esseintes calls Salome "the Goddess of immortal Hysteria" whose movements are a kind of catalepsy. She is "a monstrous Beast, indifferent, irresponsible, insensible, poisoning, like the Helen of ancient myth, everything that approaches her, everything that sees her, everything that she touches." It is the hysteria of this hypnotized and hypnotizing dancer that challenges representation: movement beyond the mind's control, beauty and horror, innocence and evil simultaneously. The dance is unrepresentable except by a union of visual, verbal, and material arts because it embodies an impossible union of calculation and madness, seduction and destruction. In this tradition, it is an art of contradiction, multiple and hysterical.

The multiple subjectivity Mallarmé finds in Loie Fuller's serial imagery is described by Jules Clarétie, novelist, journalist, director of the Théâtre Français and student of hysteria, as he watches her rehearse the *Tragedie de Salomé*, by Robert d'Humières, in street clothes, both playing her role and indicating it in a way that recalls Brechtian performance style:

There, on that evening when I saw her rehearse Salome in everyday clothes, without costume, her glasses over her eyes, measuring her steps, outlining in her dark robe the seductive and suggestive movements, which she will produce tomorrow in her brilliant costume, I seemed to be watching a wonderful impresaria, manager of her troupe as well as mistress of the audience. . . .

Then I had the immense pleasure of seeing this Salome in everyday clothes dance her steps without the illusion created by theatrical costume, with a simple strip of stuff, sometimes red and sometimes green, for the pupose of studying the reflections on the moving folds under the electric light. It was Salome dancing, but a Salome in a short skirt, a Salome with a jacket over her shoulders, a Salome in a tailor-made dress. . . . The gleam from the footlights reflected itself on the dancer's glasses and blazed there like flame, like fugitive flashes, and nothing could be at once more fantastic and more charming than these twists of the body, these caressing motions, these hands, again, these superb dream hands waving there before Herod . . . observing the sight of the dance idealised in the everyday costume.[75]

Fuller is both master of stage direction and mistress of her audience, both *regisseur* and Salome; she is hypnotized and hypnotist; the obscure hopeful and the great inventor. In the introduction to Fuller's autobiography, Anatole France describes her doubleness as that of a woman whose conversation is as stimulating as her performance; Fuller is perceived as both intelligent and instinctive, simultaneously a savvy theatrical producer and a mystic. Here Salome's duplicity is closely linked to the doubleness or multifaceted nature of the dancer's form of representation.

Fuller describes herself, throughout her autobiography, as two women: Loie Fuller the performer who is the fairy, butterfly, or flower seen and loved onstage, and Loie Fuller the producer and choreographer, a respected colleague of the artists and intellectuals of her day. Fuller frequently makes disclaimers about her public success and separates her stage persona from her everyday self, "since my personality counts for nothing."[76] In fact, she denies that she *is* the woman onstage: when a child in her audience whom Fuller "seemed to have hypnotised"[77] comes to her dressing room, she claims that she is "not Loie Fuller." In each case, Fuller heightens her stage identity and the power of her performance by putting her own name in quotation marks. And indeed, after her initial successes, she is actually confronted with other women claiming to be "Loie Fuller": "I never arrive in a town without Loie Fuller's having been there in advance of me, and even in Paris I have seen announced in flamboyant letters, 'Loie Fuller, radiant dances,' and I have been able to see with my own eyes 'la Loie Fuller' dance before my face."

Fuller seems mostly unconcerned about this separation into two selves, the bracketing of the onstage "Loie Fuller," and even the replication of her image in the dances of her imitators. Shaped by the crowd and the stage, the dancer's subjectivity is, on the one hand, negligible, and on the other, all-encompassing.[78] Her narrative swings between the poles of self-denigration and self-aggrandizement. For Fuller herself, the two Loie Fullers go hand-in-hand: the "little soubrette" with the "noble soul," the "fat lady" with the orchid and butterfly, the simultaneous self-destruction and self-creation. Her subjectivity seems to depend upon this split; she describes it as a healthy multiplication of identities rather than a disturbing fracturing of a whole. This multiple, mobile subjectivity, created by her art, becomes the subject of her art.

Fuller's subjectivity hinges on her movement between an onstage and an offstage persona, and her dance allows that doubleness to multiply. She produces, in the electric light, a series of constantly changing images: she is flower, butterfly, bird, fountain, and more abstract things—not because she pretends to be them, allegorically or metaphorically incarnating a role, but because her stage image makes it possible for the viewer to imagine them. In Mallarmé's writing, Fuller becomes an "inconsciente révélatrice" of his mystical literary system, of the visual but invisible "idée" and of the subjectivity that system presupposes: "unconscious" (307) because onstage she becomes a Sign, unaware of her literary potential and unable to manipulate language herself, "knowing no eloquence other" (306) than her steps.[79]

Fuller's choreography and her account of the choreographic process both make reference to hypnosis. *Fifteen Years of a Dancer's Life* describes how her career took off from a serious parody of the medical and paramedical vogue of hypnosis at the end of the century. Engaged to play in a New York music-hall production called *Quack, M.D.*, Loie looks for a costume for the hypnotism scene, which, she says, "we did not take very seriously" though she notes that "hypnotism at that moment was very much to the fore in New York."[80] Her remarks on hypnosis indicate her awareness of its powerful theatricality, but also read as a critique of its cultural currency. Fuller's description of the tremendous effect her dance produced in this show indicates that despite her disclaimers, she ends up taking its hypnotism quite seriously, claiming to be hypnotized herself while hypnotizing her audience. In her account, the "discovery" of her signature dance form takes shape in a series of hypnotic performances, both public and private, beginning with her success in *Quack, M.D.* At home, Fuller rehearses the hypnotic experience before her mirror,[81] and a repetition of the hypnosis scene gets Fuller her first big break:

A single gas jet lighted the empty stage. In the house, which was equally dark, the manager, seated in one of the orchestra chairs, looked at us with an air of boredom, almost of contempt. There was no dressing-room for my change of clothing. . . . Without delay I put on my costume, there on the stage and over my dress. Then I hummed an air and started in to dance very gently in the obscurity. The manager came nearer and nearer, and finally ascended the platform. His eyes glistened.[82]

If hypnosis is a culturally and medically familiar way for Fuller to describe the multiplied subject of her dance, electricity proves to be a way to enact it. Mallarmé describes Fuller as two people, an artist of inebriation and a technological wizard: "The exercise, a kind of invention without employment, involves a drunken artistry and, simultaneously, an industrial accomplishment" (307).[83] Fuller's technical accomplishment, separate from and yet simultaneous with the hypnotic inebriation of her art, is her use of electric light onstage. The double of the hypnotic performer, the producer of her multiple identities, is the Fuller who engages in electrical experiments.

Mallarmé describes Fuller's innovations—the abstraction and expansion of the body in dance, effected through the musical movement of veils, and the rhythmic production of images with them under electric light—with the word "armature": "An armature, of no particular woman, and thus unstable, across the veil of generality, draws onto such a revealed fragment of the form and there drinks the flash that renders it divine; or exhales, in return, by the undulation of fabrics, floating, palpitating, scattered this ecstasy" (311).[84] Signifying on the structural, musical, and electrical levels, "armature" is a structure supporting and protecting a fragile body, describing the involution of inside and outside in Fuller's dance; it is the key to the tonality of the veils' musical movement: "However this transition from sonorities to fabric (is there anything, better, resembling gauze than Music!") is, uniquely, the sorcery that Loie Fuller effects."[85] And finally "armature" suggests Fuller's technical genius, what Mallarmé calls the "accomplissement industriel" of her art. Like the plates of a dynamo, Fuller's spectacle builds charge; it is electrified and electrifying.

When the single gas jet of Fuller's trite audition scene is replaced by electric lights of her own design, the result is a theater revolution:

Loie Fuller has made studies in a special laboratory of all the effects of light that transform the stage, with the Dead Sea, seen from a height, and the terraces of Herod's palace. She has succeeded, by means of various projections, in giving the

actual appearance of the storm. . . . I should not venture to say how she has created her light effects. She has actually been turned out by her landlord because
of an explosion in her apparatus. Had she not been so well known she would
have been taken for an anarchist. At this theater, Rue des Batignolles . . . she has
installed her footlights, her electric lamps, all this visual fairyland which she has
invented and perfected, which has made of her a unique personality, an independent creator, a revolutionist in art.[86]

Fuller's use of electricity both makes manifest her multiple talents
and facilitates the presentation of the "other" Loie Fuller. The split or
multiple subject she describes in her autobiography—*her* Salome—is
thus not simply an effect of hypnosis or its emulation, but is produced in
and by her use of electric light. First, because the electric light produces
the hypnotized performer, making her seem, in Mallarmé's terms, "a
prestigious being . . . withdrawn from all possible life." Reinforcing the
hypnotic effect, the light falling on Fuller makes her unable to see her
audience; she seems "withdrawn," or "unconscious," before their gaze. The
electric light itself comes to represent the gaze that makes performance
possible and shapes the performer's identity. Mallarmé describes the effect of this light as that of a *"regard absolu"*: "it would be necessary to sub-
stitute for it I don't know what impersonal or striking absolute gaze, like
the light which envelops, for several years now, the dancer at the Edens,
melting an electric rawness onto the extra-carnal whiteness of makeup,
and which really makes her a prestigious being withdrawn from all possible life" (306–7).[87] Like a disembodied gaze, the electric light constitutes
dancers' performing identities; Fuller uses the light to create a *"regard absolu"* that allows her the creative projection of multiple identity and serial
imagery.

Second, the use of electricity establishes Fuller as not only a hypnotic
performer, but also a technical wizard, as the operator within or behind
her performance. Fuller's use of electricity creates the climate in which
her stage identity thrives, and allows her to control the production of her
own image. Although Fuller uses electricity in a different form and for a
different end than the clinician, her use raises important questions regard-
ing the agency of the technology and its resulting impact on the subject
which can best be understood in relation to its contemporary clinical
uses. Fuller's use of electricity onstage differs in two crucial ways from its
use in the clinic: because Fuller herself controls it, her position is not only
analogous to that of the patient, but also to that of the doctor; furthermore, in Fuller's spectacle, electricity does not touch the body directly. In

Charcot's clinic, the use of electricity clearly divides patient from doctor; it cuts through the ambiguity of hypnosis, which often puts in doubt who is in charge of the clinical "performance." Its application to the body is a direct intervention that establishes the primacy of the clinician. Yet despite these crucial differences, the two situations share a more remarkable similarity: Fuller uses electricity to create a climate in which the divided or multiplied performing subject can flourish—the very division or multiplicity that the clinician attempts to collapse in electroshock treatments of hysterical patients.

The difference between these two uses of electrical technology, and their resulting effects on hysterical personality type, is introduced by Fuller herself in an anecdote in her autobiography. If electricity works for her onstage as a counterpart to her hypnotic dissociation of self, facilitating her self-creation as a performer, it works to exactly the opposite end within the context of cure. When the control of technology passes out of her hands, and intervenes directly in the body, it works to counteract the hypnotically divided subject. In the anecdote, Fuller undergoes an electric cure in a spa at Carlsbad, in a curiously theatrical context not unlike that of the semipublic "performances" in Charcot's lecture hall. The way in which Fuller responds to this particular "performance" context illustrates in what ways her stage spectacle reproduces the clinical cure and in what essential ways it differs. The use of electricity here does not have the transformative effect her own use of it does onstage:

I was once at the Swedish gymnasium at Carlsbad, where machines with electrical vibrations shock you from head to foot. I was just about to dress myself when one of the women of the place came to me, and said: "Won't you please return to the hall, and pretend to take the electric treatment again in order that the archduchesses, who are there, with a whole crowd of court ladies, may see you?" I replied: "Tell the archduchesses that they can see me this evening at the theater." The poor woman then declared to me that she had been forbidden to mention their Royal Highnesses, and that they had bidden her get me back into the hall on some pretext or other. She was so grieved at not having succeeded that I returned to the machines, and had my back massaged, in order that the noble company might look at me at their ease, as they would survey an interesting animal.

They looked at me, all of them, smiling, and while they viewed me I never turned my eyes away from them.

The odd thing was that they did not know that I knew them. I was, therefore, as much amused by them, and without their perceiving it, as they were amused by me.[88]

Here the use of electricity on the body allows Fuller to remain herself, as if offstage, while "performing" the "Loie Fuller" a certain public wants to see. Collapsing her onstage and offstage identities, rather than allowing them to diverge, the description of this treatment directly contradicts her conclusions about the effect of her own use of electricity. Fuller's response to the treatment, even in this playful ambience, suggests that electricity applied to the body does not allow the subject the freedom that an electrified space can. Most significant in her descriptions of her performance in these two different venues is her feeling that the spa "appearance" is a performance, which gives her the unique opportunity to trick her audience; to perform without becoming the other, hypnotic, "Loie Fuller." If her own electrified spectacle creates a theater of femininity, the simultaneous presentation and representation of a woman, this episode is an animal show—not that of a creating subject, but that of an observed object.

Fuller's account suggests that the application of electricity to the body cuts through its metaphoric productions, imposing a physical reaction that shorts out the body's capacities for representation.[89] Contemporary with Fuller's performance, Charcot and his associates will use electricity for a wide range of treatments of various ills, but all produce this effect, ultimately diffusing the power of the hysterical spectacle, and putting its control into other hands.

Charcot is particularly concerned with the dramatic power of the female patient's spectacle, which can mislead the doctor's diagnosis, and the use of hypnosis in the charged theatrical atmosphere of the lectures only heightens the pathos created by the hysterical drama. The sustained electrical treatments given in the Tuesday lectures created an equally charged performance, but put the clinician more clearly in command. Though electricity is used more or less to effect the same ends as the treatments by hypnosis, it does so by passing the agency to the technology and radically reorienting the patient-doctor relationship.

Charcot used hypnosis in the clinic and in lecture-demonstrations at the Salpêtrière to free the body from psychosomatic paralyses and return its freedom of movement. In one generalizable case, presented in 1887, Charcot's demonstration proceeded in three steps: first, demonstrating to the audience that the hypnotized patient had complete freedom of movement, contrary to the paralysis manifested in the conscious state; then, implanting the suggestion of paralysis in the nonaffected limbs by tapping them; and finally, asking the hypnotized patient to learn to move the now-paralysed limbs by imitating those with free movement (originally those subject to the hysterical paralysis).[90] The use of hypnosis in these conditions emphasizes the theatrical aspect of the illness and its treatment, the imitative nature of the affliction, and the mimetism practiced in the cure.

Hysterical patients at the Salpêtrière imitated the symptoms of epileptics and others who were in the wards with them, and even those patients whose physical symptoms Charcot could prove were psychically created were often thought to be faking. By separating the mentally ill from the physically ill, and by arranging for patients to police one another,[91] Charcot hoped to thwart patients' attempts to fake. Charcot acknowledges that the history of hysteria is tied to a conception of hysterics as theatrical; but because the patient's theatrical imitation operates as a pathogen, Charcot takes it seriously:

simulation . . . is met with at every step in the history of hysteria. One finds oneself acknowledging the amazing craft, sagacity and perseverance which women . . . especially under the influence of this great neurosis . . . will put in play . . . especially when a physician is to be the victim. But it does not seem to me that the erratic paruria of hysteria has ever been shown to be wholly simulated. Though they [the women] certainly take pleasure in distorting, by exaggerations, the principal circumstances of their disorder, in order to make them appear extraordinary and wonderful.[92]

It is not only the patient, then, but the illness itself which is theatrical in nature; Charcot emphasizes the power of both, and warns that it is the physician who is the most likely victim of the patient's hysterical pathos. Yet Charcot also describes the hysteric's theatrical manifestations as an art: "the desire to deceive even without purpose, by a kind of disinterested worship of art for art's sake, though sometimes with the idea of creating a sensation, to excite pity, is a common enough experience, particularly in hysteria."[93]

In the case of one of Charcot's most famous patients, Blanche Wittman, the power of the spectacle is particularly great: one of the three original patients suffering from "massive hysteria" and brought to Charcot for treatment by hypnosis in 1878, Blanche was a favorite patient of the medical students and followers of Charcot and is recognized as the swooning woman depicted in a hypnotic state in the Brouillet painting *Demonstrating Hysteria*. Described by one of Charcot's biographers as "rather intelligent,"[94] Blanche was the subject of many of the experiments in hypnotic perception; her youth and beauty no doubt help account for her popularity with Charcot's audience. Transcriptions of sessions in which she was presented in the public lectures and accounts of her treatment by medical students reveal both her hypnotic powers and the abuse she received no doubt because of them:

Blanche Wittman, who was described as carrying out imaginary crimes with a dramatic flair equal to Sarah Bernhardt's, was much in demand for medicolegal demonstrations. On one occasion Charcot had invited a distinguished audience of jurists, magistrates, and specialists in forensic medicine to a demonstration in the lecture theatre at the Salpêtrière. Blanche, in a state of somnambulism, had obediently performed the most blood-thirsty tasks, "shooting," "stabbing," and "poisoning." The notables withdrew from a room littered with fictive corpses. The medical students who remained, being very like medical students in all times and places, then told Blanche (still in a state of somnambulism) that she was alone in the hall and should undress and take a bath. But Blanche, who had waded through blood without turning a hair, found this suggestion too infamous and came abruptly out of hypnosis with a violent hysterical attack.[95]

Other anecdotes underscore the sexual and misogynistic nature of jokes made at Blanche's expense: "Binet recounts a jest perpetrated by Londe on Blanche while she was in a state of hypnotic somnambulism. Showing her a photograph of donkeys ascending a hillside in the Pyrenées, he declared: 'Here is your portrait. You are completely naked [in it]!' Later, coming upon the plate in a waking condition, Blanche stamped on it furiously."[96] The treatment of hysterical patients in such theatrical contexts contributes to confusion about the mimetic nature of their illness and their ability to fake. In an interview after Charcot's death, Blanche explained that it was impossible to simulate diseases under his watchful eye; yet her antagonism in the face of mistreatment is read as proof of her fakery.[97]

To reduce the power of the hysteric's spectacle and to arm himself against misdiagnosis, the clinician turns to other forms of treatment. If hypnosis produces a confusion between the patient's conscious and unconscious states, it seems to produce confusion in its observers as well, making the clinician both hypnotist and dangerously hypnotized. But electricity, when applied to the body in electroshock therapy, clearly defines doctor and patient, illness and cure. The use of electricity in the clinic more clearly defines the clinician's role as that of scientist rather than mesmerist,[98] and puts in his hands the technology necessary to direct the spectacle in the amphitheater. It is significant that Freud, eventually abandoning the apparatus of Charcot's treatments, will not give up the detachment secured by medical science to protect the clinician from the patient's pathos.

Treatment by electroshock intervenes directly to control the body's movement. In one treatment carried out by Charcot's colleague Pitres at the St. André Hospital in Bordeaux, electroshock is used to address two very different muscular problems. Described in an article published in *Le Progrès Medical*, the journal of the Paris École de Médecine, in 1887, the goal of one such treatment is to return "normal sensitivity" to an "unfeeling [or paralyzed] part of the teguments";[99] physiographs charting the movements show that the muscle is restored to healthy functioning. But in another case described here, electricity renders zones that were convulsive into zones that no longer feel anything. For both problems, the goal is the same: to restore to the body its equilibrium, homogeneity, and normal range of movement through the application of electricity.

If treatment by hypnosis attempted to teach the hysteric a lesson, allowing her to learn from one half of her body the freedom of movement the other half should emulate, electricity forcibly erases bodily differences, brings the disparate halves into accord and the hysteric back from her wandering. Application of electricity to the body collapses hysterical dissociation, bringing together a divided body and the divided mind it represents. Whereas electricity can create a space in which the body's metaphoric productions of meaning can flourish, electricity in the clinician's hands, applied to the body, undoes its expressive power. Yet it is testimony to the hysteric's unfailing expressivity and mimetic powers that even the treatment is eventually incorporated into the hysteric's theater: Pitres names, on the list of *chorées*, a "chorée électrique," which reproduces as symptoms those movements produced by electrical cures.[100] The cycle of visual resemblance comes full circle as hysteria patients mime the cure and the clinician calls it illness, turning pathology into the pathological.

Charcot describes his clinical–anatomical method as nothing more than the acute observation and rigorous description of what he sees, claiming that his work of diagnosis relied primarily on visual criteria: "all I am is a photographer. I describe what I see." He describes his technique as if he were an artist drawing always from nature, or a scientist working only through experiment: "I am not of the type to suggest things that cannot be demonstrated experimentally. You know that, as a principle, I pay little attention to abstractions and have no use for preconceived notions. If you want to see clearly, you must take things exactly as they are."[101] But Charcot's reliance on a particular realist conception of the art of the photographer to describe his own work, equating "I describe what I see" with "I am a photographer," is an oversimplification belied by his own practice and by the practice of photography associated with it.

In Freud's description of his teacher's clinical-anatomical method, Charcot does much more than simply "see":

He was not a reflective man, not a thinker: he had the nature of an artist—he was, as he himself said, a "*visuel*," a man who sees. Here is what he himself told us about his method of working. He used to look again and again at the things he did not understand, to deepen his impression of them day by day, till suddenly an understanding of them dawned on him. In his mind's eye the apparent chaos presented by the continual repetition of the same symptoms then gave way to order: the new nosological pictures emerged, characterized by the constant combination of certain groups of symptoms. The complete and extreme cases, the "types," could be brought into prominence with the help of a certain sort of schematic planning, and, with these types as a point of departure, the eye could travel over the long series of ill-defined cases—the "*formes frustes*"—which, branching off from one or other characteristic feature of the type, melt away into indistinctness. He called this type of intellectual work, in which he had no equal, "practicing nosography," and he took pride in it. He might be heard to say that the greatest satisfaction a man could have was to see something new—that is, to recognize it as new; and he remarked again and again on the difficulty and value of this kind of "seeing." He would ask why it was that in medicine people only see what they have already learned to see. He would say that it was wonderful how one was suddenly able to see new things—new states of illness—which must probably be as old as the human race; and that he had to confess to himself that he now saw a number of things which he had overlooked for thirty years in his hospital wards.[102]

In Freud's explanation, visual observation was not Charcot's only method, but merely a first step, part of a process repeated constantly to trigger understanding. Observation in itself, Charcot remarks, will not lead clinicians to knowledge: for most of them, seeing something new is not the same as seeing something *as* new. This requires the special insight of the "mind's eye": a sharp eye for the schematized lists of symptoms, the insight to imagine what their combination produced, and the visual acuity to recognize it in the wards.[103]

Though Freud's description of Charcot's technique may reflect his own response to Charcot's teaching, his well-known bias against the "blindness of the seeing eye,"[104] it sheds some light on Charcot's insistence on and oversimplification of visual diagnostic and descriptive technique. Freud tells the following story to illustrate Charcot's empiricism:

Charcot, indeed, never tired of defending the rights of purely clinical work, which consists in seeing and ordering things, against the encroachments of theoretical medicine. On one occasion there was a small group of us, all students from abroad, who, brought up on German academic physiology, were trying his patience with our doubts about his clinical innovations. "But that can't be true," one of us objected, "it contradicts the Young-Helmholz theory." He did not reply "So much the worse for theory, clinical facts come first" or words to that effect; but he did say something which made a great impression on us: "*La théorie, c'est bon, mais ça n'empêche pas d'exister* [Theory is good, but that doesn't prevent things from existing]."[105]

Visualizing technologies introduced into Charcot's practice complicate the nature of visual diagnosis and theatrical treatment. The use of photography as an imaging and recording practice in Charcot's laboratory, in combination with the use of electricity, raises questions about the conception and representation of hysteria crucial to its decoding and its relation to dance performance. Like electrical technology, instruments could give the clinician a distance and agency crucial to his control of the hysterical scene.

In Charcot's laboratory, Duchenne de Boulogne used electricity in a series of experiments with muscular electrification in limbs and in the face, recorded in photographs. Such experiments—"using the true living anatomy of electromuscular exploration"—allowed Duchenne to see better into the body than was possible in morbid anatomy, and to correct "some physiological errors committed in attributing to some muscles movements that are not theirs and in failing to recognize some that are."[106] Duchenne believed that the movements of the limbs and trunk are controlled by the will, but the movements of facial expression are not. The dramatic photographs of Duchenne's electrical experiments on human physiognomy, in which only his hands are usually visible, illustrate a host of ideas familiar from nineteenth-century science and science fiction: the theatrical presentation of patients, the mostly unseen man of science manipulating a monster, the unblinking eye of science and of the camera before the patient's dramatic pathos. Though the electrical manipulation of patients' faces to test theories of mental physiology results in a certain form of hysterical expression, the effect of the experiments is more clearly the manipulation of the body's expressive capacity in a "performance" shaped by scientists wielding instruments.

In *The Birth of the Clinic*, Michel Foucault argues that the visual knowledge of the body built into nineteenth-century anatomy is paradigmatic for all nineteenth-century medicine:

The structure, at once perceptual and epistemological, that commands clinical anatomy, and all medicine that derives from it, is that of *invisible visibility*. Truth, which, by right of nature, is made for the eye, is taken from her, but at once surreptitiously revealed by that which tries to evade it. Knowledge *develops* in accordance with a whole interplay of *envelopes*; the hidden element takes on the form and rhythm of the hidden content, which means that, like a veil, it is transparent.[107]

Even with instrumentation enhancing the clinician's ability to see, touch, and hear the body's inner recesses, vision remains medicine's epistemological foundation. "Thus armed, the medical gaze embraces more than is said by the word 'gaze' alone. It contains within a single structure different sensorial fields. The sight/touch/hearing trinity defines a perceptual configuration in which the inaccessible illness is tracked down by markers, gauged in depth, drawn to the surface, and projected virtually on the dispersed organs of the corpse. The 'glance' has become a complex organization with a view to a spatial assignation of the invisible."[108] Anatomy then gives rise to two kinds of gazes: "Thus from the discovery of pathological anatomy, the medical gaze is duplicated: there is a local, circumscribed gaze, the borderline gaze of touch and hearing, which covers only one of the sensorial fields, and which operates on little more than the visible surfaces. But there is also an absolute, absolutely integrating gaze [un regard absolu] that dominates and founds all perceptual experiences. It is this gaze that structures into a sovereign unity that which belongs to a lower level of the eye, the ear, and the sense of touch."[109]

Yet although Charcot describes his method as clinical-antomical, his nosography and the experimentation carried out by Duchenne and others in his laboratories signal a significant move away from anatomical thinking. Charcot seeks to link visible behaviors to physiological disorders, perhaps verifiable in autopsy but only recognizable in the living subject. Similarly, Duchenne experiments with muscle activities analyzable only in the living body. Though the certainty provided by death remains important, the essence of the illness under investigation appears only in the living, moving patient.

In Charcot's practice anatomy becomes less and less significant as a locus of illness; in his late recognition of "la chose génitale," he reconceives anatomy, with Freud, as social destiny, reading problems with anatomy as the symptom—and not only as the cause—of deeper illness. Freud quotes Charcot in "On the History of the Psychoanalytic Movement" holding forth on a particular case of frigidity in marriage:"in such cases as this it is always the genital thing, always ... always, always [dans des cas pareils c'est toujours la chose génitale, toujours ... toujours, toujours]." Freud concludes the story by remarking his amazement at this formulation and wondering "if he knows that, why does he never say so?"[110] Jones records a 1914 account by Freud of three occasions on which practioners whom he respected had suggested that sexual factors play a part in the neuroses: Breuer, Charcot, and the gynecologist Chrobak. In "The Aetiology of Hysteria," Freud claims that both Charcot and Breuer had a "personal disinclination" to singling out the sexual factor in hysteria.[111]

What connects pathological anatomy through Charcot to Freudian psychoanalysis, then, is not anatomy at all, nor the conceptual visualization of the body, but a practice of looking that reads the surface of the body as a manifestation of processes beneath, whether the depth be identified as anatomy, neurophysiology, or the unconscious. For Mallarmé, Fuller's veiled dance requires a "transparent prolongation" of the gaze: the spectator of her dance, more like Charcot than like the clinical anatomist, looks through the body into its movements. Described in uterine terms by Mallarmé, this dance suggests a profound reconception of hymen and *hystera*, not as a site of hysterical dysfunction but as a motor of representation. But if Loie Fuller's representations bear an uncanny resemblance to a contemporary illustration of a uterus from *Le Progrès Médical*,[112] it is a wry commentary on the fact that Fuller's work de-anatomizes femininity, redefining it as movement rather than structure. In this way, her dance parallels Charcot's shift from the traditional "uterine" theory of hysteria to a neurophysiological one, in which physiological processes are not governed by hidden anatomical structures and hysteria is not corporealized in the womb. As a representation of physiological action rather than anatomical structure, representing femininity while abstracting it, Fuller's theater moves beyond visual resemblance while playing with it.

If the gaze of the dance spectator in this particular case parallels, with some differences, the medical gaze, it is partly because in fin-de-siècle France the cultural authority of medical interpretations of the body's somatic meanings can be seen to influence dance production and reception. With the rise of medical professionalism in nineteenth-century France, and the medicalization of hysteria through pathologies like Charcot's, medicine becomes a major cultural index by which the moving body's meanings are measured. But if Mallarmé's dance theory suggests an awareness of the medicine or science of his time, it is also because the dancer he most admires responds directly to medicine's interpretive authority. Loie Fuller's work confronts medical stereotypes of the hysterical body and the cultural conception of femininity it subtends, putting its pathological nature into question, and pointing to a different way of reading the body's language.

Fuller's work responds to the medical and cultural linking of dance and hysteria by using the clinician's own tools: hypnosis and electricity. Although her work thus asks to be read in the context of Charcot's cures, and she uses, significantly, those techniques that Freud would discontinue in psychoanalysis, she uses them to such radically different ends that her goals seem more closely to resemble those that Freud will adopt. Fuller's theater is situated in the passage from what Charcot constituted as a kind of movement cure for his theatrical hysterics to Freud's practice of the "talking cure," in the "private theater" of psychoanalysis.[113] Before hysteria is reduced to what Jacques Lacan calls "des affaires de foutre"[114] in Charcot's late thinking and in Freud's, the symbolic bodily expression of sexual or sexualized problems, this dance form suggests the greater expressive potential of the body, and a curative as well as symptomatic role for the somatic.

The prescription that Charcot writes himself to ease the tensions of work in the Salpêtrière sheds some light on the treatments he developed there: "Movement does me a great deal of good. It is definitely the treatment for me."[115] Freedom of movement—here he undoubtedly means travel—is his antidote to the hysterical convulsion. Yet Charcot devoted his entire adult life to the Salpêtrière and its patients, from midcentury until his death in 1893; it was Charcot's son who, taking his father's prescription, would become the famous—and famously lost—explorer.[116] One of Charcot's many professional offspring, Freud would read his prescription for movement quite differently.

Charcot's cure for himself is telling in light of the range of treatments he developed for the different kinds of patients, many of which attempted to restore freedom of movement to hysterically paralyzed bodies. Treatments by hypnosis and by electricity were part of what might be called a movement cure. Such freedom of movement, within Charcot's experiments, largely emulates the mental health it appears to guarantee or rep-

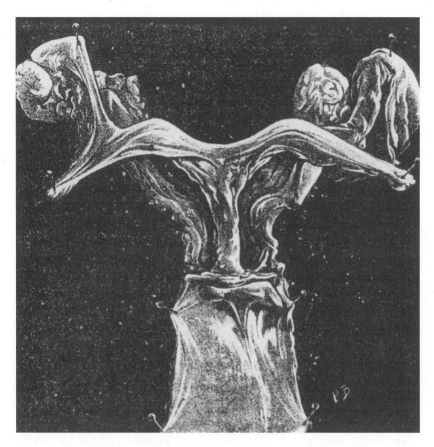

Fig. 13. (a) Loie Fuller. Anonymous photograph, reprinted by permission of the Musée Rodin, Paris [1536]. (b) "Utérus cloisonné dans toute sa hauteur" (Uterus divided along its length) *Le Progrès médical*, February–March 1887.

resent. Despite their differences, Loie Fuller's theater and Charcot's resemble each other remarkably. Reapplying "medical" technologies in very different ways, Fuller can make into art what is, in the psychiatric hospital, only symptom; she can express what the hysterical patient represses in shaping the symptoms of what Freud would name "conversion hysteria." Loie Fuller's dancing can be understood in this context as a successful or healthy theatricalization of what Freud calls, early on, "double conscience" or "hysterical dissociation (the splitting of consciousness)."[117]

Implementing the clinician's tools differently, Fuller's hypnotic and electric experiments allow her to put "hysterical dissociation" into theatrical practice. But while the hysteric's production of meaning on the body can be described as metaphoric, replacing the trauma with a physical sign that silently bears witness to it, the dancer's could be described as metonymic.[118] Slipping across the series of signifiers she produces, representing while presenting herself, the dancer has a greater detachment from her signs, a subjectivity that multiplies as it moves through them. The hysteric, speaking silently through the coded somatic mark, hides behind or inside the movement, sign, or image, using it both to hide and to name its content or intent. Imitating the pattern of hysterical conversion, translating into the body, the dancer theatricalizes "successfully" what the hysterical patient tries and fails to say. Even if Fuller's hypnotic states merely mime hypnosis, they allow the dancer the very freedom of movement, the mobile subjectivity that in other contexts develops as malady.

Like Blanche Wittman, Loie Fuller can state with clarity and surety that her dance was beyond her own control; yet unlike Blanche, Fuller can recount both of her states and is, in this way, firmly situated between the movement cure and the "talking cure." Contemporary with the founding of psychoanalysis, Loie Fuller's dance addressed the questions that psychoanalysis would address with practices differing from those of the medical treatment of hysterias. At the end of his career Charcot admits that he believes that certain kinds of psychically generated physical ailments are related to sex, and Freud's theory will develop and broaden this idea. Yet in giving up hypnosis and electricity, Freud developed an idea of cure that was closer to Loie Fuller's than to Charcot's: allowing the patient to divide, or to mime that dissociation, giving the patient room to express herself, tell her story; and providing the *regard absolu*— an internal eye, not the public arena of spectacle—in which to be seen, or heard, telling it.[119]

In 1888–89, just two years after leaving Paris, and while in the process of putting together his practice, Freud includes massage in the course of treatment of one of the patients from the *Studies on Hysteria*, given the pseudonym Emmy von N. He remarks that the massage brings out, rather than suppresses, the conversation he is hoping for. Manipulating the patient's body, Freud manages to draw free association out of it. But where Charcot's controlling and violent interventions kept the body and its story separate, Freud acknowledges their involution, understanding that words come out of the body, that the implicated organ "joins in the conversation."[120] Tapping the richer vein of the patient's dreams, fantasies, lapses, and associations, Freud's practice of hearing the patient's story—as well as reading the body—sets his method markedly apart from Charcot's.

Freud abandons Charcot's practices, but continues to read the body for signs of illness. He opens up Charcot's observation of movement as a sign of motor-neurological distress, criticizing that "blindness of the seeing eye" that the clinician depended on and interpreting the body's movements in broader cultural and psychical context. Yet Freud eventually excludes movement from cure, explaining that Dora's fingers crawl, during one session, in and out of her opened and closed reticule as a "symptomatic act."[121] Dora's freedom of movement (or the sexual freedom that it mimes) points to the physical remainder that continues to accompany therapeutic talk, a vestige of the movement cure overtaken by the talking cure.

Though Freud will assign a significant cultural role to artistic creation and phrase it in the powerful psychic terms of sublimation, the ways in which the body can speak in art will be limited, and will always lend themselves to sexual interpretations. The talking cure made the movement cure history, assigning dance to the realm of Charcot's hysterics. With the advent of the talking cure, the movement cure is marginalized: dance as metonymic self-elaboration, acting out hysteria, or practicing a kind of preventive medicine, in which the dancer is doctor as well as patient, becomes symptomatic itself of a hysterical past.

CHAPTER 4

Céline's Biology and the Ballets of
Bagatelles pour un massacre

> "Mr. Céline! . . . You've been seen frequently at the Foyer
> de la Danse [Monsieur Céline! ... On vous voit beaucoup
> au foyer de la danse]."
>
> *Bagatelles pour un massacre*, Louis-Ferdinand Céline

Rejecting romantic "idea" or its Symbolist counterpart, Louis-Ferdinand Céline reaches, in dance, for something he calls by another name: "I am not a man for ideas. I'm a man for style [Je ne suis pas un homme à idées. Je suis un homme à style]," he declared in an interview late in his life.[1] Célinian "style" is defined as the rhythm of his writing, its heartbeat, linked to the body's high and low forms of expression, to biology and to ballet. Céline published only five ballets in his lifetime, but his wife, the dancer Lucette Destouches, claims that he never stopped imagining them, and that, at the time of his death, several ballet projects were in progress.[2] Though he denied their influence, Céline's dance writing replays the legacy of both Gautier and Mallarmé, and his attempt to define his personal literary style via dance locates him squarely in their tradition. Célinian "style" is another version of what Gautier and Mallarmé, each in his own way, called the literary "idea" that dance was capable of expressing or inscribing, and like them Céline locates it in women dancing.

Céline's prose, plays, letters, and interviews attest to the dancer's position of prominence in his literary and personal mythologies. From the dedication of *Voyage au bout de la nuit* to Elizabeth Craig to the recognition of Lucette Destouches's constant grace under fire in *Féerie pour une autre fois*,[3] Céline acknowledges the powerful presence of dancers in his life as companions and muses:

Luckily Arlette, reason itself! Not divagating, not hysterical, ever! ... A harmonious good nature, a dancer in body and soul, entirely noble! She'd rather die twenty times over rather than make a fuss about her feelings ... She's a classic ... she has a kind of heroism as a dancer, an elegance and gentleness ... supreme self-control ... Never to be found maladroit, hesitating at the sound of her heartbeat.

Heureusement Arlette, raison même! Pas divagante, pas hystérique, jamais! ... La nature tout harmonie, la danseuse en l'âme et au corps, noblesse tout! Vingt fois qu'elle aimerait mieux mourir que son sentiment fasse un pli ... C'est une classique ... elle a l'héroisme comme elle danse et l'élégance et gentillesse ... la tenue suprême ... Jamais à trouver maladroite hésitante au son de son coeur.

But the dance that appears in the ballets of the 1937 pamphlet, *Bagatelles pour un massacre*,[4] is as far as possible from this "pas hystérique, jamais!" The deviance of dance and dancers in the ballets is traced to the social ills Céline complains of throughout the pamphlet, the sickness of the society that he records. The publication of Céline's first three ballets in *Bagatelles pour un massacre* signals ballet's connection for him with the social problems attacked in it; they are vehicles both for the pamphlet's ideology and its critique of ideology. "Style" and "ideas" come together in a volatile combination in Céline's ballets, as hysteria.

Developing his "style" by writing ballets, Céline never strays far from what he disparagingly calls "ideas." Although his style has been considered revolutionary, it has not—at least not since the publication of Céline's second novel, *Mort à Crédit*, in 1936 and the appearance of *Bagatelles pour un massacre* the following year—disguised how reactionary these ideas are. In the three ballets first published in the pamphlet, Céline calls on dance to serve an ideological end. These ballets reveal to what degree Céline's avowedly formal interest in dance is charged with explosive social and political content. In their conception, in their plots, and in the stories of their reception related in the pamphlet, the ballets are battlegrounds of hysteria and social pathologies.

Céline identifies himself and his work with an idealized dance world early on, as a defense against literary and political critique. But his dance writing swings violently between opposite poles: a dance theory grounded in an idealized image of dancers is belied by libretti that create menacing dances of possession, insurrection, and perversion. Céline's dance theory denies the very hysterical and disruptive element in dance that his ballets explore. His dance propoganda has misled us; because of it, his ballets have been read as fairy tales that demonstrate his passion for the dance and his idealizing admiration of the female dancer,[5] a view he himself insisted on. This view was reinforced by a reedition of the ballets in a volume of their own by Gallimard in 1959, taking the *Bagatelles* ballets—"La Naissance d'une fée," "Voyou Paul. Brave Virginie," and "Van Bagaden," out of context and adding two "fairy-tale" ballets, "Scandale aux Abysses" and "Foudres et Flèches." *Ballets sans musique, sans personne, sans rien* encouraged the misreading of their plots and purpose that Céline himself wanted; ironically, it has led to their marginalization in the Célinian opus as well as to a misunderstanding of their place within the pamphlet, their relation to Céline's fiction, and their greater significance for Céline's writing. The ballets have been misread as the frivolous or light-hearted expression of Céline's imagination, divorced from both the reactionary politics and the radical inventiveness of his prose. Such readings ignore the dark forces in the ballets as well as the dark underside of Céline's own personal interest in the dance, evident when they are considered in the context of their original publication. They also ignore the rhythmic compositional structures unique to Céline's writing and closely connected to dance and the tradition of dance pathologies within which Céline's work must be read. Despite his unmitigated praise for French classical ballet, Céline himself plays upon the institutional and social evils inherent in its nineteenth-century form. He is well aware of the ballet's unseemly past, in particular at the Paris Opéra, but conflicted about its significance. The pamphlet cries out against the corruption of the romantic ballet by certain menacing enemies of French high culture, but Céline's racially charged argument simply creates convenient scapegoats.

Céline defines his style in opposition to the "precious" language of fin-de-siècle France championed by authors he disparages as literary elites: Gide, Proust, and others. Theirs is an elitist language of the era he defines as Charcot's, a language that he will also identify as "Jewish." *Mort à credit*, in 1936, describes a character who affects this style just as Céline complains in *Bagatelles* he himself was called upon, in his work for the S.D.N. (the League of Nations), to do: "He spoke precious, careful, subtle [French], Metitpois, like people in Charcot's time [Il parlait precieux, fignolé, subtil, Metitpois, comme les gens des années Charcot]."[6] Céline's medicine and his view of dance are inflected by a rival nineteenth-century tradition that defines itself against the medical thinking and medical language of Charcot.

Céline's hysterical dances first reveal their racially, sexually, and politically troubled motivations in a parody of the romantic ballet to which he runs for shelter from the critical storm in the opening pages of *Bagatelles pour un massacre*. In what can be read as autobiographical writing, he begins by announcing a bon vivant's desire for dancers that recalls the era of Gautier: the intent to capture the dancer and possess her by means of a libretto. The three ballets included in the pamphlet refer to and parody the romantic ballet tradition, what he calls "the old themes ... all the pet subjects of the repertory ... the cavalry of the Opera ... Giselle ... Bagatelles ... " (339). Céline is criticizing the Opéra ballet tradition, but he will insist, later in his life, that his ballets "are completely sincere, without an ounce of irony."[7] Céline's denial of ironic or parodic intent suggests to what degree he considers himself a serious librettist whose ballets are of artistic merit; putting his title next to Gautier's, he allies himself to the Opéra tradition even as he seems to belittle Gautier's work and his own.

The ballet tradition that Céline ridicules is the very place he chooses to take refuge from the criticism leveled at his second novel, *Mort à crédit*. After the success of the 1932 *Voyage au bout de la nuit*, praised by the French left and nearly awarded the Prix Goncourt, the second novel had met a press angered—as if deceived by Céline's revolutionary style—by its reactionary motifs. This literary failure is dramatized in the ballets' story lines; and the ballets' failures, recounted in the pamphlet, reenact that of the novel. Against the attacks of critics whom he sees as upper-class literary snobs, Céline looks to the ballet to establish his own "refinement." In his vituperous response, Céline attempts to undermine all critics while setting himself up as an arbiter of taste: "The world is full of people who call themselves refined, and who are not, I declare, one bit refined. But I, yours truly, I know that I am refined! The thing itself! Authentically refined" (11). But the refinement authenticated by his passion for the dance threatens also to undo him: "How I was seized, strangled, agitated, by my own refinement? Here are the facts, the circumstances ... " In the first pages of the pamphlet Céline recounts to his friend Léo Gutman the revelation of this "more and more tenacious, pronounced, virulent, what am I saying, absolutely tyrannical taste for dancers that came over me [goût de plus en plus vivace, prononcé, virulent, que dis-je, absolument despotique qui me venait pour les danseuses]" (12). The obsession with dancers is a virulent, pathological possession; Céline declares himself its passive victim.

Céline claims that dancers are literature par excellence; that they are poetry themselves: "'In a dancer's leg the world, its waves, all its rhythms, its madness, its wishes, are inscribed [inscrits]! ... never written [Jamais écrits]! The most nuanced poem in the world!'" (12). But the Mallarméan tone of this description of the dancer's legs as idealized inscription—as what Mallarmé called "direct instrument of idea"—gives way immediately to flesh and blood. Céline is not content to dream of dancers' inscription of poetic images; he wants to work with them, or more precisely, to have them work for him. It is through the writing of poetry—specifically, ballets—that this involvement will become possible, and the work relationship promises amorous relationships in its wake: "Starting next week, Gutman, after the rent is paid ... I want to work only for dancers ... Everything for dance! Nothing but dance!"

The two things that Céline wants in the early 1930s—a literary reputation and the company of dancers—get scrambled together; poetry is embodied in the dancer, and more practically, provides the means for getting close to her. It is poetry that Gutman tells Céline he will have to write to get anywhere in the ballet world: "Yes, but be careful ... A poem! ... Dancers are difficult ... sensitive ... delicate ... " Gutman counsels Céline to restrain his scurrilous pen: "Ferdinand! Good sense and moderation! ... Charm ... tenderness ... tradition ... melody ... real poetry comes at a cost ... dancers!"

Both divine and carnal, then, dancers inspire the "raffiné" Céline who enters the world of the classical ballet as a refuge from the press's harsh accusations of vulgarity. But they also attract the semi-autobiographical loner Ferdinand Bardamu of Voyage au bout de la nuit, who finds himself in heaven amid the English dancers at the music hall where he is a supernumerary. As close as he is, Ferdinand finds them inaccessible: "I probably could have obtained the same coitus for myself at the 'Tarapout' with my English [women] and free of charge, but thinking about it I gave up on this opportunity because of the complications, the miserable jealous little pimping boyfriends that always hang around the dancers backstage."[8] The desire for dancers that serves as a metaphor for literary ambition swiftly brings Céline up against obstacles for which at first he finds racist, rather than misogynist, explanations.

The rivals who limit the dancer's accessibility, rather than making her less attractive, serve instead to augment her desirability; both model and obstacle, the menacing pimps of Voyage au bout de la nuit become, in Bagatelles pour un massacre, the Jewish impresarios who, Céline believes, prevent him from staging his ballets. This network of critics, conductors, and administrators, which Céline identifies as Jewish, controls Paris the-

aters. To get to the dancer, Céline must fight his way through this network of power; to do so, he believes, he must adapt his writing to its
tastes and emulate everything Jewish.

The complex power relations between Céline, a caricatured Jewish
model and rival, and the dancer are sketched throughout the pamphlet,
moving from racism to sexism and back. Céline finds the dancer in collusion with this fictionalized Jewish impresario with whom he finds himself incapable of competing, and complicated scenarios of identification
with both the rival and the object ensue. Céline's negotiations over dance
with what he perceives as the Jewish establishment take shape as conversations with his colleague Gutman. In the context of the pamphlet's anti-
Semitism, "Gutman mon ami" seems a contradiction in terms. Though
the Jewish doctor is put down at every turn, Céline excuses himself, and
Gutman, from the general tirade: "Gutman! Gutman! I've offended you
my poor man! I bet, with all these 'Jews' this and 'Jews' that ... " (15–16).
Céline's mockery at once denigrates Gutman because he is a Jew and denies him any Jewishness altogether.

On the one hand, Céline admires Gutman's position as a powerful
doctor who performs the kinds of services that public figures like to keep
quiet. Gutman boasts that, through his connections, he will be able to get
special treatment for the ballet he urges Céline to write: "I will go and
take it myself ... to the Opéra ... Mr. Rouché is my friend! ... Mine! ...
Definite! ... He does whatever I ask him to ... ." This is the kind of power
that Céline envies, and he enjoys having Gutman exercise it for him. Inspired by his offer and by the possibility of getting what he wants, Céline
falls at Gutman's feet: "Ah! Léo ... (I threw myself at his knees) ... You're
exciting me! I see heaven! Dance is paradise!" (16).

But throughout the pamphlet, "*juif*" is an adjective attached freely to
anything or anyone Céline does not like; in his paroxysms of frustrated
anger and desire, Céline uses the adjective constantly. Fearing that a Jewish conspiracy against him will ruin his chances at the Opéra, Céline ex-
plodes in anti-Semitic fury directed at its administrators: "—Jews' intim-
idation! [Bluff de juifs!] ... Imposters! I protest! ... Publicity! ... The ser-
vants have become the masters? ... The Jews are at the Opéra! ...
Théophile Gautier! tremble! dirty hirsute. You would be kicked out with
Giselle! ... He wasn't Jewish ... I was kidding [déconnai-je]" (16). Céline
imagines an Opéra where even Gautier—a model for ballet librettists—
would be rejected for not being Jewish. But if his ballet is accepted, Céline promises, he will control his hostility: "I swear! I'll say no more about

it! just so my ballet gets on!" Gutman answers him, significantly: "You exaggerate like a Jew, Ferdinand!" (16).

In *Pouvoirs de l'horreur: essai sur l'abjection*, Julia Kristeva has theorized the relations between Céline and the Jewish model-obstacle in his oeuvre, the role played in *Bagatelles* by Leo Gutman. For Kristeva, the figure of the Jew in Céline's writing is perceived both as "he who HAS" and "he who IS," enjoying the best of life and existing fully in that enjoyment.[9] Céline in contrast claims never to "enjoy" life; he hates but also emulates this "other" here represented by Jewish impresarios he categorizes as the pimps of art. In another pamphlet, the Jew is the powerful bourgeois who makes good friends in the ministries from his loge at the Opéra.[10] To have his ballets accepted, he must satisfy what he imagines to be a rigorous Jewish program; but to do so he must write in a style he describes as *"juif,"* become *"juif"* in another crucial way. In the course of the pamphlet, Céline moves between a social and political critique of what he perceives as predominantly Jewish capitalism, to assigning the negative term *"juif"* to what he considers artistic and sexual perversity. Addressing those who wish to profit *("jouir")* at the election of the new government, headed by Léon Blum, in 1936—what he calls the "big Jewish and Masonic triumph"—Céline asks: "Is your soul facing the abyss? ... within reach of every gesture? ... yes? ... I don't believe so ... I have the impression you don't see clearly ... Spectators! ... *Jouisseurs!"*

The vicious attack that he levels here and throughout the pamphlet is one of voyeurism, equated with sexual perversion and cowardice. *Bagatelles* repeatedly complains about Jewish "spectating"—rather than active involvement—during the First World War. This spectating, like critical writing, is a kind of false *jouissance*, a misplaced sexuality condemned by Céline; he pushes the category to include critics—Jews— who "jouissent en dégueulant [profit from / take pleasure in spewing]." Yet the position of voyeur is precisely where Céline first puts himself vis-à-vis the dance. Before Gutman convinces him to write for the dance, Céline claims "I prefer to remain on the look-out ... To catch a glimpse of these adorables, sheltered by some thick curtain" (13). In 1935–36, through his friend Karen Jansen, a Danish dancer, Céline obtains permission to watch the ballet class in the studio of Madame Alessandria.[11] A later remark in the pamphlet extends his voyeuristic pleasure to the realm of his work at the S.D.N.: "It's watching that interests me [C'est regarder qui m'intéressait]" (98). In a letter of 1947 he declares himself "not a violator ... but a voyeur to the death! [pas violeur ... mais 'voyeur'

à mort!]"[12] In many contradictory moves throughout the pamphlet, Céline becomes what he has denounced: he opts for the voyeurism he finds
uncreative and cowardly, and begins his attempt to profit from it as the
"raffiné" insider.

In *Pouvoirs de l'horreur*, Kristeva reads Céline's resistance to or denial
of any ideology in psychoanalytic terms. In *Voyage au bout de la nuit*,
Kristeva finds, Céline rejects the *idée fixe* as derisory and impossible for
him to achieve: "my ideas, they were kind of streetwalking around in my
head with a lot of space in between, like little candles, wavering and
blinking all life long in a really horrible universe ... ultimately, it wasn't
possible for me to imagine being able, like Robinson, to fill my head
with just one idea."[13] But this rejection of "idea" and "ideology" is belied
by what Kristeva finds in Céline, a decade later: a "mystical positivism
[positivité mystique]" that she identifies with fascist ideology. She cites,
from a 1941 source: "There is a guiding principle [une idée conductrice]
of peoples. There is a law. It begins with an idea that rises toward absolute mysticism, and that continues to rise without fear and program. If
it inclines toward politics it's all over ... an idea, a severe doctrine, is necessary [il faut une idée, une doctrine dure]."[14] Beyond the political, and
yet connected to it, is a "material positive [positivité matérielle]"; Kristeva writes: "Beyond politics, but not ignoring it, this material positive, a
full, tangible, reassuring and complete substance, will be incarnated by
Family, Nation, Race, Body [Au-delà de la politique mais sans l'ignorer,
cette *positivite materielle*, substance pleine, tangible, rassurante et heureuse,
sera incarnée par la Famille, la Nation, la Race, le Corps]." In a tone familiar from the speeches and propaganda of the Third Reich, Céline remarks that he would give all of Baudelaire for one female Olympic
swimmer ("Je donnerais tout Baudelaire pour une nageuse olympique").
Throughout Céline's dance writings, dance is linked to body, hygiene,
family, race, and nation; to a hygienic ideal and to a pathological racism.

Céline will continually link his style to dance, characterizing ballet as
the height of French culture, the ultimate in discipline, the equivalent of
the champion swimmer. But because his conception of dance is closely
linked to hysteria, the ballets inevitably dramatize the social thinking of
the pamphlets, what Kristeva has called their confessed delirium, their
"délire avoué." Céline's passion for the ballet tellingly takes him back to
nineteenth-century social pathologies, grounded in a scientific discourse
of race and rooted in a social biology. If there is a unifying, overarching

"idea" in Céline's work, it is described by him on more than one occasion as the "truth" or "fact" of biology. In his last novel, *Rigodon*, Céline names the "single truth" that has real "biological" force; this is the "biological truth" of race: "politics, speeches, nonsense! ... only one truth: biological! ... in a half-century, maybe sooner, France will be yellow, black around the edges ... "[15] The idea of contagion, of degeneration, of corruption of the individual and social body of France that is staged across *Bagatelles'* three ballets brings together the pamphlet's racism, biologism, and anti-Semitism.

Kristeva's psycholinguistic analysis of the mechanisms that Céline's writing employs to cast the Jew as his model and rival points toward the political and scientific components in the history of anti-Semitism in modern Europe. In *The Jew's Body*, Sander Gilman has studied the constructed difference of the Jew in Western culture, and how via the scientific discourse of race, such difference comes to be labeled "pathological."[16] Investigating representations of the Jew as differing from a "white" Western norm, Gilman identifies the development of a scientific racism in the nineteenth century linked to ethnology and linguistics that has continued across countries and centuries:

One can speak of the anti-Semitism of Western culture even though this term evokes a specific stage in the history of Western Jew-hatred. Coined by Wilhelm Marr as part of the scientific discourse of race in the nineteenth century, it is half of the dichotomy of "Aryan" and "Semite" which haunted the pseudoscience of ethnology during this period and beyond. . . . It is a socially constructed category which was used in Europe and the European colonies specifically to categorize the difference between "Semites" and Others. The terms were taken from nineteenth-century linguistics. This was not an accident for, as we shall see, language has played a vital role as a marker of Jewish difference.[17]

The Jew's Body elaborates how the discourse of race identified and pathologized a Jewish body—including its voice and language—and variously allied it with the Asian and African bodies also marked as different by European culture. Merging a scientific ideology with popular assumptions about the Jew's inherent, essential nature, stereotypes about Jewish appearance and judgments about personality related to skin color and physiognomy emerged:

This late eighteenth-century view of the meaning of the Jew's skin color ... saw this "black-yellow" skin color as a pathognomic sign of the diseased Jew ... James Cowles Pritchard (1808) commented on the Jews' "choleric and melancholic temperaments, so that they have in general a shade of complexion somewhat darker than that of the English people." . . . Nineteenth-century anthropology as early as the work of Claudius Buchanan commented on the "inferiority" of the "black" Jews of India. By the midcentury, being black, being Jewish, being diseased, and being "ugly" come to be inexorably linked.[18]

Gilman sets the pseudo-science preoccupied with defining race within historical context and explains that it allied itself with nineteenth-century science through its use of observation:

The Jew as a member of a different race was as distant from the Aryan = Christian as was the Hottentot, the "lowest" rung on the *scala naturae*, the scale of perfection, of eighteenth-century biological science. . . . Given the basic philosophy of late nineteenth-century science, this difference was defined in terms of observable phenomena (or phenomena suggested to be observable) by nineteenth-century ethnologists and those they influenced, such as the physicians of the period.[19]

In the overlapping of scientific and social discourses, in the development of an ideology of the "science" of race relying on biologism, and in the representations that these discourses create, Gilman finds the pathologization of Jews and other groups. Céline's thinking echoes much of this pseudo-scientific, appearance-oriented racism. Within its French context, it also echoes the ideology of the Third Republic, in particular the ethical-biological basis of its moral education, which would have been that of the young Destouches.

In *Les Livres d'école de la République 1870–1914: discours et idéologie*, Dominique Maingueneau traces the influence of texts such as Jules Payot's *Cours de Morale* published just after the turn of the century, some of whose themes resound in Céline's pamphlets and in early twentieth-century hygiene.[20] Like Payot, Céline assumes implicit connections between ethnic "others" such as Arabs (standing in for all non-Christians), "savages," "vagrants," "vagabonds," "bohemians," "sluggards [paresseux]" and "madmen."[21] Such thinking takes as its foundation what Payot calls "the collective results of contemporary science [les résultats généraux de la science contemporaine],"[22] the kind of ethical-biological thinking that supports Céline's early interest in hygiene. Biology is enlisted to confirm all kinds of generalizations about races and the differences between them, including brain size and the ability to "pay attention for a long time." Of particular interest, given Céline's passion for the dancer's physical discipline, is Payot's estimation of the physical abilities of these "others":

Our distant ancestors, and in our time the savage tribes (Negroes, Red-Skins), as well as barely civilised people (Arabs), were or are capable of violent efforts, such as those required by war and hunting. Only, we have seen . . . they had and have a horror of long-term efforts of attention. Laziness is not the incapacity to make violent efforts, but to pay attention for a long time.[23]

Maingueneau points out that the qualities that make a good citizen in an industrialized, capitalist nation—such as coordinated perseverance and intensity—come to constitute the ethical-biological paradigm. The groups deemed unproductive in industrial society, the reprobates censured by a sociological-moral critique, come to include Africans, Arabs, vagabonds, bohemians, and vagrants, who, like children, are thought to need guidance from masters. Like madmen, they are deemed passive, waiting to be told what to do; each is "incapable of motivation on his own [incapable de se mettre en mouvement de lui-même]" and destined to be a slave, an animal. Maingueneau notes the slippage from "savage" to "slave" in the passage in which Payot describes native peoples as courageous but not as courageous as the white colonizers who persevered in their long-term, coordinated efforts and who have a better use of their nervous system.[24]

Much of Céline's thinking can be traced to fin-de-siècle hygiene and writing on the social pathologies, and some of it sounds like the texts of public health without entirely reproducing their arguments. Robert A. Nye's *Crime, Madness and Politics in Modern France: the Medical Concept of Decline*, untangles connections between the social pathologies and the medical models at their core.[25] In Nye's history, texts on criminal anthropology proliferate in the 1890s along with tracts on alcoholism and pamphlets denouncing nudity in cabarets of the Belle Epoque and at the Folies Bergères, the Moulin Rouge, and the Olympia.[26] Contributing to moral decline, and—more significantly—population decline, were nervousness, fatigue, alcoholism, and other causes. Nye calls the national concern over depopulation the "master pathology" of the Belle Epoque.[27] Among the many authors of such texts, Nye isolates two major theoreticians of the fin-de-siècle thinking of decline whose writings had a French audience, Max Nordau and Richard von Krafft-Ebing. Nordau targeted literary intellectual figures, and saw madness, alcohol, suicide, and crime as symptoms of the "sickness of the age." Krafft-Ebing's *Psychopathia Sexualis* (1886) warned that "episodes of moral decay coincide always with the progression of effeminacy, lewdness, and luxuriance of the nation"; and that "exaggerated tension of the nervous system stimulates sensuality, leads the individual as well as the masses to excesses, and undermines the very foundations of society, and the morality and purity of family life."[28] Of the many branchings that French mental medicine took in the nineteenth century, Céline's medical thinking followed this tradition more closely than it did Charcot's or Freud's.

Céline's social thinking takes its cue, as public health, from what Nye has called the "medical model" of the social pathologies developed in fin-de-siècle France.[29] This model of health was appealing, Nye argues, because of alarming trends in France's vital statistics: depopulation, rising rates of syphilis—especially in the 1890s—alcoholism, mental illness, crime, suicide. The thinking of this cultural crisis of decline analogizes the individual body to the social body. Nye has described how degeneration theory "telescopes" biological and social causes; "this mode of thinking . . . encouraged the appraisal of social problems from the point of view of *national* interest, thrusting, as it were, issues of domestic health and external security into an identical frame of analysis."[30] In another formulation, Maingueneau finds a "homology between the body and the social body, between hygiene and political practice," whose aim was to maintain intact the "treasure of our energy," making a direct connection between health and national strength.[31] Concern about the decline of French character depended upon its definition according to national type: "the 'scientific' study of national character was a veritable industry in France in the thirty years before World War I."[32] In this climate, each case of individual pathology was a symptom of the syndrome of degeneracy.[33]

Céline's definition of the pathological, unlike Claude Bernard's in one nineteenth-century tradition discussed earlier, would be that which differs from the "normal" in kind as well as in degree. In this definition the ideal is not inferred from an observed "normal" state; rather, a constructed "normal" is imposed as "ideal." In many of the passages of *Bagatelles*, Céline follows the trajectory of thinkers like Payot, in which, as Maingueneau describes it, "History is a vector: biologism, psychology, everything moves toward *homo occidentalis*, the supreme ideal."

Yet Céline's significant differences from such thinking, also evident in *Bagatelles,* must be underlined. Céline envisions a physical perfection rather than a moral one.[34] Payot's and others' idealized pedagogy in which the teacher's mission is to breed the animality out of students is countered by Céline's belief that schools drain their healthy vitality.[35] He is angered by the way in which schools reduce animal spontaneity;[36] and praises the "feline quality" of American women.[37] Dance, Céline argues, belongs not to the realm of pornography but to the realm of health; dream and dance, fairy tale, create—for those allowed them—an inner life that encourages both production and reproduction. More closely aligned with Céline's views on health is the fin-de-siècle literature— much of it nationalistic in tone—emphasizing sport and its potential for revitalization or "regeneration."[38]

Although two characters in two Bagatelles ballets, Méphisto in "La Naissance d'une fée" and the title character in "Van Bagaden," complain about the idle, both caricature ineffectual attempts at mastery—perhaps only confirming that some who are masters should be slaves. Much of the anti-Semitism of Bagatelles pour un massacre critiques purported Jewish wealth, banking interests, and monopolies. Authority, hierarchy, and power, as well as the Republican insistence on the goodness of those who serve them, such as mother and soldier, and the importance of duty in general, will be cynically recast everywhere in Céline's oeuvre. If Céline's goals for France echo Republican moralistic ends—production, reproduction, hygiene, exclusion of "others," preservation of racial purity— he comes to imagine them being realized in very different ways.

Significantly, Céline's model for the kind of truth biology represents is the dramatic nineteenth-century Hungarian hygienist Philip Ignaz Semmelweis, whom he championed in his medical school dissertation. The dissertation tells the emotional story of the unrecognized genius and portrays him as a victim of the politics surrounding the medical profession, a great medical mind driven to madness and self-destruction. Céline's passion for, and eventual identification with, the individual struggling against the institution find an outlet in this story. It is an unusual one for the Ecole de Médecine, a rather renegade history of medicine that depends upon the idea of the genius of the great man, familiar from both medical and literary history, and yet makes an important distinction between science and literature.

Semmelweis is remembered in medical history for discovering a solution—without uncovering the cause—for a high rate of puerperal fever in one of the maternity wards under his direction. Céline singles out Semmelweis for his discovery of the biological "fact" governing the cause of the deaths of infants delivered by doctors coming from dissections without washing their hands. For Céline this is an action more laudable than what he calls the "literary gestures" of philosophers and politicians:

In other domains we have become habituated to declarations on the part of thinkers and politicians, solemn, but not based upon any precise or stable fact. Those are, in brief, only literary gestures. This one, on the contrary, marks a definite point in our biology.[39]

The tone of the pamphlets suggests that Céline thinks of himself, in dramatic terms, as a Semmelweis, preaching "fact" to a world that will not listen, and giving himself entirely to the cause. Céline's Semmelweis ends up infecting himself and dying to prove his point. The desire to associate his writing with scientific "fact" is paradoxically also the desire to associate himself with Semmelweis, whose work relied on observation—not biological explanation—of the high mortality rate in one of his hospital's maternity wards. Semmelweis determined the pathogenic effect of hands that had been touching corpses without the benefit of microbiology or microscopic research. The overarching truth of biological "fact," then, is closely connected for Céline to clinical observation, pathological anatomy, and—especially in Semmelweis's case—the statistical science of pre-Pasteur hygiene.

This science can be understood to have its own particular style, linked to an ethos of action rather than mere "gesture." In *Les Microbes*, Bruno Latour argues that what united nineteenth-century hygienists before Pasteur was precisely a certain "style" rather than any particular nosological approach.[40] Central to this style, Latour finds, was a rhetoric that followed no single current but tended rather to accumulate various kinds of advice, warnings, suggestions, statistics, remedies, rules, anecdotes, and case studies. This accumulation of arms was necessary to combat diseases understood—or misunderstood—as being caused by anything at all; because causes of illness were deemed myriad and mysterious, nothing must be neglected by the hygienist. Latour writes that the hygienist had to "be able to act on everything and everywhere simultaneously. This style takes shape as the action that the hygienists were getting ready for."[41]

Philippe Roussin has argued that Céline's ideology is linked early on to his medical training and practice, specifically in the hygiene developed early in the twentieth century. It is a recognizable medical idealism that Céline will never completely give up—holding on to it in the dancer's image—although it will later be tarnished by his practice among the poor. Roussin describes the nineteenth-century component in the medical science of hygiene and its relationship to the world of letters in Céline's early career. Arriving on the French literary scene with the publication of *Voyage au bout de la nuit* in 1932, Céline presented himself as a doctor diagnosing society's ills, a public health specialist in the tradition of the nineteenth-century hygienists: "Céline's medical identity, far from disappearing with his entry into the world of literature, was, on the contrary, claimed and reaffirmed by him . . . between December 1932 and April 1933, Céline chose to be regularly interviewed at the dispensary in Clichy and . . . photographs of him in his hospital whites, surrounded by his colleagues, appeared in the press at that time."[42] Using his medical degree and professional practice as his basis of authority, and medical discourse as the model for novelistic "truth-telling," Céline first negotiated the world of letters and arts by claiming an objective and professional superiority.[43] This is the superiority gained by nineteenth-century medicine; and when Céline—Dr. Destouches—first appears in the public eye in 1932, it is a resurfacing, Roussin says, of the image of the nineteenth-century societal hygienist who, like Parent-Duchâtelet, designs strategies to combat social ills.[44]

Beyond *Semmelweis*, Roussin reads Céline's medical writings as utopian treatises of medical organization, practice, and surveillance. They were written between 1925 and 1932—first at his post in the Office of Hygiene of the League of Nations (what Céline in *Bagatelles* calls his "bien joli poste" at the S.D.N.) and after 1929 at the public health dispensary of Clichy. Having recruited Céline in 1918, the Rockefeller Commission had helped to steer his medical training toward social hygiene; the various posts he held after graduating from medical school and until 1928 were Rockefeller-funded, and they made Céline into a public health propagandist for "standardized medicine." These texts describe a program in which public health must be the charge of the primary care physician, closely observing work conditions and keeping workers on the job. In his travels to the Ford plant in Michigan and elsewhere, Céline absorbed and lectured on the doctrines of Taylorism and Fordism that he then helped to proselytize in France, in the sanitarian campaign against "waste" in industry.

Roussin finds a close connection between the utopian thinking of these texts of the 1920s and the accusations made in the pamphlets of the 1930s:

One suspects that this exaltation of the physically energetic dimension of man at work, this polemic against "waste" (the denunciation of "nonproductive" social groups is implicit), is one source of the anti-Semitic and eugenic tendencies that would come to light in Céline's pamphlets of the 1930s. . . . With the help of

Taylorism and Fordism, Céline's medical writings define a utopia, a *medical utopia*, a society without sickness, in which industrial America is the model for a Europe coming out of wartime, a Europe where illness symbolized, as it were, the *symptom* of the Continent's backwardness relative to the New World and the *sign* of that anachronism, visibly inscribed on the body politic.[45]

After the 1929 crash, Roussin notes, Céline's utopian model will shift from America to the "socialist or communist state system" of Germany and Soviet Russia. Céline's dance trajectory in *Bagatelles* thus follows one of the major lines of his medical-political thought. From his fascination with an American dancer made manifest in *Voyage* and in an early play *Progrès*,[46] Céline's dance writing in the pamphlet considers the classic French romantic ballet ("La Naissance d'une fée"), then its destruction with the introduction of technology and modern dance forms ("Voyou Paul. Brave Virginie"), and then, after a hopeful attempt at selling the French romantic ballet in Russia, makes a half-hearted and parodic attempt at Stalinist social commentary ("Van Bagaden").

For Roussin, the medical discourse of these utopic texts of the 1920s bears an inverse relation to the discourse of the novels Céline published immediately following them. In the novels, Céline is the doctor recording not just social ills but the "illness of history"; the "community pathology at that moment in history." This is "the history told through the history of illness": "by exposing History, the narrative portrays illness: that of bodies affected by time, subject to history, which render time visible, whereas the hygienist writings proposed a utopia of abstract bodies, exempt from the wear and tear of time."[47] In a similar way, the delirious ballets of *Bagatelles* bear an inverse relation to Céline's idealizing dance theory.

Céline's interest in dance, especially in the years spanning the publication of his first novels, bridged his careers as public health doctor and literary figure. Across this range of medical thinking and experience stretches Céline's image of dance as discipline and illness, from the utopic thinking of public health and hygiene to the practice among the poor of Clichy. An early play, *Progrès*, features a dancer who is the image of New World hygiene. The United States's industrial and hygienic discipline is inscribed on the body of this American dancer, and her health is the sign of America's productive advantage.

This dancer is a biological marvel; she anticipates "the day when women will be covered only in muscle ... and in music ... and less in words ... "[48] The American emphasizes that this idealization of the dancer's body will be effected not only through movement or musicality, but also through simple nutrition. She herself has reached this idolized state through proper diet and exercise; the Frenchman Gaston, who worships her body, vilifies the corpulent brothel madame whom he has to deal with: "I'm bawling you out because you sell flesh and you don't even recognize good merchandise; your profit has made you a blockhead ... insolent and excessive as the *nouveau riche* are, the body of an arriviste, short and stumpy, the body of a serf. Oh, shame, short, fat, and nevertheless badly fed, fed too late, too well, ugly madame Lard ... " For Céline, the body is shaped by work, movement, diet, lifestyle, and thus can be read as an indicator not only of class but also of character. The American underlines the fact that her idealization results from hard labor for a body of flesh and bones.

This statement reveals a link between Céline's thinking about the dancer and his political and social thinking, as the early pages of *Bagatelles pour un massacre* have shown. At many moments, Céline's physical program and ideals resonate with those of the Third Reich, and the ballets carry implicit, if not explicit, political messages that can easily be identified with the politics outlined in his pamphlet. After the American dancer in *Progrès* and the Olympic swimmer, Céline's personal and erotic identification with the dance and with the dancer suggest a view of dance quite different from the fascist choreography visible in the mass military spectacle or the individual glorification of the heroic body, captured by Leni Riefenstal's films "Triumph of the Will" and "Olympia," both commissioned by the Third Reich. But much of Céline's writing on hygiene must be described as fascist in content if not intent.[49]

For Céline, dance is not only physical training but the creative exercise of spirit and imagination. Dancers' discipline allows them to turn the physical body, which constantly threatens and disgusts in the novels, into an aestheticized body. Yet in a passage from *Les Beaux Draps*, Céline recommends participatory dance for the masses, and finds it crucial to "hygiene" broadly defined. Without it people become sad, work less, and, significantly, produce fewer children: "We have to learn to dance again. France remained happy up through the *rigodon*." But whereas the dance belongs to France's fairy-tale past, the present makes people shut themselves up in cinemas to forget their own existence. It is in part the new technology that is to blame: "We will never dance in the factory, and we will never sing either. If we don't sing any more, we die, we stop making children, we shut ourselves up in the cinema to forget that we exist."[50] In this strange causality, industry will lead to the end of France; by quelling dance and song, modern technology will deprive the French of life itself. Dance thus has a specific place in the program of the hygienist: dance leads to production, to procreation, to repopulation and thus increased production, whereas the life of industrial production, without "dance" and everything it entails, curtails reproduction if it is not carefully monitored.

This thinking connecting dance to sex and, via sex, to reproduction and to productivity places Céline's hygiene in line with what Michel Foucault has called the "bio-politics of population," the "bio-power" that governments began to exercise, in particular via their administration of hygiene, when productivity and population growth became crucial to the success of industrialized capitalism.[51] Such thinking, however, is often controverted in Céline's other dance texts, which—when they connect dance to sex—either problematically idealize the dancer's sexualized body as an empty, nonreproductive and nonproductive site, or pathologize it for its sexual excesses.

The ballets of *Bagatelles* invert and subvert the utopic tone of Céline's early dance theory: they diagnose dance movements, ground them in a racialized biology, and blame them for cultural degeneration. The fascination with dancers is medical in nature: the professional fantasies of an overworked physician, the vestiges of the utopian medicine of the public hygienist. Although dance seems to illustrate the ideals of public health, the glorified body of efficiency and hygiene, the world of dancers also offers from the start an escape from medicine, a window onto the world of arts and letters that Céline so repudiates and yet is evidently proud of joining.

The ballets stage hysteria not only as upper-class European neurasthenia, the crisis of nerves in technologized society, but also as sexual possession, the disintegration of the community, the degeneration of French culture, crowd frenzy, and anarchy. In Céline's worldview, while dance constitutes work and discipline for the American in *Progrès*, the dances of Semitic, gypsy, African, and Caribbean peoples are the perverse result of excessive leisure, a leisure and excess he perceives as threatening France. Hysteria is the thread connecting the "social pathologies" the pamphlet describes in the form of dance. Whether caused by hysteria or manifest as hysteria, such social diseases call for Céline's public health expertise. Céline's view recalls late-nineteenth-century views of hysteria as a social ill closely connected to syphilis, alcoholism, prostitution, degeneration, and immigration. The metaphorical thinking of degeneration sees the health of the nation threatened by the sickness of the social body, and locates the sources of illness and infection among particular social groups.[52]

For Roussin the medical-figure-as-author-and-narrator is a social investigator, called upon to anatomize society, diagnose its ills, and "register the explosion of the social ensemble." The doctor-as-writer is also a kind of ethnographer;[53] Céline casts himself as one. The ballets provide metaphors for the perceived threat of Semitic and African cultures that comes in the form of a bad drug to which Europeans become addicted: in "La Naissance d'une fée," a gypsy's potion; in "Voyou Paul. Brave Virginie," the love potion of an island tribe; in "Van Bagaden" the frenzy of the crowd, the fête, the carnival. The plots of the ballets are transparently anti-Semitic, racist, degenerationist, blaming the decline of French culture on "others." Significantly, they also adhere to a sociobiology that extends the idea of contagion to the realm of mental health, belong to the tradition in which mental and physical illness is understood as moral affliction, and develop the idea of race as a social pathology. Reading the body and diagnosing its ills, reading society and prescribing its cures, are the doctor-writer's province. Reading the social body for signs of "health," reading class and color as signs of its sickness, Céline uses a symptomatology familiar from the nineteenth century, one in which dance figures significantly as a model.

The first ballet in *Bagatelles*, "La Naissance d'une fée" (The birth of a fairy), is the text Céline produces when Gutman tells him to grab his pen and write, the ballet for which all of this opening discussion is a pretext; it is a mise-en-scène of Céline's view of the ballet tradition and his place in it as voyeur. The set indications for "Naissance" clearly place it in the fairy-tale, romantic ballet tradition, but with more than a hint of parody: "Epoch: Louis XV. Setting: Wherever you like. Scene: A clearing in a wood, rocks, a river in the distance." The opening scenes of the ballet proceed more or less as in the openings of *Giselle* and other ballets with pastoral settings, in this case with dances of the forest spirits followed by the festive dances of the village youths. The plot is set in motion by the menacing figure of the gypsy Karalik, who, angered by their disruption of her fortune-telling, hurls a curse at the couple around whom the group—and the ballet—are centered: Evelyne and her fiancé, the Poet. In their international rather than national allegiances, the gypsy and the Jew are, to Céline, one and the same.[54] The gypsy is a thinly disguised version of the threatening Jew; she has a mystical power, connected with nature, and delivers her curse in tandem with a thunderstorm.

When a large coach arrives in front of the town's inn, its coachman turns out to be the second dark and threatening figure of the ballet—the text names him Mephisto. He is the ballet master of the troupe of ballerinas, who pop out of the coach arrayed like little dolls. But he is also, more symbolically, the impresario who drives into town with high culture in tow; he is the promoter and the procurer for Lucifer himself. Though Céline sets the ballet in eighteenth-century France, it is a nineteenth-century female *corps de ballet* which emerges from the coach. Despite their innocent looks, the ballerinas are seductresses enslaved to this devilish ballet master. He demands total submission from his pupils: "Having at last united and assembled at great pains this crazy company, he sermonizes these girls! ... And he explains to the fat innkeeper that he is the one in charge! ... That he is the master! That he must be obeyed! ... The 'Maitre des Ballets du Roi!'" This "Méphisto-coachman" drives his troupe like horses, demanding their discipline and obedience: "The little maître de ballet wants no laggards [ne veut pas de paresseuses] ... He pushes his pupils."

In their turn, the dancers enslave the men of the village who are drawn to watch their ballet class through the windows of the inn where they are rehearsing: "The poet, the fat magistrate, the notary, the doctor, the boarding-school teacher, the grocer, the blacksmith, the gendarme, the general, all the people of note, the workers, even the undertaker's apprentice ... They get excited ... Scandal of the wives trying to snatch them away from the blinds ... The worthies fidget comically, they shift their weight from one hip to the other ... " (20). The dancers turn the village upside down, as the men they have hypnotized jump onto the departing coach to follow them out of town. Even the Poet, seduced by the Prima Ballerina, turns unfaithful to his Evelyne. Abandoned by her fiancé, Evelyne abandons herself to thoughts of suicide and dances them out with the "Angels of Death" in black veils.[55]

But if the ballerina's dance is a seduction with the power to enslave, the only charm strong enough to outdo it is a dance powered by the forces of nature. Evelyne saves a forest creature from a hunter, and in gratitude is given "the Dance's great secrets"—the dances of nature, the "Leaf in the Wind," "Leaf Storm," "Autumn," "Firefly," "Zephyr," "Undulating Mists," "Morning Breeze" (22). With this power to move, Evelyne becomes divine: "Now she dances divinely ... She no longer has to fear any rival" (22). Displaying her newfound knowledge before Karalik and the gypsies, Evelyne in turn seduces the men and incites the women to jealousy; Karalik gives one of them a dagger and she stabs Evelyne in a rage. Here emerges the traditional ballet theme of the transfiguration of woman into spirit, the virgin who dies before her wedding, the abandoned fiancée, who will take her revenge dancing on the other side of the grave. Evelyne is transformed into a fairy by the forest creatures, and she joins the company of Giselle and the Wilis, the swans and Bayadères.

"La Naissance d'une fée," exactly like *Giselle,* makes the *corps de ballet,* and not the dead heroine, into vengeful monsters. Forest creatures lead Evelyne to the Château du Diable where the carnival reigns. But the revelry is grotesque: each "notable" is forced to dance not with a dancer, but with his own "damnés": "The Judge with his condemned ... The old Miser dances with his process-servers ... The General with the soldiers killed in the war, emaciated, with the war's skeletons and amputees, all bloody ... The Professor with his snotty pupils ... The fat Pimp with his whores, both the depraved and the teenagers ... The Grocer with the clients he's robbed ... The Notary with his ruined widows ... the Curate with his fickle nuns and his pederast clerics ... etc. ... " (25). Amid this orgy of punishment, the poet is chained in place: "The demon 'prima ballerina' ... dances before him ... for him ... bewitches him. But he can never touch her ... have her ... He tries ... He is in despair." Lucifer's project, as he presides over the whole scene, is to take a voyeuristic pleasure in creating and putting obstacles before the men's desire. It is a hellish eros, a male hell of temptation and frustration, where the women work for the Devil. Evelyne enters and with a single gesture brings the house down, crumbling the chateau to dust, freeing the Poet and the others. Back in the forest, the Poet begs her forgiveness; she forgives him, but as a fairy is unable to remain with him. She will disappear into the Poet's song: "He will sing ... he will forever sing of his ideal ... poetic ... impossible loves. ... For ever ... and ever ... Curtain." (26)

When the curtain abruptly brings closure to the musings on poetry at the end of "La Naissance d'une fée," the Poet's painful position mirrors Céline's own: writing legends for dancers in order to hold on to them. But Céline, as the manipulator of the curtain, also uses it to comment on the Poet's naiveté. Once the curtain falls, this kind of poetry—the song of the dancer's idealization and inaccessibility—ends. As parody, "La Naissance d'une fée" suggests what Céline and everyone else understood about what happened behind the Opéra curtain, the backstage prostitution of dancers and their image which is the complement to their idealization onstage. Just as the first act of *Giselle* represents the "real" life of a dancer flirted with by the Opéra's wealthy habitués, and the second the fantasy of sexual revenge by disappointed women, the orgy at the "Chateau du Diable" represents a sexual fantasy. Céline sees himself at the Opéra as the poet at the Chateau; he frames his failure with the ballet in sexual terms. When Gutman brings news of the ballet's rejection, Céline responds explicitly: "So I will never get any dancers? I'll never get any! you say so." "You're cutting off my pleasure ... you're busting my balls ... You'll see what a cut-off poem is like [Tu me fais rentrer ma jouissance ... Tu m'arraches les couilles ... Tu vas voir ce que c'est un poème rentré]" (41).

Thus the social and political anxieties surrounding the ballets, and dramatized in them, are staged as sexual anxieties. But the explicit sexuality of dance here, both borrowing from and parodying romantic ballet, is a kind of screen for what Céline considers to be more significant issues. To survive the withering defeat of this first ballet, which is clearly meant to replay the negative reception of *Mort à crédit*, Céline makes himself into a critic, in order to validate the work that will give him entrée into the dance world:

I myself find this comical-tragical fairy-tale entertainment very well done. It pleases me, and I have better taste, me alone, than all the pant-shitting and assholing critics [toute la critique pantachiote et culacagneuse] all together, so I decided, beating out all the commentary, that my ballet was worth far more, surpassed by far all the old themes ... all the pet subjects of the repertory ... the cavalry of the Opera ... Giselle ... Bagatelles ... Petits Riens ... les Lacs ... Sylvia ... No affectations! no miming! (26–27)

By the end of the first ballet of *Bagatelles pour un massacre*, Céline seems to have made himself into both the victimized voyeur and the triumphant critic he has complained about, emulating or internalizing the opposition, as Kristeva describes it, and strongly establishing dance as a locus not only of "style" but of his sexual and racial politics.

In a similiarly contradictory move, the second ballet—written in response to the failure of the first—conscripts for its purpose of social critique the very tradition he has just ridiculed. If "La Naissance d'une fée" mocks the French romantic tradition, "Voyou Paul. Brave Virginie" (Rowdy Paul. Worthy Virginie) defends it against "bad" ethnic and modern influences. Written after he receives Gutman's news of the rejection of the first ballet, this second one plays out the themes of Céline's social politics by staging the encounter of different dance styles and addressing the issues of high culture and low culture, the roles of technology and primitivism, in European culture.

Céline sets to writing "Voyou Paul. Brave Virginie" in a café, as an angry response to Gutman's news and to his request for another ballet, this time "absolutely appropriate for the pomp of the Exposition ... " Thus Céline from the outset is writing in a double bind: in order to get what he wants, he must please the presumed Jewish Exposition organizers. Céline's efforts result in a perversion of the classic "Paul et Virginie" story, with a sideshow of modern technology thrown in to satisfy popular taste.

In the opening prologue, in front of the "tableau romantique" of "Paul et Virginie," the appearance of a fairy godmother in tutu, with wand at hand, announces Céline's snide commentary: "The truth?" asks the character, "oh! listen! ... Not everything was told ... " We have already been warned by the title, and this tongue-in-cheek opening sets the tone. Paul and Virginie are not drowned, but wash ashore in a "Paysage Tropicale" where they find "good savages" dancing wildly under the influence of a magic potion passed around by a sorceress. In the first scene, the couple recover with the aid of the potion, and dance together: Paul drinking and dancing more and more avidly, as Virginie begins to distrust its effects.

A second prologue, again in front of the ridiculed painting, has the fairy godmother again, on tiptoe, introducing the second scene, at the salon of Virginie's aunt Odile. This aunt misses her niece; she is, comically, a great reader of *Paul et Virginie*: "She has read and reread, a hundred times now, the good Aunt Odile, every page of the great novel ... of the marvellous, tender, and terrible story" (31–32). Odile sits at the window watching for ships as she reads and rereads the novel. In contrast to the natives' wild display, the correct, charming young people in Odile's salon dance formally to celebrate the engagement of her daughter Mirella and Oscar, until a messenger brings news that precipitates the whole group toward the port.

Before they arrive, however, a third interlude with the fairy throws a comic warp into the proceedings. On the curtain is represented a monstrous vehicle, an "engine, a kind of diligence-autobus-tramway-locomotive" (33–34). It is the "FULMICOACH": "this apocalypic engine, a machine with colossal wheels ... " will later pass across the stage. A group of engineers are measuring for the event, which so frightens the fairy that she drops her wand and flees—an image of the incompatibility of legend and modern technology in Céline's eyes. When Paul and Virginie's ship docks, they are greeted with jubilation, but Paul immediately begins a disturbing dance with some of the members of the tribe who have accompanied them: "Jerky, convulsed and barbaric dances, utterly new for Aunt Odile and the rest ... Tom-tom ... Virginie, clinging to her aunt, does not seem especially thrilled at this demonstration ... " Here African or Caribbean dance comes to Europe, and the "tom-tom" takes over the port, symbolically representing what Céline sees as the conquest of Europe by musics of the African diaspora—ragtime, jazz, and blues—in the first decades of the twentieth century.[56]

Paul is drinking the sorceress's beverage, wildly dancing "danses impudiques." Abandoning herself to tears, Virginie grabs the potion and drinks it to the dregs. She begins to dance as well: "She is a fury ... a dancing fury ... Never had Paul seen her like this ... and he likes it ... it enslaves him ... " Like Evelyne's dancing in "La Naissance d'une fée," Virginie's dance has an erotic power. It arouses the jealousy of the woman Paul is dancing with—Virginie's once-modest cousin, Mirella, whom he has rapidly seduced away from her fiancé. In a scene of female jealousy and fury already familiar from "La Naissance d'une fée"—both ballets giving the mad scene borrowed from Giselle a violent twist—Mirella leaps toward a sailor, grabs his pistol, and shoots Virginie, whose body lies downstage as the FULMICOACH blazes across upstage, drawing the crowd away from her. She is abandoned finally even by Paul, and only the faithful dog remains unimpressed by the new technology, lying down by her side as the curtain falls.

The plot of "Voyou Paul. Brave Virginie" presents themes important to Céline and crucial to his pamphlet: the various threats—here identified as "barbarism"—to classical French culture, and the no less barbarous modern technology, championed at the Exposition by what Céline imagines as Jewish capitalist interests. By putting African culture and modern technology together as responsible for the ballet's evils, Céline is also making a racial link between African and Semitic peoples, a link referred to repeatedly throughout the pamphlet. Both cultures, in Céline's view, threaten the French tradition which this ballet defends.

By repeating in this second ballet the motifs of seduction and violence from "La Naissance d'une fée" but with an added social dimension, Céline is commenting on his own position as author and librettist. To make a ballet acceptable to the organizers of "l'Exposition des Arts et Techniques," he suggests mockingly, the libretto must first eroticize French art through the addition of exoticism; and second, present technological wonders at the expense of plot and character. The fabulous, ironic appearance of the FULMICOACH mocks the Exposition's fascination with technology, and the ballet's ending provides a moral for what Céline sees happening in the context of the Exposition: the machine has greater drawing power than the death of the good heroine of French romantic literature, abandoned in its wake. It is also a bitter commentary on French cultural history; it is the rise of the machine, and not the myths of Romanticism, that the twentieth century preserves, the interests of capital rather than poetry.

Though in "Voyou Paul. Brave Virginie" Céline has recourse to classic literature, seeming to defend it against national enemies, the refinement and mastery that he claims for himself in writing ballets are both established—precariously—in the face of what he disparages in French literary tradition. In its highest forms, Céline claims, French literature is perverse, overly ornate, "juif." The negative adjectives that describe it are exaggerated through an insistence on, or insertion of, the syllables "con" ("cunt" or "bastard") and "cul" ("ass"). Such writing is associated with "les académies Francongourt," a word merging "L'Académie Française," "les frères Goncourt," and "con"; it is "dialecticulant," encoding dialect, the dialectic, and "cul." For Céline, this is a language that hides and lies, a language of "finesse circonlocutoire," a false refinement connected to "con," to "circon" (the prefix for *circoncire*, "to circumcise") and to "les belles merdes." Repeatedly described through the interjection of "con," effeminized and bastardized, it is the language he must learn to write under the insistence of his Jewish boss, Yubelblat, at his post at the S.D.N.:

In the end he had me tamed, I rewrote, super-skillful, amphigorical, like a sub-Proust, quarter Giraudoux, para-Claudel ... I went along circumlocuting, I wrote Jewish, in the nice spirit much in style these days ... dialecticulating ... elliptical, fragilely reticent, inert, high schoolish, molded, elegant as shit, the Franc-assed academies and the fistulous Annales.

Je m'en allais circonlocutant, j'écrivais en juif, en bel esprit de nos jours à la mode ... dialecticulant ... elliptique, fragilement réticent, inerte, lycée, moulé, élégant comme toutes les belles merdes, les académies Francongourt et les fistures des Annales. (111)

Yet writing the accepted French threatens to ruin Céline's style: "Of course that hampered me. This diligence, this abuse, obstructed my development ... " (111). In a burst of what he calls "héroisme," Céline sacrifices his "very nice post" at the S.D.N. in order to save his writing "for the violence and liberation of French Belles-Lettres ... " (111).

The dance offers a model for this liberation of language from the "con," and it brings with it the romantic illusion of free expression that Gautier cast in the terms of "saying everything." If authoring libretti is an attempt to get closer to dancers, the style Céline will develop and identify with his "raffinement" is an attempt to shape a writing that emulates the physics and poetics of dance. This shift from writing that prescribes action—the libretto, the pamphlet—to writing that inscribes action involves two interconnected ideas. On one level, Céline conceives of the dancer's body as poetry, inscribed rather than described ("inscrits! ... Jamais écrits!"), the most nuanced poem in the world. On another, Céline reverses the relationship between writing and dancing: now, poetry resembles the dancer's body, and this poem-body is godliness itself: "The unprecedented [unheard-of] poem, warm and fragile as a dancer's leg in moving equilibrium, is in line, Gutman my friend, to hear the greatest secret of all, it is God! Himself! That's all! That is what I really think! [Le poème inoui, chaud et fragile comme une jambe de danseuse en mouvant équilibre est en ligne, Gutman mon ami, aux écoutes du plus grand secret, c'est Dieu! lui-même! Tout simplement! Voilà le fond de ma pensée!]" (12).

The goal is to make writing itself resemble a dancing woman, whose feeling is restored to her, and who feels more than she reasons: "to *resensitize language*, so that it *palpitates* more than it *reasons* [*resensibiliser la langue, qu'elle palpite plus qu'elle ne raisonne*]."[57] In the tradition of Charcot and Duchenne restoring sensitivity to hysterically anaesthetized bodies, Céline the writer is going to doctor the language of French literature. Thus he shifts his focus from a writing that can be put into action to the writing of action he characterizes as "style." He adopts the dancer as a stylistic model; claiming to create a style simultaneously prosaic and poetic, he uses everyday language in a rhythmically structured text, as the dancer makes the prosaic raw material of the working body into poetry. Céline defines his working-class poetics both in reference to, and in opposition to, Mallarméan poetics. *Bagatelles* mocks this tradition: "Poet? I said ... Poet? ... Poet like Mr. Mallarmé?" (13). But the later Céline does not: "I am a stylist, a colorist with words, but not like Mallarmé of words with extremely rare meanings—rather of common words, everyday words [Je suis un styliste, un coloriste de mots, mais non comme Mallarmé des mots de sens extrêmement rare—des mots usuels, des mots de tous les jours]."[58] Yet there is an identifiable Mallarméan tone to much of what Céline says about dance, in particular a remark that the dance is a poem which can be read: "It is dancers that I read. I am Greek that way—oh, not by sex! by gesture ... by their very emanation [Ce sont les danseuses que je lis. Je suis grec par ce côté—ah, pas par le sexe! par le geste ... par leur émanation même]."[59] "Reading" dance means understanding the dancer's movements as if they were words: as Mallarmé "read" the dancer's signs and imagined her as Sign itself. Here it inspires a poetics which attempts to make words signify as movements.

Such a poetics relies on rhythm to carry meaning, and Céline's rhythms—perhaps even more than the "everyday words" he uses—are the ultimate mark of his "style." In the ballets, the rhythmic patterns of the writing aptly imitate the movement of groups and individuals onstage. The omnipresent ellipses give a continuous movement to the action, running up into exclamations or series of exclamations and then dispersing again. In Céline's description of the overall effect of "La Naissance d'une fée" the rhythm of the descriptive text becomes very dancelike, repeating the rhythms that the dancing might enact: "everything in sequence ... in the pleasure, the charm ... spins ... becomes still ... variations ... reprises ... everything weaves together ... in the pleasure ... soars ... even higher ... Dance, anyone? [tout s'y enchaîne ... dans l'agrément, le charme ... tourbillone ... se retrouve ... Variantes ... reprises ... tout s'enlace ... dans l'agrément ... s'élance ... s'échappe encore ... Qui veut danser!]" (27). The dance's seduction is a rhythmic one; for Céline, the rhythm integral to dance and its writing is not illusion or ornament, but rooted in the body whether dancing or writing. The act of writing is itself a kind of dance because movement, timing, and rhythm are of primary importance.

Examining Céline's manuscripts, Henri Godard has noted that almost without exception, Céline wrote no outlines, no plans, no notes to himself, rarely marginalia or supporting texts; when he sat down to write he wrote, as if performing, the work itself. During work sessions, he never paused too long on any single passage, and the movement and rhythm of the act of writing, producing the movement and rhythm of the text itself, shapes the short, separate passages that structure the novels:

At every moment, Céline privileges movement over immediate completion. . . . If he slows down this movement, to pursue however briefly the development of a single page or series of pages, he never immobilizes it. . . . The essential remains the movement in which the work must remain caught up. . . . Terms such as "movement" or "run" [séquence] used to describe these sections, seem best to indicate the exigencies of sequence [enchaînements] and of rhythm fundamental to Céline's writing.[60]

Although the freedom of his style gives the appearance of ease, Céline considers writing, like dancing, to be physical labor. He describes the process of composition as a painstaking lace-making; he calls himself "a worker [un ouvrier]" and "a crazy artisan [un artisan maniaque]."[61] His close control of the text parallels the dancer's precise and rigorous work, and it, too, is work that disappears in the final product. Only the most disciplined body can give the illusion of improvised, free movement; as the American dancer of "Progrès" emphasizes: "it is four hours of work everyday, branded, there, of work like that ... not on 'my flesh' but in the muscles themselves."[62]

Through repeated rewriting, Céline's prose imitates the daily work of dancers. A close examination of one of these rewritings sheds light on the way in which Céline attempts to make later versions both tighter and freer, organized not by considerations of clarity or logic but by the exigencies of rhythm. In a passage from *D'un château l'autre*, the image of a dance is evoked in an unexpected context; in the transition from manuscript to the published text, some of the details of this comic dance are dropped. The scene dramatized is one in which Céline approaches the Russian border with a "delegation" of what he casts as political refugees in his escape from France at the end of the war.

From a discussion of food—the group is not only cold, but hungry, and dreams of being fed—the conversation turns toward the topic of their possible destination. Have they arrived in Russia? Céline wonders. Are they in fact headed there? While the others are talking about food, Céline imagines their arrival at the border: all that would be necessary, he boasts, would be to present him to the Russian authorities as Céline, the author of *Voyage au bout de la nuit*, which Trotsky had called the first communist novel:

salted lard! they know what we're going to eat! me, I'd love to! ... all of a sudden I deliver to them too, the Delegation, that I am the author of the first communist novel ever written ... that they'll never write another! never! ... that they don't have the guts! ... that they'd better let the Russians know! ... and the proof: Aragon and wife, translators! they'd better not disembark just any old way! ... they'd better let them know who they are! ... and with whom! ... they'd better do more than talk to them about bortch! maybe dance them a sad dance? with sobbing? ... a little "stricken impromptu"?

lard salé! ils savent ce qu'on va s'envoyer! moi je veux bien! ... du coup je les affranchis aussi, la Délégation, que c'est moi l'auteur du premier roman communiste qu'a jamais été écrit ... qu'ils en écriront jamais d'autres! jamais! ... qu'ils ont pas la tripe! ... qu'il faudra bien leur annoncer aux Russes! ... et les preuves: Aragon, sa femme, traducteurs! qu'ils débarquent pas n'importe comment! ... qu'ils leur disent bien qui ils sont! ... et avec qui! ... qu'il suffit pas de leur parler de bortch! peut-être leur danser une danse triste? avec sanglots? ... un petit "impromptu accablé"?[63]

The revised passage confuses the linearity of the first draft and conflates two separate strands of narrative. The two narrative threads intertwine with no explanation and no indicators to tell the reader when the subject changes. The two strands are further twisted by the repeated use of the single pronoun "ils," for a double referent, two different groups whom Céline is talking about—the "delegation" with whom he is traveling through the German winter, and the group of French communist writers he sees as his competitors and critics.

The passage then shifts suddenly to a third scene: Céline's comic staging of the arrival at the border of this group, swathed in funeral crêpe to keep out the cold. He imagines them, dressed in this way, fit to dance. An earlier draft of this passage describes the dance in more detail:

salted lard! me too after all ... I tell them ... to your health! "you will only eat (sun seeds) of sunflowers!" ... I too have been to Russia! ... salted lard-borsch! ... (sunflower) not as long as they the ministers had! ... but all the same! all the same ... under Stalin and at my own expense! ... the Voyage is translated into Russian! shit! by Aragon and Triolet! ... and even (their) Trotsky said to them: it's the only communist novel ever written! and that the bastards are still in awe of it! that they'll never get over it! that they will never write another! that they no longer have the guts! I deliver this to them the ministers! so they know before disembarking who they are with! (how they should present me to the Russians!) Delegation of mousseline! "you're not going to dance a number? Loie Fuller? or Duncan?" ... they would be pretty as a picture on the snow! ... A sad little dance? A funeral dance! ... with sobbing ... they have already ... and the shivers! ... they have the shivers! ... a little "stricken impromptu"?

lard salé! moi aussi après tout ... je leur dis ... salut! "vous boufferez que (des graines de soleil) du tournesol!" ... j'y ai été aussi en Russie! ... lard salé-bortch! ... (tournesol!) pas si longtemps qu'eux les ministres! ... tout de même! tout de même ... sous Staline et à mes frais! ... le Voyage est traduit en russe!

merde! par Aragon et Triolet! ... et même (leur) Trotsky leur a dit: c'est le seul roman communiste qu'a jamais été écrit! et qu'il sont encore tout cons devant! qu'ils n'en reviennent pas! qu'ils en écriront jamais d'autres! qu'ils ont plus les tripes! je les affranchis moi les ministres! qu'ils sachent avant de débarquer avec qui ils sont! (comme il faut me présenter aux Russes!) Délégation la mousseline! "vous allez pas danser quelque chose? Loïe Fuller? ou Duncan"? ... ils seraient à croquer sur la neige! ... une petite danse triste? (d') des obsèques! ... aux sanglots ... ils ont déjà ... et la tremblote! ... ils l'ont la tremblote! ... un petit "impromptu accablé"?

Céline parodies the dances of Loie Fuller and Isadora Duncan to mock the "délégation" both for its theatrical shabbiness and for its overly dramatic attitude. The "danse triste" he imagines is comic in its melodrama. Yet the reference to dancers is important, even if belittling; trying to fix his identity in the barren snowbound no-man's-land between political borders, Céline suddenly imagines a dance. The "stricken impromptu," the simple dance of great emotion, is a much better description of some of Duncan's choreographies than of Fuller's, and it is an image that dates from the era of the First World War and not the Second. But Céline knew Fuller's choreographies and may also have had in mind a 1915 photograph of a soldier in Fullerian costume and wig, performing her famous "Serpentine Dance" to a group of uniformed soldiers at the front.[64] The elision of Céline's literary persona into the creator of dances confirms the link in his mind between the internationally known "political" writer and the creator of ballets, which Bagatelles repeatedly affirms, both in the context of Russia and of France.

The draft is much more specific than the final text on several points. It names more names: Triolet, Trotsky, Fuller, and Duncan are all left out of the later rewrite. It indicates more clearly the shift from the mention of Céline as the "first communist novelist" to the comic-tragic dance—announcing it with the phrase that merges politics and the dance: "Délégation la mousseline." In the final text, the movement between Céline's literary status in Russia and the dance he envisions happens with no connectors, sliding across the famous trois points: "that they be sure to say who they are ... and with whom ... that it's not enough to talk to them about borscht! maybe dance a sad dance for them? with sobbing? ... a little 'stricken impromptu'? [qu'ils leur disent bien qui ils sont ... et avec qui ... qu'il suffit pas de leur parler de bortch! peut-être leur danser une danse triste? avec sanglots? ... un petit 'impromptu accablé'? ...]".

In the published text, the dance is brought up without any introduc-

Fig. 14. A soldier performing Loie Fuller's "Serpentine Dance" during a break on the front, 1915. Courtesy of Editions Stock; all rights reserved.

tory or explanatory phrase, and its presence is hard to understand. Why should the delegation's pathetic performance be likened to a dance? Cé-line's literary reputation, he believes, should earn them honorable entry into Russian territory. What Céline fails to say here, but does say in *Bagatelles pour un massacre*, is that his reception in Russia is unlikely to be warm, owing to the publication in 1936 of his pamphlet *Mea Culpa*, which was extremely critical of Stalinist Russia.[65]

In the reworked passage, the text becomes more difficult, more closely knit; it progresses by stylistic tricks—rhythm, meter, the stychomythia of a single voice. It takes on a nonlinear dimension which relies extensively on rhythm or movement, rather than grammar or syntax, for its meaning. But this style, of course, comes with its own set of "ideas" attached. Céline's use of everyday vocabulary and the rhythms of spoken French create a consummately popular text, early on considered one of the first examples of a "communist" writing so sought after by French writers of the period. In *Poétique de Céline*, Henri Godard locates Céline's poetic prose with the stylistic efforts of the writers of the French left. Godard cites Malraux's comment at the Congrès des Écrivains Soviétiques in Moscow in 1934 that the literary problem which most concerned French writers at the time was "The problem . . . of spoken language that would nevertheless merit the title of style [Le problème . . . d'un langage parlé, atteignant cependant à la qualité du style]." In 1964, Aragon would speak of "this syncopated speech, this oral French, typical of my generation [ce parler syncopé, ce français oral, qui est de ma géneration]."[66] Céline's justification of his own writing, against what he perceives as the formless formalism of writing he describes as Jewish, seems then to depend upon raw, visceral presentation rather than ornate figural representation. Though he calls himself a stylist rather than a writer of "ideas," his style is structured by or organized around rhythm, which permits a rapprochement of the physical to poetics, the recuperation of the body in writing. Rhythm allows the formalization of the body's less appealing physical aspects—those most frequently found in Céline's novels.[67] The cornerstone of Céline's style, rhythm is not without political significance; it is what facilitates the connection of "style" and "ideas" in dance.

In the writing of the second novel, *Mort à crédit*, and the pamphlets, Céline's rhythms, worked out syllable by syllable, become the identifying mark of his prose; for some critics this is a kind of unconscious imitation of Mallarmé.[68] Henri Godard notes that all of the elements of Céline's writing—punctuation, word choice, use of short phrases separated by ellipses, elision or non-elision—are regulated by the demands of rhythm as the "organizing principle," the formal structuring element of the prose. For Godard, Céline's rhythms not only organize the text from a formal point of view, but exist in a complex relationship to passages' meanings;

sometimes coinciding with the animation of the scene being represented, at other times, existing as poetry seemingly for its own sake. The rhythm, often octosyllabic, can emphasize pure sound or onomatopoeia, but it varies depending upon the rhythmic exigencies of each particular sequence. Godard notes that a rhythmic pattern used in one passage to establish calm can be used in another to animate the scene. The rhythmic line can "accompany the meaning, underline it and follow its articulations. Elsewhere, it imposes its own groupings at the cost of what would be demanded by meaning, substituting its particular movement for meaning, making up for what it lacks, or else enters into a relationship with meaning that is the opposite of the superficial adequation sometimes achieved."[69]

The rhythm Céline finds essential to good writing is more than a musical sense and takes more than a good ear. The constraints of style demand not simply a rhythm that, like music, can be heard, but a rhythm he finds rooted in biology. The text must echo not only in the ear, but in the entire nervous system: "Not just in the ear! ... no! ... in the intimacy of the nerves! right in the nervous system! inside the head [Pas simplement à son oreille! ... non! ... dans l'intimité de ses nerfs! en plein dans son système nerveux! dans sa propre tête]."[70] Everyone possesses this rhythm as a function of his biology: "Every man who has a beating heart also has his own song, his humble personal music, his entrancing rhythm down in his 36.8 degrees, otherwise he could not live."[71]

Céline seems particularly proud of his "personal music." Just as he will ultimately describe his prose as a dance and himself as a dancer in the concluding Marinsky episode of *Bagatelles pour un massacre*, he describes his prose as music and himself as a musician in a passage from *Guignol's Band*, I: "It has to run! ... that's the great secret ... never slowing never stopping! it has to be strung out like the seconds, each one with its little malice, its little dancing soul, hurried, but goddammit the next one pushing it!"[72]

The racism underpinning Céline's definition of rhythm and his biology, Godard has argued, sheds light on Céline's ideology rather than his style: "For anyone seeking to outline the reality of a style and its power, not only is it not illuminating, but its result is to trap rhythm in the ideological system whose basis is biology. Yet another illustration of well-known partisanship, it has nothing to add to a reflection on literature [Pour qui cherche à cerner la réalité d'un style et de son pouvoir, non seulement elle n'est pas éclairante, mais elle a pour effet de prendre le rythme au piège du système idéologique auquel la biologie sert de base. Illustration supplémentaire de partis pris déjà bien connus, elle n'a guère à apporter à une réflexion sur la littérature]."[73] But Céline's biologization of rhythm is crucial to understanding the role of the body in his rhythmic writing, in particular the female body, and his relation to it in the figures of dancers. It is the thread that connects his medical career, his passion for dance and dancers, his politics, and his literary style.

The poetry of rhythm is Céline's solution to the problem of the public world of music; it is his way to triumph over external opposing forces. The major obstacle to the production of the ballets, as Céline perceives it and cites in example after example, is not simply a conspiracy of Jewish impresarios, but the lack of music that this conspiracy brings about. Without the aid of a musical score and the collaboration of a composer, the ballets cannot hold their own with administrators. In the final pages of *Bagatelles pour un massacre*, Céline laments this lack; introducing "Van Bagaden," he calls for the lights to come down, and for Dream to come and take him and his audience away. But without music, such transport is not possible:

But the Music? ... Ah! This is my whole problem ... I have a relapse, I'm completely hampered! ... Music! ... the wings of Dance! Without music everything collapses and grovels ... Music the edifice of Dreams! ... Once again I'm screwed ... If you should happen to hear, from your connections ... of some passably delicate musician ... who wants only to do his job well ... I beg you ... let me know ... I will make a deal with him ... between death and life ... an easy job ... We could surely come to some understanding [Nous pourrons sûrement nous entendre]. (374)

Playing on the double meaning of *entendre*, Céline points to his solution to the problem of music: lacking a musician, Céline makes his own music. Céline's theory of rhythm based in the body ultimately connects his music and style to his conception of biology, his theories of race, and the scapegoat-thinking of degeneration. Far from transcending this thinking, the ballets are as trapped in it as Céline himself.

In an approach that could be called psychobiological, Julia Kristeva points out that Céline claimed to write as he did because of the body he lived in. Kristeva notes the degree to which Céline identifies his head wound from the First World War as the founding point for the pain narrated in his stories, exaggerating it and blaming it for headaches, earaches, arm aches, vertigo, inner-ear noise, vomiting: "At the throbbing peak of *his* pain, Céline goes looking for a history, a probability, a myth. It is the famous story of his head wound from the First War, a wound whose seriousness, according to most biographers, Céline exaggerated."[74] The hysteria provoked by the wound—and the hysteria of the war that created it—connect Céline to World War I's tradition of male hysteria.[75]

For Kristeva, it is Louis-Ferdinand Destouches's physical pain that is the source of Céline's written "music." The expression of this vertiginous pain and the emotion it creates shape the rhythm of his sentences: "Beyond the story, vertigo finds its language: it is music in the breath of words, in the rhythm of sentences and not only as a metaphor [Au-delà du récit, le vertige trouve son langage: c'est la musique, comme souffle des mots, comme rythme des phrases et pas seulement comme métaphore]."[76] Céline's cult of emotion becomes glorification of sound; Céline is writing affect and thus writing the body.[77] But the writing itself comes out of the body, out of his own body, and its hysterical wound. Thus for Céline, the dancer is a model to imitate: moving to make art out of pain, out of the body's rhythms, out of its nervous system.

Kristeva's poetics of *chora* link Céline's writing—its rhythmic and emotional qualities—to the maternal body. In *Pouvoirs de l'horreur*, Kristeva identifies in his style the writing of a maternal "abyss" (*gouffre*), a version of what she has called the semiotic chora. "Chora" is a term used by Kristeva to describe poetic forms that seem to rebel against the symbolic function of language. This semiotic element, Kristeva proposes, exists simultaneously with and within symbolic language, and is present in writing such as Mallarmé's or Céline's.[78] For Kristeva, this writing is close to the physical body and to affect, which can be understood as existing prior to or outside of language. Like a current running underneath or inside symbolic language, this semiotic chora runs parallel to, and sometimes against, what Jacques Lacan calls the symbolic order, identified with paternal interdiction organizing and controlling the accession to language. It is thus identified with the maternal body, and with the body's drives, which are themselves identified as feminine. Michèle Montrelay glosses one psychoanalytic view in the debates on femininity, in which femininity—not "woman"—is defined by drives: "by femininity we understand the ensemble of 'feminine' drives (oral, anal, vaginal) inasmuch as they resist the process of repression."[79]

In keeping with ballet tradition, the dancers of Céline's texts are denied motherhood, and remain at the far end of the spectrum from the women of his dissertation on Semmelweis. The women of Semmelweis's wards are described as the passive victims of the medical community's errors; just as Semmelweis himself is represented as the victim of the closed-mindedness of the medical establishment.[80] But Céline finds both a kind of maternal comfort and hysteria in the dancer's body, and connects both to rhythm and to the body's rhythmic drives. Céline's oeuvre gives us, in general, two stereotypical female bodies: the idealized dancer and the terrifying, possessed, perverse, or diseased figure familiar from the ballets and from the novels. The American dancer masters the body for the purposes of art; the dancers of the ballets in *Bagatelles* frequently fall into convulsive submission to bodily excess. But these two kinds of bodies in Céline's work simply incorporate two different views of the female body; and they coexist in the dancer desired in the early pages of *Bagatelles*, simultaneously seductive and threatening, promising pleasure and a disturbing loss of identity, sex, and death:

Life grabs them, the pure ones ... carries them away ... at the slightest transport, I want to go lose myself with them ... all of life ... quivering ... wave-like ... Gutman! ... They call me ... I'm no longer myself ... I turn myself in ... I don't want to be rocked in infinity! ... at the source of everything ... of all the waves ... the world's reason is there ... Nowhere else ... to perish by the dancer!

La vie les saisit, pures ... les emporte ... au moindre élan, je veux aller me perdre avec elles ... toute la vie ... frémissante ... onduleuse ... Gutman! ... Elles m'appellent ... Je ne suis plus moi-même ... Je me rends ... Je veux pas qu'on me bascule dans l'infini! ... à la source de tout ... de toutes les ondes ... La raison du monde est là ... Pas ailleurs ... Périr par la danseuse! (12)

The siren call that tempts Céline brings him close to danger and death with a body that is a maternal space of origin, "la source de tout" and the origin of the waves which typify what Céline most loves, "de toutes les ondes." Its power to carry him away on these waves is also a terrifying power of the empty space of "l'infini," the terrifying threat of loss of identity in union with this body. "Périr par la danseuse" represents both his desire and his fear, both the pleasurable rocking of the waves and the death they can bring.

For Kristeva, Céline's writing brings his reader closer to the kinds of meaning that travel through sound or rhythm, poetic elements of language: "at the exact point of the overturning of emotion into sound, at this threshold between body and language, in the catastrophic fold between the two [au lieu précis du renversement de l'émotion en son, à cette charnière entre corps et langue, dans le pli-catastrophe entre les deux]."[81] Through the use of slang, through his particular rhythm and punctuation, through his incorporation of music and dance, the writing "approaches this void of meaning that Céline seems to aim at [approche ce vide du sens que Céline semble viser]."[82] Céline's development of a rhythmic prose, and his move toward music and dance, ultimately open up onto a terrain of emptiness: "But in reality, this emotion sliding toward music and dance gives way, in its final form, to the void. At the end of the voyage is thus unveiled the full trajectory of language's mutation into style under the impulse of an unnameable alterity that begins as a passion, becomes rhythm, and then empties itself out [Mais en réalité, c'est sur le vide que débouche, en dernière instance, ce glissement de l'é-motion vers la musique et la danse. A la fin, au bout du voyage, est ainsi dévoilé le trajet complet de la mutation du langage en style sous l'impul-sion d'un altérité innomable qui, passionelle pour commencer, se rythme ensuite, avant de se vider]."[83] This emptiness is the feeling of abjection, fascination, and disgust in Céline's writing. Thus the writing both ex-presses and rejects what Kristeva calls abjection; Céline's style can be read as a challenge to and defiance of abjection ("défi à l'abjection").[84] By naming and writing this abjection, Céline attempts to write his way through and past it.

The writing ultimately expresses emptiness; but it is an emptiness Céline describes as full. Like Mallarmé, he finds the nothingness of the void to be the locus of the artist. During a difficult period in his life, he would write: "I only feel good in the presence of nothing, of the void [Je ne me trouve bien qu'en présence du rien du tout, du vide]."[85] This "presence of nothing, of the void"—like the presence of the dancer—is comforting as well as terrifying; and elsewhere in his writing it is associ-ated with the feminine. Like the maternal chora or womb, like the waves of dance and dancer, this full emptiness is feminized.

But Céline defines his writing in respect to two views of femininity. If the "vide" is where the artist belongs, or where he feels best, the lan-guage used to bring the reader there makes him "tout con." Defined against the idealized feminized of emptiness, the reader is assigned the slang word for the female sex ("cunt"), more generally used as a deroga-tory term for men (translated here as "bastard"). The female sex does not escape Céline's brutal language: "Slang is a language of hate that puts your reader in his place ... annihilates him! ... at your mercy! ... he re-mains an idiot! [L'argot est un langage de haine qui vous assoit très bien le lecteur ... l'annihile! ... à votre merci! ... il reste tout con!]."[86] Like the writers of the French left mentioned in the passage from *D'un château l'autre*, the "bastards" or "idiots" who are "tous cons devant" Cé-line's novels, the reader of Céline's slang is incapable of reproducing what the writer produces.

"Con" and "vide" then, both crucial to writing, are both attached to the female body, as its negative and positive poles, or as the "masculine" and idealized "feminine" of femininity.[87] Those who are "con"—the rival writers and critical readers—remain impotent while Céline flourishes in the "vide." He uses the "vide" to make others "con"; his talent, as a writer, is the art of "déconner." Through her alternate language of music and movement, the dancer transforms what is potentially "con" into an idealized "vide," giving form without losing the passion of the unformed. Such passion is the hysterical "idea" at the core of Célinian "style."

The link between Céline's politics and his creation of dances, between style and ideas, and the suture between the writer and the dancer within him, is finally acknowledged in the sections of *Bagatelles pour un massacre*, which introduce the pamphlet's third and final ballet, "Van Bagaden." The concluding pages explicitly address the questions of socialism and style addressed in the pamphlet. Céline's merging of popular prose with the poetry of the body is staged in the context of Céline's visit to Russia, his presentation of "La Naissance d'une fée" to the directors of the Marinsky theater, and the ballet they then commission, which remains unfinished and, like the others, unperformed.

The introduction to "Van Bagaden" mockingly suggests that this "Grand Ballet Mime et quelques paroles" is too long and boring to be reproduced in full in the pamphlet; and that though commissioned in Leningrad, it will not be delivered:

And then this ballet? ... It was finished ... I was fairly pleased with it ... Always a matter of ghosts ... I intended it for Leningrad. ...And then there you have it! ... The circumstances ... too bad ... that's that! I'm going to read you the beginning of this long entertainment ... a bagatelle! All? ... I would bore you. ...Is it a plausible epic? ... with very profound intent? ... No! ... A simple somersault between death and life ... exactly our size ... it dances between death and life exactly ... it distracts ... takes you away! ... Are you following me? ... Just some lights and OK ... The Dream is taking us away.

"Van Bagaden" is set in the busy Antwerp of 1830—the same date and setting as "Voyou Paul. Brave Virginie"—and again uses the past for the purposes of contemporary social commentary. The curtain goes up on a hubbub of activity: workers and goods, dock hands hauling and loading, officials checking and double-checking bolts of fabric, baskets of grain, every possible kind of cargo. The stage space represents a huge hangar, throbbing with commercial activity. A group of *parfumeuses* take up one corner with their precious wares and petty arguments. Equally attractive, the *cigarières* take up the opposite corner. With the constant movement of dock workers back and forth from the ships the scene is "humming with activity ... work ... disputes ... " and the air is filled with the music of the port: "sirens ... calls ... the songs of men slaving away ... the songs of men at work ... hauling ... etc. ... and then other music ... street organs [des orgues de Barbarie] ... street musicians ... " Out of this cacophony leaps an African dancer whose dancing is described like that of the islanders arriving at the port in "Voyou Paul. Brave Virginie": "short savage interlude."

This bustle of activity is overseen by the powerful Van Bagaden hidden behind a screen: "deep in his formidable armchair, very brittle, gouty, peevish." No longer able to move from his chair, where he sits sleeping, eating, spitting, and guarding his gold, Van Bagaden is "tyrant of the seas and seamen," "shipowner on all the world's seas." Van Bagaden's personal secretary and slave, Peter, sits chained to his stool, hovering over the accounts, never going fast enough for the boss, who curses and beats him continually. Van Bagaden smashes his cane on the floor in discontent with all his workers: "Van Bagaden is upset about this ... So his workers are having fun instead of working! ... So he no longer has any authority! He's too old! ... All these little scoundrels are defying him! escaping him! ... He can no longer make them obey him! Damnation!" (377).

A captain enters with information for Van Bagaden, whispers it in his ear; and a mysterious unloading of cargo begins. Peter is unlocked, and brings in a heavy net of pearls as big as oranges; another net of jewels of all kinds, larger, heavier. No one helps him. The crowd looks on. Peter takes the treasure to Van Bagaden, who locks it up in a coffer behind him, beneath his "throne." Peter chains himself back to his stool once more, and the workers return to their labor, when a brass fanfare ("fanfare très martiale") is heard outside, drawing closer and closer. Van Bagaden's dictatorship is threatened, affronted, as the parade enters, a joyous crowd with banners, music, even a "miniature 'saint' on a palaquin" and gigantic cut-out puppets. This is an odd demonstration—part festival, part military parade, part carnival. Van Bagaden, who has never had fun in his life, reacts in fury to the display of joy, the outburst of music and dancing. Trying to raise himself from his armchair, he demands that

Peter fight off the intruders with his cane, and Peter is sent out alone, charged to "beat them! ... kill these hooligans for me! ... " (378). Van Bagaden's fight against the popular fête ends with the image of his lackey trying single-handedly to suppress the "immense farandole." The text breaks off with this image of the mass popular movement and the paranoid violence of the authoritarian ruler.

The ballet not only dramatizes the failure of power in the hands of the corrupt individual, but also suggests a criticism of the Front Populaire's institution of the forty-hour work week. In *Bagatelles pour un massacre*, Céline ascribes this reduction of labor to what he perceives as the sloth of the alcoholic and pleasure-seeking masses under the control of Jewish interests promoted by a liberal Jewish government.[88] On one hand, Céline wants, like Van Bagaden, to drive off the corrupting forces of popular culture—their raucous drunken music and display. But on the other hand, he also sees himself as the tyrant's slave. The character of Peter recalls that of Ferdinand in *Mort a crédit*, an autobiographical stand-in for the young Louis Destouches working for a jeweler in Paris and Nice, charged with important deliveries. Céline's introduction to the ballet denies it any serious merit, referring to it as a "bagatelle"; yet "Van Bagaden" visibly refers both to the autobiographical characters of his novels and the personal issues they dramatize, as well as to the pamphlet's disturbing social and political commentary.

The ballet's ability to treat such "ideas" is explicitly at issue in the writing of "Van Bagaden." Sitting at the ballet in Leningrad night after night, during his visit in 1936, Céline is heartened by the discovery that the Russians understand the timeless importance of the fairy tale: "Ballet means fairy tale ... The most irreparable, the most ignominious catastrophes aren't those in which our houses collapse but those that decimate our fairy tales ... " (347). When he has seen every program at the Marinsky two or three times, the desire to be a successful librettist returns to him, and he decides to present his ballets to the administration: "In the end I couldn't resist. The idea took me over again [L'idée me reprit] ... the obsession ... It seemed to me that I, after all ... To try my luck ... He who risks nothing ... My poems? ... if these Russians should go for them? ... Who ever knows? A flop in Paris ... maybe a hit in Russia" (348).

Céline enthusiastically presents "La Naissance d'une fée" to a room of thirty unmoved Marinsky people; redoubling his enthusiasm, Céline acts out the entire ballet, finally earning their "Murmurs! ... approbation! ... clamors! ... and they compliment me! ... Flatter me! ... Celebrate me! ... Vidi! Vici! Vici!" (350). But at the director's request, Céline slowly rereads certain passages, and finally the entire libretto; the director is confirmed in his opinion that certain elements in "La Naissance d'une fée" simply will not play to a Soviet audience. He indicates that a ballet by Céline would be welcome, but only if it treats less "frivolous" themes. Céline summarizes the director's critique: "Ah! He desired nothing more than to stage such a show by a foreign author ... of such importance! ... Very desirous ... However, one not quite on this theme ... If I might keep in mind ... Perhaps using some other poem ... less uncommon ... less frivolous ... less 'archaic' ... a less dreamlike formula ... some more realist structure ... a bit brutal, even violent ... " (350).

The commissioned ballet must also satisfy particular stylistic requirements: "Perhaps in addition, I could provide several passages of dialogue in my story ... Ah! that would be innovative! ... dialogue! dancing words! [des paroles dansantes!] ... A dancer by word ... by letter! [Une danseuse par mot ... par lettre!]" (351). Socialist art depends on dialogue: the director wants some in the ballet in order to avoid the Parnassian mythologies of romanticism, the familiar themes of the romantic ballet: "Ballets must make people 'think'! like all other kinds of performance! ... and think 'sozial'! Move ... certainly! ... charm ... but charm 'sozial' you see? The better a poem is, the more it is 'sozial'! [Les ballets doivent faire 'penser'! comme tous les autres spectacles! ... et penser 'sozial'! Emouvoir ... certes! ... charmer ... mais charmer 'sozial' n'est-ce pas? Plus le poème est réussi ... plus il est 'sozial'!]" (351). The director emphasizes that a ballet like Céline's might have played in Russia in 1906, or even 1912, but no longer.

As if he has chosen ballet for its wordlessness—when in fact his ballets are only words—Céline declares himself incapable of dialogue. He takes the director's comments as a sign of his failure: "Insensitive to ridicule, not at all humiliated, I felt after this failure only a very sincere sorrow ... At the entrance to the Temple I gave up ... I got myself kicked out, by perfect connaisseurs, like a wretched skirt ... I could have cried ... " (351). Rather than responding in anger, he seems to take the board's opinion seriously; at first glance, "Van Bagaden" looks like an attempt to fulfill the program outlined by the Marinsky director. The "several words [quelques paroles]" announced in the title of "Van Bagaden. Grand Ballet Mime et quelques paroles," however, mock the Soviet's request for social realism in the ballet, and a critique of Stalin is implied in the authoritarian figure of Van Bagaden. The text of *Bagatelles* breaks off after the opening of "Van Bagaden"; perhaps losing faith in it, Céline stops himself because he wants the ballet to remain a "féerie," and not a vehicle for "sozial" thinking. The longer account in the pamphlet of Céline's presentation of "La Naissance d'une fée" to the Marinsky board reveals how much more closely he wants to identify his work with the fairy-tale element in ballet—even when it carries a hidden social or political message—than with social "ideas."

But ideas are an inextricable part of style, in writing as in dance; and style for Céline is inextricably bound up with language, culture, race, and nation. Facing the formidable audience of Marinsky judges, engaged in trying to sell his ballet, he himself becomes a performer trying to make his audience believe in his story:

I throw myself into the story without further ado ... the "Birth of a Fairy" ... They all understand me perfectly ... but not one of them moves a muscle ... perfectly inert, atonic. I provide all the action ... I put new heart into it! ... the whole show! ... I'm putting myself into it! ... I mime ... I'm giving it all I've got ... how I'm shaking! glib! ... conjure up so much and more! cavalcade! ... I'm outdoing myself! ... I am theater, orchestra, dancers! all the "ensembles" at once ... all by myself! ... I impersonate the entire "Birth of a Fairy" ... All the joy, the sadness, the melancholy ... I'm everywhere [Je suis partout!] ... I imitate the violins ... the orchestra ... the rousing waves ... and now the "adagios" ... (349–50)

Reenacting the ballet with words and mime, Céline demonstrates physically the rhythms and gestures of his writing. Far exceeding simple gesticulation, Céline's performance shows the degree to which his writing translates dance, reproducing its action. It also suggests the degree to which he himself, as a storyteller, thinks of himself as a dancer. Performing his text, Céline becomes "théâtre, orchestre, danseuses!" Sometimes using ballet terminology, he describes his tours de force as dance movements:

Nobody holds me back! ... I lunge ... develop ... other entrances! ... quadrilles! ... I bounce to the other end ... rebound ... a kid! ... multiplied, all in arabesque, around these enigmas! I emerge possessed! innumerable ... throw myself into it again ... Ah! and then suddenly! stop! ... backbend [cambré] ... whirlwind! ... in sequence [enchaînant], I begin again ... unfurling ... the plot's meandering ... underline in passing the thousand graces of the theme ... on demi-pointe ... in relevé ... Very good! ... two arabesques! ... In the airborne humming of a waltz ... two more "fouettés" ... very en dehors ... I make my escape ... intrigue ...

slip away ... volta! ... return ... In attitude! piqué ... Sarabande ... I land in a great "fifth"! within reach of the director ... I dive ... toward the delighted audience ... *grande révérence!* (350)

Céline describes his initial victory with the Marinsky group as if it were his dancing—the visible fireworks of his presentation—that wins them over: "Vidi! Vici! Vici! It's very clear! ... What a gift! ... What soaring! ... The spirit! ... The take-off! ... Taglioni! ... They are in heaven! ... It is visible!" (350).

What is evident in Céline's danced version of his text is the element of possession injected into the classical ballet entrances, variations, and positions he prescribes. Though Céline always blames the authorities, Jewish or Stalinist impresarios and directors who encourage and then reject his work, the hysteria is here clearly situated in the writer himself, and it finds expression in the performance of dance and words. Significantly, this performance includes the very dialogue that the Stalinist administration has solicited. Céline himself is the perfect "sozial" show, as he divides and multiplies, playing all the roles, representing dancers, musicians, and audience. The dialogue played out in the passage is one between dancer and ballet master, whose encouraging "très bien" and commanding "deux arabesques!" "En attitude!" can be heard in the narration. The passion for the dance, the desire to please and to perform, feed on one another, and what Céline began by describing in the opening of the pamphlet as the haven of the classical ballet is revealed to be at the eye of the storm.

By describing his art in the terms of an idealized as well as denigrated femininity—identifying himself with the first and his public with the second—Céline repeats the simultaneous idealization and degradation of the dancer familiar from the nineteenth-century tradition. Simultaneously separating the dancer from hysteria while producing hysterical dances, and distancing her from writing while imagining writing itself to be a dancing woman ("il faut que ca palpite"), Céline creates two female bodies in his work that ultimately come to represent the writer's own doubleness, the contradictions that structure the work, the writing divided against itself.

Lacking dancers as well as music, Céline comes to emulate the dancer not only in his art but in his very person. By the end of *Bagatelles pour un massacre*, the desire to possess the dancer, and to write her, is transformed into the desire to become her. As the writing comes to emulate dance, so does the body of the writer. In the various shapes it takes,

Céline's desire for dance is a desire based on identification rather than object-possession, like that defined by Mikkel Borch-Jacobsen: "desire . . . does not aim essentially at acquiring, possessing, or enjoying an object; it aims (if it aims at anything at all) at a subjective identity. Its basic verb is 'to be' (to be like), not 'to have' (to enjoy)."[89] Becoming rather than possessing the dancer would be, in Borch-Jacobsen's revision of Freud, another expression of desire or wish fulfillment. "Identification is not a means for the fulfillment of desire, it is that 'fulfillment' itself."[90] In Freud's terms, it is in the identification itself that hysterical symptoms are expressed:

Identification is a highly important factor in the mechanism of hysterical symptoms. It enables patients to express in their symptoms not only their own experiences but those of a large number of other people; it enables them, as it were, to suffer on behalf of a whole crowd of people and to act all the parts in a play single-handed. I shall be told that this is not more than the familiar hysterical imitation, the capacity of hysterics to imitate any symptoms in other people that may have struck their attention—sympathy, as it were, intensified to the point of reproduction. Thus identification is not simple imitation but *assimilation* (or appropriation, *Aneignung*) on the basis of a similar aetiological pretension; it expresses a resemblance and is derived from a common element which remains in the unconscious.[91]

This identification, more pronounced than in Gautier's or Mallarmé's responses to dance, becomes pathological with Céline. Like the nineteenth-century men of letters he repudiates, Céline is drawn to the theater early in his writing career, with some desire to make his name in it. But what interests Céline, more than the dramatic form, is a self-dramatizing that he will develop in the largely autobiographical characters that color the novels so vividly. Céline's early attempts at play writing are as far as possible from his later mode of quasi-autobiographical narration, but the pamphlets are dramatic in the way that the novels will become, in that he dramatizes himself in them. Godard notes: "By moving the 'I' into the realm of essay and polemic, the pamphlets inevitably overtake the 'I' of the novels. . . . From one book to another, we see him creating ways to be ever more present in the text."[92] The ballets do not exclude their author; within the context of *Bagatelles pour un massacre* they include him as narrator, presenter, and quasi choreographer. Because the ballets themselves have never been danced, they have never existed as dances with performers whose practice, subjectivity, and interpretation we might consider. Without dancers they remain only texts unchanged by the performance of real bodies.[93] The principal performer of the ballets—as at the Marin-sky—is thus Céline himself. Identifying with the dancer, and conceiving of himself as a performer, Céline connects his "style" to the tradition of performative madness familiar from nineteenth-century medical history.

When Céline describes himself, at the beginning of *Bagatelles pour un massacre* mouthing his critics, as not "crazy" or "mad," but "hysterical" and "cunning," he demonstrates a familiarity with the medical tradition that defines hysteria as a calculated, simulating disease: "Mr. Céline is not even mad ... this hysteric is cunning ... [M. Céline n'est même pas fou ... cet hystérique est un malin ...]" (14). Identifying himself as hysterical, he parodies the pseudo-psychological tone of criticism he had received.[94] For E. H. Kaminski, writing at the time of *Bagatelles'* publication, it is the social dimensions and implications of this "madness" that are most signif-icant: "Is he mad? ... Probably. But there are dangerous madmen and they are even more dangerous when they live in an era where madness easily becomes widespread ... That is why the case of Céline concerns not—or not only—alienists, but also and above all, society [Il est fou? ... Proba-blement. Mais il y a des fous dangereux et ils le sont encore plus quand ils vivent dans une époque où la folie se généralise facilement ... C'est pourquoi le cas de Céline ne regarde pas—ou pas seulement—les aliénistes, mais aussi et avant tout la société]."[95]

Latter-day critics have tended to see Céline's madness, if not that of the pamphlets, as more complex and often, in retrospect, less dangerous. In "Les crises d'identité du racisme Célinien: entre prédications xéno-phobes et désir d'exil," Yves Pagès reads Céline's novelization of his pathological wandering against the nineteenth-century psychopathology of the wandering Jew.[96] Pagès believes that the way in which the young Destouches is portrayed, in particular in *Guignol's Band*, as a wanderer and exile, transposes this "Jewish" stereotype onto himself. Pagès's sug-gestion of Céline's identification with the Jewish figures against whom the pamphlets rage builds on Kristeva's analysis of the Jew as rival and model and finds it indicative of the contradictions at the heart of Céline's ideology and writing.

But the diagnosis of madness or paranoia has often been used, Isabelle Blondiaux argues, to avoid the critical problem of the pamphlet's politics. In "Louis-Ferdinand Céline et le diagnostic de paranoïa,"[97] Blondiaux analyzes what critics have variously called his "fictionalizing fantasy," his "moral vice," his "psychological troubles," his "playful talent for provocation." Whatever the diagnosis, what Blondiaux finds most significant is that "if there is paranoiac pathology, Céline seems to manipulate it rather than be manipulated by it, whether adopting a medical or literary point of view."[98] For Blondiaux, a clinical reading of Céline such as Milton Hindus's suppresses the ideological stakes of the work. She calls this a "délire à deux" in which Hindus lends (in some ways, his own) madness to Céline; not so much calling him "mad" as describing him as behaving "like a prima donna."[99]

Blondiaux—herself both a psychiatrist and a literary critic—agrees with the diagnosis of Céline as a kind of actor using his knowledge of pathology to create a "simulated paranoid delirium." Céline was a "writer-doctor who ultimately resorted to data constituting the field of mental pathology rather than to some ineffable personal experience."[100] While other critics have read Céline's sometimes semi-autobiographical fiction as a mise-en-scène of his experiences, Blondiaux invents the term "retrofiction" to describe how Céline's fiction rewrites his past as "a pseudobiography based on data borrowed from the novels."[101]

Semmelweis can be seen as something of a model for the Dr. Destouches who entered the literary world as a hygienist; treated with electricity for paralysis following his head wound, choosing medicine as a career, declaring himself hysterical to outdo the opposition's diagnosis.[102] Although *Bagatelles* speaks the doctor's language, detailing society's ills, Céline's writing ultimately belies medicine's claims to authority and truth. Despite the doctor's connection to nineteenth-century medical traditions in which the hysteric is not crazy but cunning, not male but female, not French but alien, his writing derives its power and appeal from the everyday medical practice that diagnoses the sickness of the age everywhere, and in everyone.

According to Philippe Roussin, Céline "makes illness an interpretive mechanism of History"; he is an "anatomist" of culture like the writers of nineteenth-century realist fiction:

As a figure of authority, the "doctor" of the early 1930s invoked the serious, realist textuality of the nineteenth century; he was the authorial figure who conveyed meaning, whose work was indicative of both a genesis and an attempt to achieve a sound semantic conclusion. He invoked the medical model of realism and naturalism by way of a *semiotics*, through his sense of coherence, his attempt to present an ordered, meaningful world, his ability to read signs (symptoms, detail, metonymic digressions, inessential motifs created by narrative chance, clues).

Symptoms and clues: that is, whatever signified, attested to the existence of meaning, of true, objective reality, and justified the medical model of the novelist, who knew how to recognize and organize symptoms as signs of a reality that could be charted and described.[103]

Like a doctor and as a doctor, Céline reads symptoms and practices his own nosography. Along these lines, Fredric Jameson has described Céline's narrative technique as akin to the detective story: like the doctor, the detective moves easily into people's lives and gathers from them significant details. But for Jameson it is the French *moralistes*, and not the writers of the realist novels, who are Céline's real literary antecedents; unlike nineteenth-century realism, Céline's novels do not focus on the "empirical, the contingent, and the ephemeral" but on "the convulsions of human nature."[104] The writing of obsessional human nature calls for a frenzied language that, Jameson says, "fills the narrative void," blurring the distance between observer and observed, doctor and patient, good guys and bad guys. Within the limits of the form Céline mastered, "there are no villains, since human beings are all by definition maniacs." But "when Dr. Destouches gives in, as conventionally and stereotypically as any other classical petit-bourgeois, and identifies the Jews and the Bolsheviks as the ultimate sources of all suffering and evil, then we have left the novels behind, and returned to history and its different ideological pathologies."[105] Jameson connects Céline's writing of history not to objective accounts of doctoring, but to a kind of moralism gone berserk, a pathology turned pathological.

Blondiaux identifies in Céline's prose the polarized swinging between "saying everything" and "saying nothing" that makes this a "psychotic writing": not the writing of a psychotic, but one produced by a writer negotiating psychosis.[106] Extending Kristeva's analysis, Blondiaux isolates in the opening pages of Céline's first novel these poles of "everything" and "nothing": "Me, I had always said nothing. Nothing. [Moi, j'avais jamais rien dit. Rien.]"; "I will have to tell all without changing a word, about the most vicious stuff seen in men [faudra raconter tout sans changer un mot, de ce qu'on a vu de plus vicieux chez les hommes]."[107] In Blondiaux's analysis, with reference to Kristeva and psychoanalytic theory, Céline's discourse moves between the paranoid retentiveness of the first and the explosive "defecation" of the second, between the nothingness that language comes out of and the "all" it tries desperately to enunciate through the void.

For Roussin the poles of Céline's writing represent sickness and cure;

Céline's discourse is "ambivalently situated between the therapeutic—at the normative center of ordinary communication—and the pathological—the place most distant from ordinary communication." Roussin connects this need for "telling all" with the indiscreet spreading of secrets that the doctor is supposed to keep to himself. Céline is the doctor who listens, who "hears complaints," but then reveals them in the novels: "what is the narrative of the doctor—doctor for the poor, doctor of the suburbs—if not a breach of the private, secret, and non-symbolic discourse that the professional physician is supposed to keep safe and sealed, but that he now communicates at the margins of legitimacy?"[108] Yet if the need to "tell all" is pathological, telling all also brings a certain comfort, and a distinctly therapeutic potential for cure: "There's nothing terrible inside us or on earth or possibly in heaven itself except what hasn't been said yet. We won't be easy in our minds until everything has been said once and for all."[109]

Roussin and Alice Kaplan have called Céline's a "vitalist conception of language and literature, by which words are perceived as a means of perpetually renewing experience."[110] It takes words to express feelings. "What's left for the novelist to do then? ... Emotion can't be captured and transcribed except through spoken language ... remembrance of spoken language!"[111] It is only when the unique voice that Céline creates, projecting itself into dialogism, excludes other voices that it becomes the voice of paranoia.[112] The turn toward ballet is at once a move toward such "vitalist" living expression and against the confinement of words—loaded as they are with "ideas." Words translate somatic experience and communicate emotion; dance translates words—ideas—back into the body, into movement. But without words, the dance absorbs any political meaning—even opposite, contradictory meanings. It is as if, for Céline, staging ballets would allow him to represent his ideas in a form that would bypass censorship, allow him to name names and diagnose ills without suffering the consequences that print entails. Dance offers an opportunity to dramatize a political and social program without words. And without words, dance functions like a symptom, open to broad cultural and medical interpretation, the perfect vehicle for the representation of society's sickness.

Although Céline, in writing ballets, seems to move beyond words—ridiculing the commission for "quelques paroles"—the Céline ballets are *only* words and remain so. To write a literature that diagnoses society's ills, that "speaks reality,"[113] Céline turns to dance, to the traditions of

Gautier and Mallarmé, romantic and Symbolist poetics, and the history
of medicine that dance invokes. Céline himself will call it diversion, entertainment, and escape; but his desire for dance, and its influence on his
writing, cannot be divorced from his medical, social, and political views.
To write dance when he does, as a doctor, is to write the contemporary
history of a particular sociomedical tradition, a history of dance's pathologization and pathology's socialization.

Céline's ballets consistently ascribe symptomatic expression to "others," and blame them for the symptoms of degeneration as if they were
contagious. Despite their fictional and fantastic nature, the ballets of
Bagatelles, with their name-calling, their accusational, "real-life" commentary, belong not simply to Céline's medical utopia, but to history's "different ideological pathologies." Inserted into a medical-social tradition that
typed hysteria as a somatic, inherited, and contagious illness, inherent in
and spread by social groups deemed dangerous to the public health, and
used to subtend biological theories of race, Céline's dances fit a familiar
symptomatology. The ballets of *Bagatelles pour un massacre* are documents
of the age in which the ballet tradition meets new forms of dance. Significantly, the very dance forms that Céline, as a hygienist in the nineteenth-century mold, associates with sickness and the social pathologies,
the twentieth century will, over time, associate with health and freedom
of expression. They will be seen as expelling the demons of modern nervous life—until the appearance of new epidemics.

REFERENCE MATTER

Notes

Introduction

1. Boethius, *The Consolation of Philosophy*, 4–5 (translation modified).

2. Michel Foucault, *Madness and Civilization: A History of Insanity in the Age of Reason*, ix.

3. On the iconography of the *danse macabre*, see Philippe Ariès, *The Hour of Our Death*, 116–18.

4. See, among others, Carlo Ginzburg, *Ecstasies: Deciphering the Witches' Sabbath*.

5. On the idea of Christianity *as* madness, see M. A. Screech, "Good Madness in Christendom."

6. Jan Goldstein, *Console and Classify: The French Psychiatric Profession in the Nineteenth Century*. An alternate opinion about the religious climate of late nineteenth-century France is advanced by Mark Micale, who finds a continuity between religious and medical cultures in France. The great success of Lourdes around the turn of the century suggests to Micale that France was not desacralizing. Micale describes similarities between Lourdes and the Salpêtrière that suggest how Mediterranean Catholic countries "accommodated" differences between the church and psychiatry. See Micale, *Approaching Hysteria*, 262.

7. Mark Franko has shown how this tradition is subverted in the burlesque ballets of the 1620s, suggesting that disorder—in the form of carnivalesque reversals of class, race, and sex—is featured in the foreground, not the background, of this particular form of court ballet. See Mark Franko, *Dance as Text: Ideologies of the Baroque Body*, and "Double Bodies: Androgyny and Power in the Performances of Louis XIV."

8. Examples of literary studies that discuss dance texts without problematizing performance contexts include Barbara Johnson's work on Mallarmé, to be discussed in Chapter 2; Françoise Meltzer's *Salome and the Dance of Writing*; and

Emily Apter, "Figura Serpentinata: Visual Seduction and the Colonial Gaze." While Apter problematizes the performance context by considering the North African dancer as subject to a commodifying colonial gaze, she makes no attempt to consider dancers' resistance or response to that commodification, relying solely on the colonial texts' descriptions of dancers and accepted Western cultural notions about the belly dance. Her conclusion discusses representations of women in a text of postcolonial theory in a way that suggests their resistance to such photographic representations, but does not attribute this component of active response to dance performance or to the dancers who were represented in dance writing. Examples of dance studies that do problematize performance contexts include the essays collected in *Bodies of the Text: Dance as Theory, Literature as Dance*, ed. Ellen W. Goellner and Jacqueline Shea Murphy.

9. In remarks at the University of Sydney in July 1995, Ludmilla Jordanova, describing trends in the current research of cultural historians, noted that "music and images" have begun to receive attention but made no mention of dance. In fact, much significant work has been published recently in cultural studies of dance and relevant publications are noted throughout this book.

Chapter 1

1. Albert Smith, *The Natural History of the Ballet Girl*, 7–8.

2. Ibid., 5, 6, 7.   3. Ibid., 19.

4. Ibid., 46–47.   5. Ibid., 47.

6. Susan Foster, *Choreography and Narrative*.

7. Ibid., 230.

8. Ibid., 264. Foster discusses the work of modern dance pioneers Isadora Duncan, Loie Fuller, Ruth St. Denis, and Maud Allen, 261.

9. Ibid., 263.

10. Ibid., 262.

11. Karl Marx, *The German Ideology*, part 1, 154: "In direct contrast to German philosophy which descends from heaven to earth, here we ascend from earth to heaven." In this section, Marx critiques both the "Old Hegelians" and the "Young Hegelians."

Although I am using the word "ideal" here in a general sense, its philosophical definitions and implications are complex. For my purposes, the two philosophical precursors whose thinking is significant for the writers in question are Plato and Hegel. Although they make no specific mention of philosophical traditions of idealism in the texts I am reading here, the work of both Gautier and Mallarmé needs to be read with these traditions in mind. Resemblances between Mallarmé's conception of a literary "Idea" and Platonic *eidos* and the doctrine of Forms are discussed by Philippe Lacoue-Labarthe in *Musica Ficta: Figures of Wagner*, and below in Chapter 3. One Plato commentator writes that in *The Repub-*

lic, chap. 19, Socrates demonstrates that "the realm of ideas is the *real* world, un-changing and eternal, which can be known by thought. The visible and tangible things commonly called real are only a realm of fleeting appearance, where the ideal is imperfectly manifested in various degrees of approximation." Plato, *The Republic*, 176. In Hegel, "ideal" is also defined in complex relation to the "real": "Hegel often uses the term *reell* to mean relatively self-subsistent being, and con-trasts it in this sense with *ideell*. In this contrast *reell* applies to a stage of the di-alectic so long as that stage presents itself as self-subsistent, as, so to say, the last word. But as 'sublated' in a higher stage, the stage which was *reell* has now itself only an *ideell* being." G. R. C. Mure, *An Introduction to Hegel*, 135.

12. Judith Butler, *Gender Trouble: Feminism and the Subversion of Identity*, 134–49, describes "gender performatives." Sue-Ellen Case critiques and com-ments on these pages in "Performing Lesbian in the Space of Technology: Part I," 1–18, esp. 5–8.

13. See Frank Kermode, *Romantic Image*, and "Poet and Dancer Before Di-aghilev," in *What Is Dance? Readings in Theory and Criticism*, ed. Roger Copeland and Marshall Cohen. My book uncovers and analyzes the operations that make Kermode's romanticized view of the dancer possible, evident in statements like the following: "There is no disagreement from the fundamental principle that dance is the most primitive, non-discursive art, offering a pre-scientific image of life, an intuitive truth. Thus it is the emblem of the Romantic image." "Poet and Dancer," 147–48.

14. In *De la prostitution dans la ville de Paris*, originally published in 1836, Alexandre Parent-Duchâtelet characterizes prostitutes as morally corrupt, hys-terically inclined sexual deviants. See Jann Matlock, *Scenes of Seduction: Prostitu-tion, Hysteria, and Reading Difference in Nineteenth-Century France*, for an explo-ration of diagnoses of sexual perversion in hysterics, and analysis of a nineteenth-century understanding of hysteria *as* sexual perversion, considered to symbolize, mime, or even enact it.

15. Among the proliferating studies of Charcot, I am thinking especially of Georges Didi-Huberman, *L'Invention de l'hystérie: Charcot et l'iconographie pho-tographique de la Salpêtrière*; Ludmilla Jordanova, *Sexual Visions: Images of Gender in Science and Medicine between the Eighteenth and the Twentieth Centuries*; Sander Gilman, "The Image of the Hysteric," in Gilman et al., *Hysteria Beyond Freud*; and the seminal Michel Foucault, *The Birth of the Clinic: An Archeology of Medical Perception*.

16. On this misconstrual of Hippocrates, see Helen King, "Once Upon a Text: Hysteria from Hippocrates," in Gilman et al., *Hysteria Beyond Freud*. Throughout the eighteenth and nineteenth centuries, "marriage"—sexual inter-course—was often recommended as a cure for some hysterical-type afflictions.

17. I am alluding here to Jonas Barish, *The Anti-Theatrical Prejudice*.

18. Mark S. Micale, *Approaching Hysteria; Disease and Its Interpretation*, 200.

19. Ibid., 201.

20. Ibid., 217.

21. I am thinking, for example, of the series Studies in the Social History of Medicine, and the Wellcome Institute Series in the History of Medicine.

22. See, for example, Janet Beizer, *Ventriloquized Bodies: Narratives of Hysteria in Nineteenth-Century France*. I agree that "it is impossible to isolate scientific from popular discourses, given their common ideological bedrock" (240) and that "novelists and physicians are formed in a common cultural pool, and in turn mold similar cultural products; or, more radically yet . . . novelists might have intuitions about cultural phenomena (including pathology) that precede or contradict medical 'knowledge'" (94). But when the pathology in question is not only a cultural but also a scientific phenomenon, the culture of science and scientific method must be brought into consideration. Although I have done so here only schematically, I have attempted to underline not only the similarities between medical and literary texts that Beizer has identified in the literature on hysteria, but—in spite of these cultural similiarities—their significantly different cultural status and positioning. Thus I am attempting to bring into the discussion not only medical practice but also medical theory; both private and "public" medicine; the medicine of experimental science and the medical folklore.

23. For the nineteenth-century history of this problem in France, see Anne Harrington, *Medicine, Mind, and the Double Brain: A Study in Nineteenth-Century Thought*. On the connection between neurology and the hysteria diagnosis, see her "Metals and Magnets in Medicine: Hysteria, Hypnosis, and Medical Culture in Fin-de-Siècle Paris."

24. Lester S. King, "Medical Philosophy, 1836–44," 144: "A medical system was a body of doctrines which had certain characteristics. In the seventeenth and eighteenth centuries a system came into being when its author tended to generalize widely from one or two observations, drew further inferences quite recklessly, and then proceeded to arrange and interdigitate the whole series of inferences without paying much attention to the immediate 'facts' on which the inferences rested and without concerning himself much with verification."

25. See, for example, David Armstrong, "Bodies of Knowledge / Knowledge of Bodies," 20: "According to Foucault, changes in medicine were simply one facet of a wider cognitive revolution: certainly diseases were 'fabricated' by medicine but so were the bodies that contained the diseases; and this production of bodies was common to a range of techniques deployed through schools, prisons, workshops, barracks, and hospitals."

26. Of the three texts on medical philosophy King studies, two of them are French: J. Bouillau, *Essai sur la philosophie médicale*; and T. C. E. Edouard Auber, *Traité de philosophie médicale*.

27. King, "Medical Philosophy," 144.

28. Ibid., 145.

29. This chapter in the history of Paris medicine and the rise of various theories is discussed by Ian Dowbiggin, "Degeneration and Hereditarianism in French Mental Medicine"; Claude Quétel, *History of Syphilis*, chap. 7: "Madmen and Hérédos"; and Alain Lellouch, "La Méthode de J. M. Charcot, 1825–93."

30. Claude Bernard, *An Introduction to the Study of Experimental Method*, 26.

31. Ibid., 27.

32. Foreword by I. Bernard Cohen in Bernard, *Introduction*, xiii, citing an 1878 obituary by Paul Bert.

33. Bernard, *Introduction*, 3.

34. Georges Canguilhem, *The Normal and the Pathological*, 289.

35. Ibid., 77, 126.

36. Ibid., 76.

37. Ibid., 78. Canguilhem points out that, strictly speaking, a norm does not exist, because Bernard believed it possible always to give an experimental content to the concept of the normal (77).

38. Ibid., 76.

39. Françoise Loux, who has described a "polysemic culture of the body," explains the relation between medicine and culture this way: "there existed a culture, a set of traditional knowledge pertaining to the body, with its own coherence and mode of transmission, which, however, doesn't imply that it is completely independent from learned culture." "Popular Culture and Knowledge of the Body," 84.

40. Exceptions must include studies of hysteria as feminist self-expression within institutional and social constraints. See especially Matlock, *Scenes of Seduction*, chap. 9: "Doubling Out of the Crazy House: Gender, Autobiography and the Insane Asylum System." Matlock describes the theatrical "doubling" strategy used by a female performer to bring attention to her illegal incarceration, and her ultimately successful use of that strategy of mistaken identity in writing her way out. In the field of performance theory, see Joseph Roach, *The Player's Passion: Studies in the Science of Acting*, which explores the links between historical theories of acting and concurrent medical constructions of the body.

41. Lellouch, "La Méthode," 66.

42. For a detailed bibliography of both the classical hysteria histories and recent work, see Micale, *Approaching Hysteria*, 295–316.

43. Micale, ibid., traces at length the gradual shift to mentalist or psychological explanations of hysteria in the eighteenth, nineteenth, and twentieth centuries. Micale describes the work of Willis and Sydenham (22), the complexities of Jorden's text (48), and of Reynolds's (127).

44. Foucault, *Madness and Civilization*, 178, 181, 197.

45. Ibid., 197   46. Ibid., 196–97.

47. Ibid., 182.   48. Ibid., 198.

49. John Harley Warner claims that to assess the role of science in modern medicine, we need to take into account the "multiple meanings of science and the diversity of medical practices." Paper delivered at the Australasian Association for the History, Philosophy, and Social Studies of Science, University of New South Wales, July 10, 1995. See Warner, "Science in Medicine."

50. Roselyne Rey, *The History of Pain*, 221.

51. Lellouch, "La Méthode," 44, citing Charcot, "La Médecine empirique et la médecine scientifique": " ... cette anatomie pathologie première que j'appellerai volontiers empirique ... se limite volontairement et par systeme à constater, à décrire les lésions, sans chercher à saisir le mécanisme de leur production, ni les rapports qui les unissent, aux symptômes exterieurs."

52. See Stanley Joel Reiser, *Medicine and the Reign of Technology*, 25: "linking symptoms during life with findings at autopsy," Laennec believed anatomical lesions to be "the least variable and most positive of the phenomena of local disease."

53. Lellouch, "La Méthode," 51: "Plus vite que ses collegues français, Charcot avait donc pris conscience du declin de la médecine française d'hôpital et du 'chaos méthodologique' qui régnait dans la pratique parisienne, au milieu du dix-neuvième siècle. Il n'eut alors de cesse que d'ordonner ce chaos. Les contributions medico-scientifiques de Magendie et de Claude Bernard paraissaient en France, sans doute, encore trop marginales. Charcot regarda alors de l'autre cote du Rhin et voulut introduire à Paris les nouveaux outils méthodologiques qui se forgeaient dans les pays germaniques."

54. Ibid., 49.

55. "L'idée du mouvement est déjà le mouvement en voie d'execution; l'idée de l'absence de mouvement est déjà, si elle est forte, la paralysie motrice réalisée; tout cela est parfaitement conforme aux idées de la psychologie nouvelle. La paralysie motrice réalisée peut donc être dite idéale, psychique, par imagination (mais non imaginaire)." Ibid., 67–68, quoting Charcot.

56. Carlo Ginzburg, "Clues: Morelli, Freud, and Sherlock Holmes."

57. Ernest Jones, *The Life and Work of Sigmund Freud*, 218.

58. Daphne de Marneffe makes this observation in "Looking and Listening: The Construction of Clinical Knowledge in Charcot and Freud," to be discussed in Chapter 3.

59. Foucault, *Madness and Civilization*, 198.

60. Foucault, *The Order of Things*, xxii.

61. Ibid., xxii.

62. Ibid., x.

63. Elizabeth Kendall, *Where She Danced: The Birth of American Art-Dance*.

64. Hillel Schwartz, "Torque: The New Kinaesthetic of the Twentieth Century."

65. I am thinking of recent performances by Karen Finley, the Split Britches

company, Australasian performance artist Chin Kham Yoke, and others. See also *A Sourcebook of Feminist Theatre and Performance*, ed. Carol Martin.

66. Micale, *Approaching Hysteria*, 170–71, 220.

67. "On the one hand all labour is, speaking physiologically, an expenditure of human labour-power." Marx, *Capital*, vol. 1, 312.

68. Foucault, *Madness and Civilization*, 288–89.

69. One of the early "hysterical" patients Freud attempted to cure entirely with the psychoanalytic method (the patient having previously undergone various treatments, including electroshock therapy), Dora (Ida Bauer) staged, in her symptoms, the entire process of conversion hysteria and its relation to the talking cure. Unable to find a sympathetic ear and never listened to by her family, Dora had prolonged episodes of aphonia (loss of voice), by which she acted out her social and personal predicament. Dora's symptoms translated into her body (often quite literally) what she could not say, expressing in another register the content of her difficult situation. Hélène Cixous's play *Portrait de Dora* develops the theatrical material of the case while giving freer reign to Dora's own self-expression and imagining her point of view. In *The Politics and Poetics of Transgression*, Peter Stallybrass and Allon White have described turn-of-the-century hysteria as a bourgeois preservation of carnivalesque performance.

70. Elaine Showalter, *The Female Malady: Women, Madness, and English Culture, 1830–1950*.

71. William Shakespeare, *Hamlet* (III, ii, 142–44), in *The Riverside Shakespeare*, 1163.

72. Julia Kristeva, *Revolution du langage poetique*, 22–30.

73. See, for example, Kristeva's *Powers of Horror: Essays on the Abject*, to be discussed at length in Chapter 4.

74. In *Gendering Bodies, Performing Art*, Amy Koritz describes the twentieth-century social and artistic positioning of performers in the English public. This particular problem of negative dance reception in what I am describing here in its "pathological" form is as old as the antitheatrical prejudice, but I believe the twentieth-century form Koritz analyzes is shaped in the nineteenth century. I will discuss this problem further in Chapter 2.

75. See, for example, Roach, *Player's Passion*.

76. I am thinking in particular of what Paul Ricoeur calls "l'action semantique," the text as a model for signifying action, and of Jacques Derrida's description of mime as "écriture" or "différance" in "The Double Session," in *Dissemination*. See also Ricoeur, *Du texte à l'action*, *La Metaphor vive*, and *Hermeneutics and the Human Sciences: Essays on Language, Action, and Interpretation*.

77. Tzvetan Todorov, *Théories du symbole*.

78. See Dan Sperber, *Rethinking Symbolism*.

79. Here I am thinking of the double nature of the sign according to Saus-

sure, and the application of structuralist linguistics to psychoanalytic theory in Jacques Lacan's conception of a divided signifying subject. See Ferdinand de Saussure, *Cours de linguistique générale: Saussure's Third Course of Lectures on General Linguistics, 1910–1911*; and Jacques Lacan, *Ecrits*.

80. Paul Robinson, *Freud and His Critics*, 233.

81. Modern dance has explored in choreography the idea of disrupting and reconfiguring narrative structures of meaning. Much recent work in dance history and performance studies has addressed dance's narrative qualities. See, for example, Susan L. Foster, *Reading Dancing: Bodies and Subjects in Contemporary American Dance*; and Ellen W. Goellner and Jacqueline Shea Murphy, "Introduction: Movement Movements," in *Bodies of the Text*. Mark Franko has pointed out to me that this allegorical or narrative reading of dance does not hold for what he calls the critical-creative tradition of absolute dance.

82. Richard Terdiman, *Present Past: Modernity and the Memory Crisis*, 268–69.

83. For Terdiman, the Saussurian sign fails to capture the temporal relation between signifier and signified in the storage of memories, their somatic expression, and their eventual retrieval in analysis: "Memory implicates the *directionality of time*. . . . Understanding memory requires being able to model time. Semiotic paradigms based upon the Saussurian dyad of 'signifier' and 'signified' cannot manage this. For them time is simply not a dimension. . . . A dyadic semiotics is blind to temporality. . . . A Saussurian semiotics must thus inevitably experience trouble with psychoanalysis" (283).

84. Ibid., 310.

85. Ibid., 291.

86. Josef Breuer and Sigmund Freud, *Studies on Hysteria*, 41.

87. I am thinking in particular of the work of Melanie Klein. That of Karen Horney, Anna Freud, and Joan Rivière also belongs on this list. The more recent work of feminist psychoanalysts and theorists of literature will be referred to throughout this book.

88. Foucault, "The Incitement to Discourse," from *The History of Sexuality*, vol. 1, reprinted in *The Foucault Reader*, 309–10.

89. Foucault, *Madness and Civilization*, 100.

90. Matlock, *Scenes of Seduction*, and Beizer, *Ventriloquized Bodies*, are two of the best recent examples of this feminist view. But whereas Beizer focuses exclusively on the "uterine theory" and the misogyny of medical texts, Matlock "attempts to move beyond accounts of victimization to a history of resistance" to the power of the medical establishment (12).

91. Recent scholarship has explored dance's influence—whether direct or indirect—on writing of all kinds. Following the lead of Selma Jeanne Cohen are dance studies scholars Ellen Goellner, Jacqueline Shea Murphy, Sara Cordova, and many others. It should be noted that, whereas some of the dance writing considered in this book is also dance theory, a new field of dance theory or

dance studies, influenced by and merging literary theory, psychoanalytic and feminist theory, performance studies, cultural studies, and cultural history, is now taking shape, making "dance writing" a broad category that includes not only historical texts like libretti, poetry, theory, and reviews, but also contemporary research in dance.

Chapter 2

1. Marie-Hélène Huet has persuasively argued that any revolution in French theater would have to be dated to the French Revolution itself, the trial and execution of Louis XVI. This disposal of the king is significantly more radical than *Hernani*'s essentially conservative, Christian plot. See Huet, *Rehearsing the Revolution*.

2. The day of Gautier's funeral, Edmond de Goncourt recorded him for posterity as "l'auteur de *Giselle*." *Journal des Goncourt* 10, 116 (Oct. 25, 1872), quoted in Edwin Binney III, *Les Ballets de Théophile Gautier*, 383. The original 1841 edition of *Giselle* published by the Librairie de l'Opéra (in the collection of the Bibliothèque Nationale, Paris) is authored by Saint-Georges, Gautier, and Coraly [*sic*], in that order. But the same text of *Giselle* is reprinted in the 1872 edition of Gautier's writings for the stage: *Théâtre: mysteres, comedies, et ballets*. Studies of Gautier invariably assert that the libretto was his, and that Saint-Georges lent his name in order to sway the Opéra administration in favor of its production, Saint-Georges being at the time better known and respected at the Opéra than Gautier.

3. Evelyn Gould has called one such tendency in French writing "virtual theater." See her *Virtual Theater from Diderot to Mallarmé*.

4. See Victor Hugo, *Hernani*, with a "Notice" and "Documentation Thématique" by Pierre Richard, 13–15 and 180–209.

5. "Ce n'est pas Racine ou Voltaire qui peuvent faire cela." Stendhal, cited by Henri Martineau in the preface to *Racine et Shakespeare*, iii.

6. Brooks, *The Melodramatic Imagination: Balzac, Henry James, Melodrama, and the Mode of Excess*.

7. Cyril Beaumont, *The Ballet Called Giselle*, 87–88.

8. Jean-Pierre Pastori, *La Danse: du ballet de coeur au ballet blanc*, 67.

9. Ibid., 67, quoting a letter of Stendhal's dated Oct. 24, 1818: "Si Vigano trouve l'art d'écrire les gestes et les groupes, je maintiens qu'en 1860, on parlera plus de lui que de Mme de Staël, donc j'ai pu l'appeler grand'homme."

10. "*L'écrivain qui ne savait pas tout dire*, celui qu'une idée étrange ... *prenait au dépourvu et sans matériel pour lui donner corps, n'était pas un écrivain.* ... Tout homme qu'une idée, si subtile et si imprévue qu'on la suppose, prend en défaut, n'est pas un écrivain. L'inexprimable n'existe pas." Charles Baudelaire, *L'Art romantique*, 90, 103, quoting Gautier. This first meeting must have taken place

sometime in the 1840s; Baudelaire's article "Théophile Gautier" was first published in *L'Artiste* in 1859.

11. "La plastique animée, voilà le véritable élément chorégraphique, et le littéraire qui écrit un livre de ballet ferait bien de prendre pour collaborateur un peintre ou un statuaire habitués par leur art muet à rendre la pensée visible." Gautier, in *Le Moniteur universel*, July 18, 1864; quoted in Claude Book-Senninger, *Théophile Gautier: auteur dramatique*, 118.

12. Ibid.

13. Gautier, "Solitude," in *Oeuvres érotiques: poésies libertines; lettres à la Présidente*, 54.

14. Philippe Perrot, *Les Dessus et les dessous de la bourgeoisie: une histoire du vêtement au dix-neuvième siècle*, 260.

15. Though Gautier eventually married Carlotta's sister Ernesta Grisi, a singer, his enduring love for the dancer is apparent even in his late letters to her.

16. Review of "Le Zingaro" at the Théâtre de la Renaissance, dated Mar. 2, 1840, reprinted in Gautier, *L'Histoire de l'art dramatique en France depuis 25 ans*, vol. 2, 34. "Elle a du feu, mais pas assez d'originalité; elle manque de cachet à elle; c'est bien mais ce n'est pas mieux"; "autant qu'on peut le distinguer sous le fard, le teint coloré naturellement; elle est de taille moyenne, svelte, assez bien prise, sa maigreur n'est pas excessive pour une danseuse."

17. Text dated Mar. 7, 1841, reprinted in *L'Histoire de l'art dramatique*, vol. 2, 103. Gautier seems to have lost track of the time, or else tried to excuse his earlier, less favorable review, by suggesting that Carlotta had had two years to improve: "Vous vous rappelez assurément cette charmante femme qui chantait et dansait, il y a deux ans ... elle danse aujourd'hui merveilleusement. C'est une vigueur, une légèrté, une souplesse et une originalité qui la mettent tout d'abord entre Elssler et Taglioni."

18. Text dated July 5, 1841, written in the form of a letter to Heine, reprinted in Gautier, *L'Histoire de l'art dramatique*, vol. 2, 135.

19. "Giselle ou les Wilis," originally collected in *Les Beautés de l'Opéra*, 1844; reprinted in *Souvenirs de théâtre, d'art et de critique*, 110.

20. Gautier, "Giselle ou les Wilis," in *Souvenirs*, 96–97.

21. In *Giselle: A Role for a Lifetime*, 61, Violette Verdy, a ballerina who danced the role, notes that Giselle seems not only frail, but particularly refined; and nobody ever says who her father is. Verdy's interpretation suggests that Berthe knows something about Giselle's parentage that should prevent her involvement with Albrecht, and that her warnings are related to it.

22. This is the libretto version. An alternate version addressed by Gautier to Heine is discussed below. For a record of the various versions of the ballet staged in the nineteenth and early twentieth centuries and their origins, see Cyril Beaumont, *The Ballet Called Giselle*.

23. Heinrich Heine, *De l'allemagne*, as quoted by Gautier, *Giselle* (1841). Ac-

cording to Cyril Beaumont, *The Romantic Ballet as Seen by Théophile Gautier*, Heine's text, written in French, first appeared in the journal *Europe littéraire* in 1833 and was published as *De l'allemagne* in 1835.

24. First published in 1852 and republished six years later, the volumes date from roughly the same period as Gautier's ballet libretti.

25. For Gautier, the *ballet blanc* merges the whiteness of the unwritten page and that of the dancing chorus. In a letter to Heine, Gautier writes: "In a rush of enthusiasm [after reading Heine's *De l'allemagne*] I even took a large, lovely sheet of white paper and wrote at the top, in a superbly clear script, LES WILIS, ballet." Cited and commented on in Verdy, *Giselle*, 11. Twentieth-century feminist readings of the white female body in poetic and novelistic traditions of the nineteenth century include Barbara Johnson, "The Dream of Stone"; and Sandra M. Gilbert and Susan Gubar, *The Madwoman in the Attic*. My reading is also informed by Michel Serres's investigation of *blanc* as both blankness and whiteness, in *Genèse* and *Rome*.

26. Frank Kermode, in *Romantic Image*, speaks in these terms about the dancer in the work of Yeats.

27. Ivor Guest, "Parodies of *Giselle* on the English stage, 1841–1871," in *Theater Notebook* 9, 2 (Jan.–Mar. 1955), 39, quoting Moncrieff's advertisement. Its author, William Moncrieff, had neither seen nor read the ballet, but constructed his liberal adaptation from Charles Lewis Gruneisen's account of the Paris premiere in the *Morning Post* of July 9, 1841. Moncrieff called the account "too perfect and complete" to need any further elucidation; his version was perhaps not so much a parody as an adaptation whose melodrama seems parodic to today's reader. Moncrieff's second act includes a hermit of St. Walburg, a nearby chapel of St. Walburg, a rosary of St. Walburg, worn by Giselle, an icon of the saint brought by the hermit from the chapel to save her at the last minute, and a heroic Hilarion who ends up winning the (living) heroine's heart. This version's evildoer is the Wili Queen; Giselle is kept in chains in her "Palace of one hundred fountains, the translucent retreat of Myrtha, beneath the bosom of the Wili lake, in the Witch-Wood." Myrtha is done in twice, by the sacred image and by a well-timed thunderbolt.

28. Ibid.

29. One recent critical discussion of the resonance of the term can be found in T. J. Clark, *The Painter of Modern Life: Paris in the Art of Manet and His Followers*, 109. Clark includes a discussion of Gautier's reaction to Manet's *Olympia*, to be discussed later in this chapter.

30. Claude Quétel, *History of Syphilis*, 233, 239. Despite the fact that more men carried syphilis, its spread in Europe was deemed to be principally the result of unregulated prostitution (239).

31. Quétel, ibid., discusses this theme in works by Maupassant, Barbey d'Aurevilly, and Huysmans (124–26). It is interesting to note a contemporary

notion of the pox as an aristocratic disease of luxury, a holdover from the eighteenth century; and of upper-class syphilitics as marked by an artistic sensitivity or genius. Maupassant's reaction to his infection is cited by Quétel as an example:"I've got the pox . . . and I am proud of it" (130).

32. See Gautier, *Oeuvres érotiques*; see also Quétel, *History of Syphilis*, 123–24.

33. Text dated July 5, 1841, in the form of a letter to Heine, reprinted in *L'Histoire de l'art dramatique*, 140.

34. Gautier and others frequently made the comparison between dancers and racehorses. In *L'Art romantique*, Baudelaire writes that during his first meeting with Gautier " ... il ait tiré je crois, quelques comparaisons de la vie des danseuses et des chevaux de course [. . . he made, I believe, several comparisons between the lives of dancers and racehorses]" (90). The narrator of Albéric Second's *Les Petits Mystères de l'Opéra* remarks: "Oh! combien j'enviai l'aplomb de tous ces superbes habitués qui allaient et venaient autour de moi, appellant ces demoiselles par leur nom, les tutoyant, leur pinçant la taille, se posant victorieusement devant elles, et les considérant le lorgnon dans l'oeil, comme s'il se fût agi d'estimer une jument [Oh! how I envied the aplomb of all these magnificent dandies coming and going around me, calling these girls by their name, speaking intimately to them, putting their arms around their waists, victoriously standing before them and looking them over with an eyeglass, as if it were a matter of appraising some racehorse]" (290). A contemporary account speaks of Véron's Foyer de la Danse in the broadest sexual and economic terms: "The opera . . . provides them with their amorous pleasures, just as the Pompadour stud-farm provides them with their equestrian pleasures; they consider it as a store-house for remounts, no more." Quoted in Guest, *The Romantic Ballet in Paris*, 28.

35. Second, *Petits Mystères*, 158–59. In order to make it possible for these fans to meet the least important dancers at the Opéra, the *rats*, the Opéra started a waltz class. Second records that for 5 francs, the young man could waltz with a chair, and for 10 francs, with a *danseuse*.

36. Louis-Désiré Véron, *Mémoires d'un bourgeois de Paris*, 48. Between 1830 and 1854, the Opéra no longer enjoyed the privilege of government subsidy, collected as a tax on commercial theaters, and was forced to compete with them. Véron's position was commercial; the Ministry of the Interior statement announced that "l'administration de l'Académie royale de musique, dite Opéra, sera confiée à un directeur-entrepreneur qui l'exploitera pendant six ans à ses risques, périls, et fortune." Véron got the job, he admits, because in the aftermath of the July Revolution, when cash was tight, he was able to pay a *caution* of 250,000 francs to guarantee his directorship.

37. Ibid., 52.

38. See René Girard, *Deceit, Desire, and the Novel*.

39. Charles de Boigne, *Petits Mémoires de l'Opéra*, 100, collection of the Bibliothèque Nationale.

40. Contemporary accounts such as de Boigne's speak of the public vying for seats with a good view, and disappointment when a particular dancer does not show up, or show off, enough. See also Guest, *Romantic Ballet in Paris*, 115, quoting Jules Janin on the claques in the *Journal des débats politiques et littéraires*, Aug. 24, 1832.

41. Contract dated Aug. 6, 1841, collection of the Archives Nationales, Paris (dossier no. AJ^{13} 194). Grisi's salary before *Giselle*, set forth in a three-year contract dated May 24, 1841, was to be 5,000 francs for the first year, 10,000 for the second, and 13,000 for the third. After *Giselle's* successful opening season, a new contract was drawn up, dated August 6 of the same year, setting her annual salary at 12,000 and increasing it to 15,000 the following year.

42. Alexandre Parent-Duchâtelet, *De la prostitution dans la ville de Paris*, 3d ed. See Alain Corbin, *Les Filles de noces: misère sexuelle et prostitution aux dix-neuvième et vingtième siècles*, for commentary on and reproduction of some of the documents collected in Parent-Duchâtelet's multivolume study.

43. Parent-Duchâtelet lists dancers not as a separate category, but under the heading of "artistes dramatiques." By 1902, the survey of former professions of prostitutes registered in the departments of Seine-et-Oise and Var lists "Artistes lyriques et danseuses." Reproduced in Corbin, *Filles de noces*, 80.

44. This practice is noted by, among others, Baudelaire, in the 1861 essay "Richard Wagner et Tannhäuser à Paris." Louis-Désiré Véron writes in his memoirs of the "moeurs plus que légères des demoiselles de la danse" (1856 ed., vol. 3, 226), and describes the prostitution of dancers. The list of those admitted backstage or to the Foyer de la Danse was not long; one example from 1859 contains just over 100 names. It was kept at the door to the coulisses; only those who had bought the right to be on it, and had been approved by Véron, were allowed to enter. Reproduced in *Le Foyer de la danse*, 38–40.

45. Parent-Duchâtelet, *De la prostitution dans la ville de Paris*, vol. 1, 171.

46. From "Grise-aile: parodie de 'Giselle ou les Wilis,'" in the *Musée Philipon: périodique dit Album de Tout le Monde*, collection of the Bibliothèque de l'Opéra de Paris.

47. Guest, *Romantic Ballet in Paris*, 22.

48. Abigail Solomon-Godeau, "The Legs of the Countess," 90. Skirts were shortened from mid-calf to knee length, though longer skirts were worn for certain roles.

49. Text dated July 5, 1841, a review in the form of a letter to Heine; reprinted in Gautier, *L'Histoire de l'art dramatique*, vol. 2, 141.

50. Ibid., vol. 2, 138.

51. Guest, *Romantic Ballet in Paris*, 224. Compare A. Gann, "La Genèse de *La Péri*," in *Théophile Gautier, l'art et l'artiste*, 212. Gann finds in this dance a

purely visual symbolism: "stung by her contact with man, the heavenly Peri lets fall one by one her veils, that is, the constraints that prevent man from knowing the unknown. It is only then that the union of artist and art can be effected." This kind of reading, and the tradition of symbolic interpretation of the dance to which it belongs, focus on "the symbolic, entirely visual quality" of the dance and will be critiqued later in this chapter.

52. Ivor Guest cites one account of a fascination with the dancer's stocking clasp in "Dandies and Dancers," 12, cited and commented on by Solomon-Godeau in "Legs of the Countess": the dancer "drawing innumerable glasses to a common centre, decked in flowers and a confusion of folds of gauze scarcely secreting that particular part of the leg whereon the fastening of the stocking is generally clasped and smiling and making others smile to see her pirouette as the star of the ballet" (87).

53. Janin, *Journal des débats politiques et littéraires*, Aug. 24, 1832: "La bouffante est une ruse du vieux temps de la danse, qui s'emploie beaucoup de nos jours, et qui s'emploiera encore long temps pour l'edification de nos derniers neveux. Quand une danseuse noble a été en l'air noblement et qu'elle s'est noblement montrée sur toutes les faces ... elle termine son assaut par une pirouette sur la pointe du pied. Cette pirouette commence vivement et va en s'affaiblissant; alors la robe de gaze de la déesse s'enfle comme un ballon; l'attention est immense à l'orchestre et au parterre; c'est cette enflure que j'appelle une bouffante. La bouffante ne manque jamais son effet; elle est suivie d'ordinaire d'un murmure approbateur, elle sauve la médiocrité, elle protège le génie, elle ôte des années et des rides, elle est le but de toute danse noble. ... La bouffante, c'est la chanson à boire de la danse noble." He complains of one dancer, "Not one little bouffante for this poor public that adores it!": "La nouvelle arrivée, si pleine de naive passion et de bouderies charmantes, et d'élégans [*sic*] caprices de toutes sortes, qui pourrait tout se permettre, ne s'est pas permis une bouffante. Pas une pauvre petite bouffante pour ce pauvre public qui l'adore! C'est être dure et bien sûre! Grand merci!"

54. "Ces déhanchements, ces mouvements de croupe, ces gestes provoquants, ces bras qui semblent chercher et étreindre un être absent, cette bouche qui appelle le baiser, tout ce corps qui tressaille, frémit et se tord, cette musique entraînante, ces castagnettes, ce costume bizarre, cette jupe écourtée, ce corsage échancré qui s'entr'ouvre et par dessus tout la grâce sensuelle, l'abandon lascif, la plastique beauté d'Essler [*sic*], furent très-appréciés des télescopes de l'orchestre et des avant-scène. Le public, le vrai public, eut plus de peine à accepter ces témérités chorégraphiques, ces excès de prunelles, et l'on peut dire que cette fois ce sont les avant-scenes infernales qui ont forcé la main au succès. La Cachucha française n'est point un goût naturel; c'est un goût acquis." De Boigne, *Petits Mémoires de l'Opéra*, 132. The passage most likely refers to an 1837 performance.

55. Letter cited by Guest, *Romantic Ballet in Paris*, 208.

56. "C'est le secret des attentes exaspérantes nécessaires pour convaincre le mortel de la suprême faveur qu'il va recevoir; c'est le dé mantè lement de la forteresse, les stations amoureuses du désir." Comtesse de Tramar, *Le Bréviaire de la femme: pratiques secrètes de la beauté*, 8th ed., 115, cited in Philippe Perrot, *Les Dessus*, 261.

57. Perrot, *Les Dessus*, 293. Perrot also cites Pierre Dufay, *Le Pantalon féminin*.

58. Ibid., 263.

59. Second, *Petits Mystères*, 180.

60. Guest, "Parodies of *Giselle*," 231. See also Bruce Seymour, *Lola Montez: A Life*, 72–73. Seymour recounts that at her Opéra debut, largely engineered by letters of introduction from Liszt and the support of powerful journalists, Lola's performance was remarked not for the level of her dancing but for her removal of a garter that she threw to the audience.

61. Review dated July 1, 1844; reprinted in Gautier, *L'Histoire de l'art dramatique*, vol. 3, 225. The text reviews Marie Taglioni's final performance, focusing on the role played by *La Sylphide* in the creation and popularity of the romantic repertory, and reflects on how the romantic ballet differs from its classical precedents while keeping its pink tights: "A dater de *La Sylphide*, les *Filets de Vulcain*, *Flore et Zephyre* ne furent plus possibles; . . . et l'on ne commanda plus aux décorateurs que des forêts romantiques, que des vallées éclairées par ce joli clair de lune allemand des ballades de Henri Heine. Les maillots roses restèrent toujours roses, car, sans maillots, point de chorégraphie; seulement, on changea le cothurne grec contre le chausson de satin."

62. Baudelaire, "Eloge du Maquillage," in "Le Peintre de la vie moderne." Johnathon Mayne translates "le maillot" as "the legs of the dancer" in *The Painter of Modern Life and Other Essays* (London: Phaidon, 1964). The metonymy is worth noting; though the *Robert Dictionnaire* defines "maillot" as equivalent to "maillot de danseuse" as early as 1820, it specifies a garment covering the top half of the body: "1. Vêtement souple, généralement de tricot, porté à même la peau et qui moule le corps ... 2. Vêtement collant qui couvre le haut du corps" (only the *maillot entier, maillot de jambes* would cover the legs). The *Petit Larousse Illustré* gives "*Maillot académique* (Chorégr.), maillot d'une seule pièce qui enserre le corps, des peids jusqu'au cou, ainsi que les bras" (no date). The modern French word for leotard, the dancer's garment covering the upper part of the body, is *justaucorps*, a word used to describe the seventeenth-century tightly fitted coat, according to the Larousse. Since *justaucorps* was already in use in the seventeenth century, *maillot* may have been used to describe the bottom half of the dancer's costume, specifically, the *caleçons*, or tights.

63. Solomon-Godeau has argued that in the decades following *Giselle*, the pose carries erotic overtones in the context of the development of photographic pornography and its "repertory of pose and display": "traditionally, pornography

had privileged sexual activity; with photography, the emphasis came more and more to be on the presentation of the woman or of parts of her body, a spectacular display for scopic consumption." Solomon-Godeau's study of these photographs in the Second Empire shows that the held pose became the essence of this new pornography: "On the level of technique, the intractability of the tripod-mounted camera, the relative slowness of exposure, and the resistance of real bodies to positions possible for the graphic artist all tend to enforce a repertory of pose and display." "Legs of the Countess," 96–97.

64. A further parallel with photography is suggested by Solomon-Godeau: by the early Second Empire, much daguerreotype pornography was stereoscopic, and viewing through a stereopticon, which blocked out everything but the image, made this kind of image the "acme of verisimilitude" (ibid., 95). This private, boxed-in, three-dimensional viewing gives "the illusion of being *in* the picture," by making the picture space seem to be contiguous with the space of the viewer. The theatrical aspect of this kind of viewing can be considered a development of, and even an improvement on, public viewing from the *loges* of the Opéra.

65. Ibid., 85, quoting from *Illustrated London Life*, Apr. 16, 1843.

66. Review dated Mar. 2, 1840, reprinted in Gautier, *L'Histoire de l'art dramatique*, vol. 2, 34.

67. Janin, *Journal des débats politiques et littéraires*, Mar. 2, 1840. The costume described is Eugène Lami's design for *La Sylphide* (1832): "Vous savez peut-être que nous ne sommes guère les partisans de ce qu'on appelle les grands danseurs. Le grand danseur nous parait si triste, si lourd! Il est à la fois si malheureux et si content de lui-même! Il ne répond à rien, il ne représente rien, il n'est rien. Parlez-nous d'une jolie fille qui danse, qui deploie tout à l'aise les grâces de son visage, l'élégance de sa taille, qui nous montre d'une façon si fugitive tous les trésors de sa beauté; Dieu merci, je comprends cela à merveille; je sais ce que nous veut à tous cette belle personne, et bien volontiers je la suivrai tant qu'elle voudra dans le doux pays des amours. Mais un homme, un affreux homme, aussi laid que vous et moi, méchant lapin vidé, qui sautille sans savoir pourquoi, une créature faite tout exprès pour porter le mousquet, le sabre et l'uniforme! cet être-là, danser comme ferait une femme, c'est impossible! Ce porte-barbe qui est le chef de la communauté, un électeur, un membre du conseil municipal, un homme qui fait et surtout qui défait des lois pour sa bonne part, venir à nous en tunique de satin bleu de ciel, la tête ornée d'une toque dont la plume flottante lui flatte amoureusement la joue: une affreuse danseuse du sexe masculin, venir pirouetter à la plus belle place, pendant que les jolies filles du ballet se tiennent respectueusement à distance, certes voilà qui était impossible, qui était intolérable, et aussi a-t-on bien fait d'effacer de nos plaisirs ces grands artistes. Aujourd'hui, grâce à cette revolution que nous avons faite, la femme est la reine du ballet. Elle y respire, elle y danse tout à l'aise.

Elle n'est plus forcée de couper la moitié de son jupon de soie pour en revêtir son voisin."

68. Ibid.

69. Lynn Garafola, "The Travesty Dancer in Nineteenth-Century Ballet," 37.

70. Gautier, review of *La Volière*, by Therèse Elssler, dated May 1838, reprinted in *L'Histoire de l'art dramatique*. The choreographer, says Gautier, had the good taste "de ne point donner de *pas* aux acteurs mâles de son oeuvre chorégraphique."

71. Review dated April 1838, reprinted ibid., 127–28.

72. Jules Janin, *Journal des débats politiques et littéraires*, Aug. 24, 1832, 3.

73. Ibid.

74. See Solomon-Godeau, "Legs of the Countess," 91; and Garafola, "Travesty Dancer," 39. It should be pointed out that the partnering of women by women made reference to another category of the erotic, female homosexuality in the gaze of a male spectator. The lesbian tradition in dance is less well documented but part of the cultural stereotype; in a critical attack on La Fanfarlo, Baudelaire's Samuel Kramer tries to slur her character by printing that "elle aimait trop les petits chiens et la fille de sa portière—et autres linges sales de la vie privée . . . " Baudelaire, "La Fanfarlo," in *Oeuvres complètes*, 282. In addition, it should be noted that with the travesty dancer, the dandy can perceive the female figure both as object and as object of identification. This dandyesque identification with the female dancer can be found in *La Fanfarlo* and in Oscar Wilde's play *Salome*.

75. Fanny Elssler was partnered by her sister *en travesti*, and appeared in travesty herself. Gautier, *Les Beautés de l'Opéra*, 3–4, quoted in Guest, "Legs of the Countess," 151.

76. Cyril Beaumont, *The Ballet Called Giselle*, 127.

77. See Richard Sieburth, "Poetry and Obscenity: Baudelaire and Swinburne."

78. La Fanfarlo's fall from artistic glory is a fall into what Baudelaire and others perceived as the mill of motherhood. At the Opéra during this period, the pregnancies of stars and the births of their children were never acknowledged publicly. Most dancers hid their children, as well as their marriages. A dancer was always supposed to be billed as "mademoiselle," although Grisi herself went by "madame" during the years of her relationship with Perrot. The injury that prevented Taglioni from dancing for an extended period was in fact a pregnancy, and the subsequent birth of her daughter was never made public, though Taglioni herself referred to the girl as "my knee injury." In Baudelaire's aesthetic, the dancing body is not supposed to bear children; its power for him is that of "la froide majesté de la femme stérile."

79. Quétel, *History of Syphilis*, 113, cites the correspondence of Auzias-Turenne, a doctor who developed the postulate of syphilization (proposed as an

immunization against syphilis). Auzias-Turenne describes the symptoms on the skin as a "label" or a "signature"; he urges not only reading these visible signs but unearthing syphilis even when it "feigns absence." But in general brothel prostitutes were allowed to return to work when their visible symptoms disappeared. See ibid., chap. 9.

80. Ibid., 111. In an article of 1838, Philippe Ricord determines, from clinical observation, that syphilis is caused by a virus. The 1836 *Dictionnaire de médecine et de chirurgie pratiques*'s article on syphilis, by Cullerier and Ratier, denounces doctors who ascribe to syphilis any affliction that does not respond to normal treatment (109).

81. Baudelaire, "Les Femmes et les filles," in "Le Peintre de la vie moderne," *Oeuvres complètes*, 563.

82. This is Parent-Duchâtelet's view, although it should be noted that nineteenth-century regulation measures were ineffective in stopping the spread of the disease. See Quétel, *History of Syphilis*, chap. 9: "The Pox and the Prostitute."

83. Quétel gives statistics for 1859 to 1888 (ibid., 226). No information about the contribution of homosexual liaisons to the spread of the disease is given. Parent-Duchâtelet's thinking is inflected by class; he wonders if higher-class prostitutes constitute less of a risk; and the statistical answer is affirmative. Some explanations—about higher rate of venereal disease among those with greater number of clients, are given in a later Belgian single-volume edition of *De la prostitution dans la ville de Paris*, 225, collection of the Bibliothèque Nationale.

84. Corbin, *Women for Hire: Prostitution and Sexuality in France after 1850*, 204.

85. See Judith Walkowitz, *Prostitution and Victorian Society*.

86. Corbin, *Women for Hire*, 204–5.

87. Parent-Duchâtelet, *De la prostitution dans la ville de Paris*, vol. 1, 363.

88. "Aux yeux de beaucoup, il suffirait de passer et de rire; c'est une erreur. M. Manet n'est pas peu de chose; il a une école, des admirateurs, des fanatiques même; son influence s'étend plus loin qu'on ne pense. M. Manet a cet honneur d'être un danger. Le danger est passé maintenant. Olympia ne s'explique d'aucun point de vue, même en la prenent pour ce qu'elle est, un chétif modèle étendue sur un drap. ... Nous excuserions encore la laideur, mais vraie, étudiée, relevée par quelque splendide effet de couleur. Ici, il n'y a rien, nous sommes fâchés de le dire, que la volonté d'attirer le regard à tout prix." Gautier quoted in Georges Bataille, *Manet*, 62.

89. T. J. Clark, "Olympia's Choice," in *The Painter of Modern Life: Paris in the Art of Manet and His Followers*, 79–146.

90. In *The Painter of Modern Life*, Clark points out that Georges Bataille attributes Gautier's particular "angoisse" in this passage to the surprise that the courtesan's are eyes which look without seeing. It is her contradictory demand for regard (in the sense of estimation as well as mere attention), coupled with her apparent refusal to return that "regard," that Gautier finds scandalous.

91. Gautier, in *La Presse*, Nov. 2, 1836.

92. "Son dur réalisme qui, pour les visiteurs du Salon, était la laideur du 'gorille,' est pour nous le souci qu'eut le peintre de réduire *ce qu'il voyait* à la simplicité béante, de *ce qu'il voyait*." Bataille, "Manet," 146, quoted in Clark, "Olympia's Choice," 138.

93. Stéphane Mallarmé, *Correspondance II, 1871–1885*, 37.

94. Baudelaire, "Théophile Gautier," in *L'Art romantique*, 90.

95. Walter Benjamin, "The Work of Art in the Age of Mechanical Reproduction," in *Illuminations*, 221.

96. Benjamin, "On Some Motifs in Baudelaire," in *Illuminations*, 188.

97. The dancer of this period, Garafola points out with a contemporary illustration, appears to look back at her audience. See Garafola, "Travesty Dancer."

98. Second, *Petits Mystères*, 310. Second's book includes a print by Gavarni illustrating a dancer looking through one of these "binocles." In his essay "Gavarni," Gautier notes that the illustrator paid close attention to detail, and that in general his renderings were carefully exact. But it seems impossible, if Gavarni's illustration is accurate, that a dancer could be identified through such a small aperture, or could signal through it.

99. See Véron, *Mémoires d'un bourgeois*, for his account of these rival schools.

100. The term *jouissance*, used in Lacan's theory of feminine sexuality in *Encore*, is discussed below. The notion of the "inner eye" developed by dancers and outlined in the manuals of ballet masters can also be analogized to what Lacan calls "the gaze" beyond intersubjective looking that is fundamental to subjectivity. See Lacan, *The Four Fundamental Concepts of Psychoanalysis*, where Lacan distinguishes between the function of the eye (seeing and desiring what we see in the visual realm) and the "gaze" (being seen, not purely or only in the visual realm). In the gaze, "that eye is only the metaphor of something that I would prefer to call the seer's 'shoot' [*pousse*]—something prior to his eye. What we have to circumscribe . . . is the pre-existence of a gaze—I see only from one point, but in my existence I am looked at from all sides" (72).

101. Gautier, in *La Presse*, Nov. 2, 1836.

102. The dancer whose effort is visible is no longer anything but a dancer, and should retire. Gautier writes of Taglioni's performance in 1838: "la sueur perle sur le front, les muscles se tendent avec effort, les bras et la poitrine rougissent; tout à l'heure c'était une vraie sylphide, ce n'est plus qu'une danseuse." Review dated Sept. 17, 1858 [*sic*; misprint for 1838], *Histoire de l'art dramatique*, 175.

103. Second, *Petits Mystères*, 153, collection of the Bibliothèque Nationale (1844). The physical hardship of the dancers of this period has been recorded by contemporary balletomanes, who tend to exaggerate or discount it. The character of the dancer Léila in Second's chronicle remarks that grueling training and continual poverty not only defeated the social and artistic ambitions of most

dancers of the *corps de ballet* but frequently killed them off: "Pour combien qui arrive à se faire un nom et une position, combien sont mortes à la peine!" Second's account of the poverty, hunger, and illness of dancers paints them as romantic victims of their art rather than as working-class urban women subject to poor sanitary, economic, and social conditions.

104. Quéant, *Encyclopédie du théâtre contemporain*, vol. 1, 11.

105. This critique of Gautier and his theater will be made by Stéphane Mallarmé in *Crayonné au théâtre*, a text published two decades after Gautier's death, to be discussed in the next chapter.

106. See the discussion of the relationship between the feminine and art, style, and truth in Jacques Derrida, *Eperons: les styles de Nietzsche*.

107. Baudelaire, "Les Femmes et les filles," in "Le Peintre de la vie moderne," *Oeuvres complètes*, 563. See also the discussion of femininity and artifice, the relation between "elle se donne" and "elle se donne pour," in Derrida, *Eperons*.

108. Jacqueline Rose, "Femininity and Its Discontents," in *Sexuality in the Field of Vision*, 83–104.

109. Ibid., 97.

110. Ibid., 95, quoting from Breuer and Freud, *Studies on Hysteria*.

111. Ibid., 86.

112. The "supplice quotidien" of the *danseuse* is related in Second, *Petits Mystères*, 149–51. Turn-out was an element carried into ballet from the baroque dance and was created for the frontal spectator, sitting in the "king's place" (center front), presenting this ideal spectator with a longer-looking and more elegantly turned leg. Turn-out continued to be a crucial part of ballet technique, even in the nineteenth-century Opéra house rounded *à l'italienne*, in which some seats offered a view of dancers from the side. Twentieth-century ballet technique has pushed turn-out to such an extreme that its effect has been to completely reorganize the dancer's body.

113. See Breuer and Freud, *Studies on Hysteria*, and Freud, *Five Lectures on Psychoanalysis*.

114. Kermode, *Romantic Image*.

115. In a review of *Giselle*, dated July 5, 1841, written in the form of a letter to Heine and reprinted in *L'Histoire de l'art dramatique*, 140, Gautier gives a different version of the scene. When Albrecht's duplicity is revealed, Giselle first dances a little distractedly; "bientôt ses forces s'épuisent, elle chancelle, s'incline, saisit l'épée fatale par Hilarion et se laisserait tomber sur la pointe si Albrecht n'écartait le fer avec cette soudaineté de mouvement que donne le désespoir. Hélas! c'est une précaution inutile! le coup de poignard est porté; il a atteint le coeur et Giselle expire." The sexual symbolism of this version is more explicit. As it diminishes the difficulty of the mad scene for the dancer dancing Giselle, and also provides a simpler motivation for her sudden death, it may have been

adopted during rehearsal, or devised by Coralli or Perrot as a better choreographic solution to the end of the scene. Grisi is praised throughout the reviews for her excellent pantomime, but dance historians have generally noted that Elssler was the first to perform the mad scene without dancing, entirely in mimed acting. Both variants have been performed in the many reconstructions of the original ballet. It is interesting to note that Coralli's name on the first printed edition suggests to what extent the ballet as a production of the Opéra was ultimately a collaboration between writer and choreographer. Later in the century, Alphonse Duvernay would describe how "between the poet and the dancer a close collaboration was formed." Ivor Guest, *The Romantic Ballet in Paris*, 11, quoting Alphonse Duvernay.

In an analysis of Adam's score for the ballet, Marian Smith concludes that the original production most likely staged her death "of a broken heart." See Marian Smith, "What Killed Giselle?"

116. See, for example, Violette Verdy, *Giselle: A Role for a Lifetime*.

117. Mark Micale, *Approaching Hysteria*, 191.

118. Ibid., 215.

119. Foucault describes this phenomenon and its medical status in *Histoire de la folie à l'âge classique*, 299: "Bien souvent l'hystérie a été perçue comme l'effet d'une chaleur interne qui répand à travers tout le corps une effervescence, une ébullition, sans cesse manifestée dans des convulsions, et des spasmes. Cette chaleur n'est-elle pas parente de l'ardeur amoureuse à laquelle l'hystérie est si souvent liée, chez les filles en quête de maris et les jeunes veuves qui ont perdu le leur?"

120. Verdy, *Giselle*, 1.   121. Ibid., 3.

122. Ibid., 7.   123. Ibid., 59.

124. Ibid., 4.

125. Pierre Legendre, *La Passion d'être un autre: étude pour la danse*, 254. In Legendre's Lacanian terms, dance has a special access to the symbolic, to what he calls "la passion d'être un autre."

126. Jacques Lacan, "Dieu et la jouissance de la femme," in *Le Séminaire*, vol. 20: *Encore*.

127. Ibid., 71

128. Ibid., 70–71. Lacan complains that women analysts, asked to explain this feminine *jouissance*, attribute it to "vaginal orgasm" (69–70).

129. Lacan, "Dieu et la jouissance de la femme": "pour Sainte Thérèse — vous n'avez qu'à aller regarder à Rome la statue de Bernin pour comprendre tout de suite, qu'elle jouit, ca ne fait pas de doute. Et de quoi jouit-elle? Il et clair que le témoignage essentiel des mystiques, c'est justement de dire qu'ils l'éprouvent, mais qu'il n'en savent rien" (71). An alternate translation of Lacan's remark has been suggested to me by Richard Sieburth. Reading Lacan's language as more precise and more vulgar, Sieburth translates *foutre* as sperm or

ejaculate, and suggests that Lacan is indirectly alluding to Freud's "hydraulics" and to the way in which Charcot, after Mesmerism, remains obsessed with the circulation of magnetic fluids and the ectoplasm of late nineteenth-century occultism, all forms of psychic life-fluid or "des affaires de foutre." Personal communication to the author, September 1, 1995. On the nineeenth-century link between hysteria and possession, see Cristina Mazzoni, *Saint Hysteria*.

130. I am thinking of modern dancers Isadora Duncan, Michio Ito, Jacques Dalcroze, Ruth St. Denis, and others, many of whom debuted or worked in Paris at some point in their early careers. I am also thinking of the modern ballet innovations of Serge Diaghilev's Ballets Russes de Monte Carlo, and especially of choreography and performance by Nijinsky.

Chapter 3

1. Stéphane Mallarmé, *Oeuvres complètes* (Pléiade ed.), 313. References to this edition will be indicated throughout the text by a page number appearing in parentheses. All translations are my own except where noted. Any reader of French understands the complexity of Mallarmé's language, his turns of phrase, his invention, and knows that the passages here translated say much more than their translations can. For those who cannot follow the French I have attempted to render Mallarmé's text as plainly and literally as possible, and have thus lost much of the nuance of his writing while attempting to preserve the richness of vocabulary and ambiguity of syntax. I have often chosen to use English cognates that may not carry the exact meaning of the French but have a similar resonance. The words that English and French share, and their broadly shared fields of signification, often including obsolete or arcane meanings, were certainly in Mallarmé's mind when writing.

2. These elements of Mallarméan theater are addressed by Philippe Lacoue-Labarthe, *Musica ficta: figures de Wagner*, 95–160.

3. This reading of the gesture as one of verification is Lacoue-Labarthe's.

4. Among the many discussions of this aspect of Mallarméan writing, see Julia Kristeva, *La Revolution du langage poétique*; Roger Bellet, *L'Encre et le ciel*; and Barbara Johnson, "Les Fleurs du Mal Armé: Some Reflections on Intertextuality," and "Erasing Panama: Mallarmé and the Text of History," both in *A World of Difference*.

5. Meaning is suspended in her work, even more than in the mime's, who depends both on coded gesture, specifically imitative in nature, and on audience collusion with this code. Like the romantic ballerina, the mime is incomplete without his audience; his story refers to and depends upon them. See the famous discussion of "Mimique" in Jacques Derrida, "La Double Séance," in *La Dissémination*. See also Mark Franko, "Mimique," in *Bodies of the Text: Dance as Theory, Literature as Dance*.

6. For a slightly different translation of this passage and commentary, see Barbara Johnson, "Les Fleurs du Mal Armé," in *A World of Difference*, 127.

7. Emile Benveniste, *Problèmes de linguistique générale*, vol. 1, 327–35.

8. For a résumé of uterine theories of hysteria and their nineteenth-century developments, see Janet Beizer, *Ventriloquized Bodies*, "Introduction," and chap. 2: "The Doctor's Tale: Nineteenth-Century Medical Narratives of Hysteria." On the origins of the uterine theory as a misreading of a Hippocratic text, see Helen King, "Once upon a Text: Hysteria from Hippocrates," in Gilman et al., *Hysteria Beyond Freud*, 3–90.

9. This disappearance or death of the poet, described by Mallarmé in letters written during the composition of the first version of "Hérodiade" and later theorized in "Crise de vers" (366), is also linked by Johnson to the impersonality of the female dancer. See "Les Fleurs du Mal Armé," in *A World of Difference*, 126.

10. These letters are cited and analyzed at length by Leo Bersani, in *The Death of Stéphane Mallarmé*, 5–9. My argument here summarizes many of his points.

11. Mallarmé's relationship to this poem is thus not unlike Leonardo da Vinci's relation to La Gioconda, which Mallarmé thinks of as one of the three most beautiful works in the history of art; the Venus de Milo, which he attributed to Phidias, and his own, unwritten *Oeuvre* are the other two. See Mallarmé, *Corréspondance I, 1862–1871*, 246. Gardener Davies, in *Mallarmé et le rêve d'Hérodiade*, reports that *Igitur* was also originally conceived for the stage (94) and thus the original "scène" of "Hérodiade" would have been included in it.

12. See "The Man Dies," in Bersani, *Death of Stéphane Mallarmé*, 1–24.

13. The letter, dated Feb. 18, 1869, reads in part: "'Non, non, Satan, tu ne me tenteras pas.' J'ai fait un voeu, à toute extrémité, qui est de ne pas toucher à une plume d'ici à Paques. Je pourrais te dire seulement—ne t'en prévenais-je pas dans ma dernière lettre?—que le simple acte d'écrire installe l'hystérie dans ma tête." *Corréspondance I, 1862–1871*, 301.

14. Letter to Aubanel, dated Nov. 27, 1864, in *Oeuvres complètes*, vol. 1 (Flammarion ed.), 211.

15. Letter dated Dec. 30, 1864, ibid.

16. Cited ibid., 212.

17. Ibid., 233. A letter of 1867 to Cazalis links its three poems with four prose poems on the spiritual conception of the "Néant." Cited ibid., 234.

18. Cited ibid., 212.

19. Ibid., 233. He identifies his work with that of the alchemists, "nos ancêtres," who created the Grand-Oeuvre. Ibid., 234.

20. Ibid., 213.

21. Ibid., 212.

22. Mallarmé, *Les Noces d'Hérodiade: mystère*, 13; Henri Mondor, *Mallarmé: documents iconographiques*, 78. Mallarmé's letter to Cazalis is dated May 14, 1867.

23. Cited in *Oeuvres complètes*, vol. 1 (Flammarion ed.), 234.

24. Letter to Lefébure, cited in Bersani, *Death of Stéphane Mallarmé*, 7.

25. Bersani, *Death of Stéphane Mallarmé*, 16–17.

26. Cited in *Oeuvres complètes*, vol. 1 (Flammarion ed.), 213. Mallarmé is caricatured as the Faune by Luque in an undated print reproduced in Mondor, *Mallarmé: documents iconographiques*, pl. 65, as well as in a caricature by Cazals, pl. 66. The caricatures probably date from the late 1870s, as the "Faune" was not published until 1876.

27. Nijinsky's openly erotic movements for the piece provoked a mixed reception at its premiere on May 29, 1912.

28. Cited in *Oeuvres complètes*, vol. 1 (Flammarion ed.), 214.

29. Ibid.

30. Ibid., 163.

31. Ibid., 213–14.

32. The passage is commented on by Bersani, *Death of Stéphane Mallarmé*, 25.

33. Letter dated Mar. 31, 1865, reprinted in *Oeuvres complètes*, vol. 1 (Flammarion ed.), 212.

34. Cited ibid., 213.

35. Bersani develops this reading in *The Death of Stéphane Mallarmé*, esp. 1–25.

36. Jean-Pierre Richard has called this the "retour oculaire à soi même" in *L'Univers imaginaire de Mallarmé*, 96. Bersani, *Death of Stéphane Mallarmé*; Sylviane Huot, *Le Mythe d'Hérodiade chez Mallarmé: genèse et évolution*; and others have discussed Hérodiade as the heroine of specular reflection. Huot, 50–51, cites R. de Montesquiou, *Diptyque de Flandre, triptyque de France*. Montesquiou believed that Hérodiade's secret is that she is waiting for "la future violation du mystère de son être par un regard de Jean qui va l'apercevoir et payer de sa mort ce seul sacrilège. Car la farouche vierge ne se sentira de nouveau intacte et restituée tout entière à son intégralité qu'au moment où elle tiendra entre ses mains la tête tranchée en laquelle osait se perpetuer le souvenir de la vierge entrevue."

37. The term is Jean-Pierre Richard's, in *L'Univers imaginaire*, 427.

38. See Jacques Derrida, "La Double Séance," in *La Dissémination*, for a deconstructive reading that comments on Richard's.

39. See, in addition to Bersani, Julia Kristeva, *La Révolution du langage poétique*; and Barbara Johnson, "Mallarmé as Mother," in *A World of Difference*. In *L'Enigme de la femme: la femme dans les textes de Freud*, Sarah Kofman offers an alternate view of a productive female narcissism.

40. The studies mentioned above provide in-depth readings of Mallarmé's poetics, themes, the story of his life, the history of his work. Rather than re-

viewing them or extending them to make an argument about "Hérodiade," I would like to consider the writing of the poem in relation to the dance "theory" in *Crayonné au théâtre*.

41. Bersani, *Death of Stéphane Mallarmé*, 9.

42. Cited in *Oeuvres complètes*, vol. 1 (Flammarion ed.), 212.

43. Ibid., 211.

44. These translations are by Barbara Johnson; these texts are connected to the "disparition élocutoire du poète," translated and commented upon by Johnson in "Les Fleurs du Mal Armé," in *A World of Difference*, 127–28.

45. One of the many symptoms of an overdetermined cultural construction of hysteria, "kleptomania" becomes a clinical category of hysteria in the final quarter of the nineteenth century. See Mark Micale, *Approaching Hysteria*, 214, for a discussion of the history and historiography of kleptomania and hysteria.

46. Compare the several discussions of the imagery of "Hérodiade" and "Les Noces d'Hérodiade" in Richard, *L'Univers imaginaire*.

47. Johnson, "Les Fleurs du Mal Armé," 130–31. Johnson notes that creating such a voice, or writing from such a position, is not the same as the actual participation of women in the critical conversation. As I noted in the introduction to this book, Johnson's superbly clear and useful readings nevertheless do not consider real dancers.

48. Ibid., 213.

49. Michèle Montrelay, *L'Ombre et le nom: sur la féminité*, 70.

50. Johnson, "Les Fleurs du Mal Armé," 130.

51. See Lacoue-Labarthe, *Musica ficta*, chap. 2: "Mallarmé."

52. Lacoue-Labarthe, *Musica ficta* (French ed.), 112–13; Mallarmé, *Oeuvres complètes*, 391.

53. Kristeva's notion of *chora*, first developed in *La Révolution du langage poétique*, 22–30, will be discussed in greater detail below. I have also been influenced by Michel Serres's reading of chora in *Genèse* ("Le corps du danseur est la *chóra* platonicienne," 74) and of Platonic *ekmageion* in *Rome: The Book of Foundations*, 54. For an alternate reading of Plato's *chora*, see Jacques Derrida, *Khôra*.

54. Lacoue-Labarthe, *Musica Ficta* (English trans.), 82.

55. *Les Noces d'Hérodiade*, 87. Henri Mondor notes that Valéry tried to convince Mallarmé that he could not pick up and write in the same tone he had written in twenty years earlier. Mondor, *Vie de Mallarmé*, 739, cited in Huot, *Le Mythe d'Hérodiade*, 194.

56. *Oeuvres complètes*, vol. 1 (Flammarion ed.), 450.

57. It is not clear that Mallarmé considered the poem finished; his final note on the text, written to his wife and daughter the day before his anticipated death, asks them to burn his unfinished work and the drafts of manuscripts: "Ainsi, je ne laisse pas un papier inédit excepté quelques bribes imprimées que

vous trouverez, puis le *Coup de dés* et *Hérodiade* terminé s'il plaît au sort ... " Letter reproduced in Henri Mondor, *Mallarmé: documents iconographiques*, 55–56.

58. This is the issue even in the biblical versions. See René Girard, "Scandal and the Dance."

59. A copy of the original 1893 deluxe edition of *Salomé* inscribed by Wilde to Aubrey Beardsley, its illustrator, reads: "For Aubrey: for the only artist who, besides myself, knows what the dance of seven veils is and can see that invisible dance. Oscar." Cited in Oscar Wilde, *Letters*, 348n. It is important to note that Beardsley's illustration depicts a simple belly dance with no veils. Huot, *Le Mythe d'Hérodiade*, suggests that Wilde's *Salomé* helped Mallarmé get back to his original project; yet the "Finale" of "Les Noces" is far from the Mallarméan poetics of the 1860s. And although Wilde's play is fin-de-siècle, it is more remarkable for the coldness of the dialogue, reminiscent of Mallarmé's "Scène," than for the "fait divers," which remains undescribed in the text itself.

60. *Les Noces d'Hérodiade*, 93–94.

61. Ibid., 113.

62. Ibid., 106.

63. Ibid., 44: "symbolise ... aux yeux de Mallarmé l'assujettissement réciproque du génie et de son rêve de beauté, qui est la condition de l'oeuvre pure." Davies equates the "splendide nudité" of Hérodiade without her veils with "la beauté pure" (42); even if such a conflation is Mallarméan, it suggests a reading that takes Mallarmé literally and misses a crucial half of the significance of that body.

64. *Les Noces d'Hérodiade*, 113.

65. Ibid., 114. Gardner Davies believes this "lieu nul" to be the space "ou doit se dé rouler la crise." *Mallarmé et le rêve d'Hérodiade*, 26.

66. Richard calls the "lieu nul" the site of Hérodiade's body, a reading which seems to link her body to the idealized empty space of the Livre; but I read in it the opposite of the space of *Un Coup de dés*: "RIEN ... N' AURA EU LIEU ... QUE LE LIEU." This particular dance *happens*, it is banal spectacle, and thus renders the site of its performance uninteresting, rather than potentially pure, the locus of creation.

67. *Les Noces d'Hérodiade*, 118.

68. Ibid., 111.

69. Girard, "Scandal and the Dance," 323. On the relation of ritual, sacrifice, and mimesis, see also Girard, *Violence and the Sacred*, and *The Scapegoat*.

70. *Corréspondance III*, 83. Letter to V. Pico dated Jan. 1887.

71. See chap. 2: "Mallarmé," in Lacoue-Labarthe, *Musica ficta*.

72. Bersani, *Death of Stéphane Mallarmé*, 79.

73. See Amy Koritz, *Gendering Bodies / Performing Art*.

74. All following citations are from J.-K. Huysmans, *Against Nature*, 63–77.

75. Loie Fuller, *Fifteen Years of a Dancer's Life: With Some Account of Her Distinguished Friends*, 287–88, quoting the article of November 5, 1907, in *Le Temps*. For a detailed biography of Fuller, see Giovanni Lista, *Loie Fuller: danseuse de la belle époque*.

76. Fuller, *Fifteen Years of a Dancer's Life*, 137.

77. Ibid., 138. After the performance, when brought to Fuller's dressing room, the child complained that this was not the woman she had seen onstage: "'No, no that isn't her. I don't want to see her. This one here is a fat lady, and it was a fairy I saw dancing.' . . . I endeavoured therefore to be equal to the situation, and I said to the child: 'Yes, my dear, you are right. I am not Loie Fuller.'" Another child, Fuller writes, became so enthralled with her that he "ended by making wax figurines, representing 'Loie Fuller.'"

78. Ibid., 63–64. Fuller's autobiography even reveals a sense of humor about her public image. With relish she tells a story of being so enraptured by the stained glass windows in Notre Dame de Paris that, waving her handkerchief in the beams of colored light, she is nearly arrested; she reports the policeman on duty as having said, "Tell that woman to go away; she is crazy." But her descriptions of her performances are marked by an exaggerated sense of her power as a performer, receiving ovations "such as, I suppose, never another human being has received. . . . The uproar of the applause became something fantastic in the dead of night. It was like the beating of a single pair of hands, but so powerful that no noise in the world could be compared with it."

79. "[Cette] inconsciente révélatrice … silencieusement écrira ta vision à la façon d'un Signe, qu'elle est [(This) unconsious revealer . . . will silently write your vision in the manner of a Sign, which she is]." *Crayonné au théâtre*, 307.

"Le librettiste ignore d'ordinaire que la danseuse, qui s'exprime par des pas, ne comprend d'éloquence autre, même le geste" (306).

80. Loie Fuller, *Fifteen Years of a Dancer's Life*, 28, 25.

81. "I put the garment on and looked at myself in a large glass, to make sure of what I had done the evening before . . . the sun shed into the room an amber light, which enveloped me completely and illumined my gown, giving a translucent effect. . . . This was a moment of intense emotion. Unconsciously I realised that I was in the presence of a great discovery, one which was destined to open the path which I have since followed." Ibid., 33–34.

82. Ibid., 37–38.

83. "L'exercice, comme invention, sans l'emploi, comporte une ivresse d'art et, simultané un accomplissement industriel." *Crayonné au théâtre*, 307.

84. "Une armature, qui n'est d'aucune femme en particulier, d'où instable, à travers le voile de généralité, attire sur tel fragment révélé de la forme et y boit l'éclair qui le divinise; ou exhale, de retour, par l'ondulation des tissus, flottante, palpitante, éparse cette extase." *Crayonné au théâtre*, 311.

85. Ibid., 308–9: "Or cette transition de sonorités aux tissus (y a-t-il, mieux, à une gaze ressemblant que la Musique!) est, uniquement, le sortilège qu'opère la Loïe Fuller."

86. Fuller, *Fifteen Years of a Dancer's Life*, 285–86, quoting Jules Claretie's review in *Le Temps*, Nov. 5, 1907. Claretie's 1881 novel, *Les Amours d'un interne*, set in the Salpêtrière, is discussed by Beizer, *Ventriloquized Bodies*, chap. 1: "The Textual Woman and the Hysterical Novel."

87. "Il y faudrait substituer je ne sais quel impersonnel ou fulgurant regard absolu, comme l'éclair qui enveloppe, depuis quelques ans, la danseuse d'Edens, fondant une crudité électrique à des blancheurs extra-charnelles de fards, et en fait bien l'être prestigieux reculé au-delà de toute vie possible." *Crayonné au théâtre*, 306–7.

88. Fuller, *Fifteen Years of a Dancer's Life*, 169–70.

89. Despite major scholarship on the history of electricity, and on philosophical and scientific conceptions of electricity as the life force, to my knowledge a cultural history of electricity has yet to be written that would address the specific ways in which it has shaped subjectivity. Is it generally true, as my example suggests, that a very different subject of electricity is produced depending upon (1) who controls its use (i.e., whether it is requested by the subject, paid for, imposed, etc.) and (2) the conditions of its use (whether it interacts directly with the body's physiological processes, in public or private, etc.). Such a study would need to take into account the development of the dynamo and electricity's changing force; its leisure or "spa" uses versus "state" institutional or public uses; the dangers of the domestication of direct current and Edison's solution to it; the spectacles of illumination in streets and Paris department stores (contemporary with the stage spectacles considered here) and their popular appeal. To be considered as well is the changing medical view of electricity's use as therapy, especially debates concerning the amount and type of current used, which continue at the present time. For a detailed exposition of the way in which physiologists considered the working of electrical devices as true representations of nervous and muscular activity in the later nineteenth century, see Timothy Lenoir, "Models and Instruments in the Development of Electrophysiology, 1845–1912." For a case history of how these scientific instruments were introduced into English medicine before Charcot, see Iwan Morus, "Marketing the Machine: the Construction of Electrotherapeutics as Viable Medicine in Early Victorian England." On the philosophical and scientific literature of electricity as the life force and as death-bearing, and on the connection between "nerve circuits" and electrical systems discussed by Eduard Von Hartmann's *Philosophie des Unbewußten* (1869), see Christoph Asendorf, *Batteries of Life: On the History of Things and Their Perception in Modernity*. On the relation between neurasthenia and modern technologies, see Anson Rabinbach, "Neurasthenia and Modernity," and *The Human Motor: Energy, Fatigue, and the Origins of Modernity*. And on the popularization of

electrical lighting in public and performance spaces, see Wolfgang Schivelbusch, *Disenchanted Night: The Industrialization of Light in the Nineteenth Century*, 200.

90. Charcot, "Polyclinique," in *Leçons du mardi à la Salpêtrière I, 1887–88*. Rare book collection, UCLA.

91. The misogyny underlying Charcot's positions on the social and gender issues raised in the treatment of hysteria—relatively liberal for his time—here becomes pronounced: "The best possible police, women over women, for you are aware that if women enter into any plot between themselves they rarely succeed." Quoted in A. R. G. Owen, *Hysteria, Hypnosis and Healing: The Work of J.-M. Charcot*, 73. Statistics from the Salpêtrière show a majority of female patients admitted to the hospital during Charcot's tenure there; on Charcot's diagnosis of male hysterias, see Mark Micale, "Charcot and the Idea of Hysteria in the Male: Gender, Medical Science, and Medical Diagnosis in Late Nineteenth-Century France."

92. Charcot, "Nervous System," cited in Owen, *Hysteria*, 72–73. Roy Porter has recently noted the pathetic nature of Charcot's own desire for mastery of the hysterical patient: "Hindsight reveals the deep pathos in Charcot's boast that the 'province of the physician' is 'to dissipate chicanery.'" See "The Body and the Mind, the Doctor and the Patient: Negotiating Hysteria," in *Hysteria Beyond Freud*, 259.

93. Charcot, "Nervous System," 76. Charcot's pupil Richer writes: "It's important to know that certain nervous subjects fake with the greatest detachment. The hysteric . . . fakes for no reason, just for the sake of faking [Il faut savoir que certains sujets nerveux trompent avec le plus grand désintéressement. L'hystérique ... trompe sans motif, uniquement pour tromper]." Paul Richer, *Etudes cliniques sur la grande hystérie ou hystéro-epilepsie*, 515n.

94. Owen, *Hysteria*, 187.

95. Goetz, in *Charcot the Clinician*, 189–90, cites Pierre Janet, *Psychological Healing*, vol. 1, 184, as the source for this anecdote.

96. Owen, *Hysteria*, 187, citing Alfred Binet, *The Psychology of Reasoning Based on Experimental Research in Hypnosis*, 59–60.

97. Blanche maintained that rumors that the patients faked hysterical states "are lies. We had these spells and were in these lethargic states because we could not do otherwise. Besides, it wasn't a bit of fun. Simulation! Do you think it would have been easy to fool Dr. Charcot? O yes, lots of fakes tried; he gave them one look and said 'Be still.'" A. Badouin, "Quelques souvenirs de la Salpetrière," 517–20, retold in *Charcot the Clinician*, 120–21. Porter, "The Body and the Mind," notes that "without the electric atmosphere of Charcot's clinic, Blanche Wittman and other stars of hysteria would have wasted their swoonings on the desert air" (242). At issue here is the validity of "hysterical" self-expression, whose value as theater—whether conscious or unconscious, faked or not—has not been recognized.

98. For a case history in which the acceptance of electrical treatment in

English medicine depended upon the technology's scientific credibility and use in laboratories, see Morus, "Marketing the Machine."

99. "Effets de l'electrisation statique sur quelques phénomènes hystériques," by M. Blanc-Fontenille under the direction of A. Pitres, Hôpital de St. André, Bordeaux, in *Le Progrès médical*, Feb. 19, 1887.

100. A. Pitres, *Leçons cliniques sur l'hystérie et l'hypnotisme faites à l'Hôpital Saint-André de Bordeaux*, vol. 1, 316.

101. Charcot, "Hysteroepilepsy: A Young Woman with a Convulsive Attack in the Auditorium, February 7, 1888," reprinted in *Charcot the Clinician*, 107.

102. Sigmund Freud, "Charcot," in *The Freud Reader*, 49–50.

103. Ibid.

104. Freud, *Studies on Hysteria*, 117.

105. Freud, "Charcot," in *The Freud Reader*, 50.

106. G.-B. Duchenne de Boulogne, *The Mechanism of Human Facial Expression*, 23.

107. Foucault, *The Birth of the Clinic*, 165–66. Foucault adds a footnote on the veil: "This structure does not date from the beginning of the nineteenth century, far from it." Mallarmé's metaphysics of the veil follows the tradition identified by Foucault here as dominating "the forms of knowledge and eroticism in Europe from the mid-eighteenth century onwards" (173).

108. Ibid., 164.

109. Ibid., 165.

110. *Standard Edition of the Complete Psychological Works of Freud*, vol. 14, 13–14.

111. Jones, *Life and Work*, 220–21; and Freud, "The Aetiology of Hysteria," in *The Freud Reader*, 100–101.

112. *Le Progrès médical*, Feb.–Mar. 1887.

113. The two terms are coined by the patient Anna O., whose case history is included in Breuer and Freud, *Studies on Hysteria*.

114. "Ce qui se tentait à la fin du siècle dernier, au temps de Freud, ce qu'ils cherchaient, toutes sortes de braves gens dans l'entourage de Charcot et des autres, c'était de ramener la mystique à des affaires de foutre." Jacques Lacan, "Dieu et la jouissance de la femme," in *Le Séminaire*, vol. 20: *Encore*, 71.

115. Charcot, cited in Owen, *Hysteria*, 230.

116. See Jean Malaurie, "J.-B. Charcot, Father of French Polar Research," 191–96.

117. In the first of the "Five Lectures on Psychoanalysis" delivered in 1909, Freud writes: "The study of hypnotic phenomena has accustomed us to what was at first a bewildering realization that in one and the same individual there can be several mental groupings, which can remain more or less independent of one another, which can 'know nothing' of one another and which can alternate with one another in their hold upon consciousness. Cases of this kind, too, appear

spontaneously, and are then described as examples of '*double conscience.*'" *Five Lectures on Psychoanalysis*, 16.

118. The idea that dance expresses the desire to be other, in a Lacanian formulation of desire as metonymy, is the thesis of a book on ballet by Pierre Legendre, *La Passion d'être un autre: étude pour la danse.*

119. What Foucault calls the "regard absolu" of nineteenth-century pathological anatomy seems more closely assimilable to what Lacan calls "the gaze": an absolute or internalized gaze beyond the intersubjective, public eye of the medical amphitheater, and functioning within the subject of psychoanalysis.

120. Daphne de Marneffe cites and discusses this idea in "Looking and Listening: The Construction of Clinical Knowledge in Charcot and Freud," 100. De Marneffe argues that Freud's technique differs significantly from Charcot's by including (up to 1900) the subjective accounts of his patients and acknowledging his own subjective contribution to the analysis; and that Freud's attitude toward women and the body changes after the *Studies on Hysteria*, particularly around the Dora case.

121. Freud, "Fragment of an Analysis of a Case of Hysteria ('Dora')," in *The Freud Reader*, 215.

Chapter 4

1. Louis-Ferdinand Céline, *Le Style contre les idées*, 67. On this question, see also Philippe Almeras, *Les Idées de Céline.*

2. This statement, published in an interview given after Céline's death, was confirmed in conversation with the author.

3. See Alphonse Juilland, "Elisabeth Craig vous parle."

4. All references to Louis-Ferdinand Céline, *Bagatelles pour un massacre* (Denoël ed.), appear as page numbers in parentheses in the text.

5. For example, Philip Day writes: "Toutes les vérités inexorables que Céline ressasse dans les romans s'opposent aux thèmes délicats et à l'ironie bienveillante des récits qui nous occupent à présent. En effet, l'ambiance torride des enfers céliniens est momantanément raffraichie et même égayée par les Ballets ... Ils vont donc nous permettre de reconnaître un côté léger et précieux de l'auteur que celui-ci devait nécessairement dissimuler ailleurs." Philip Stephen Day, *Le Miroir allégorique de Louis-Ferdinand Céline*, 196. In an attempt to counter such readings, this chapter focuses exclusively on the ballets originally published in *Bagatelles pour un massacre* in the context of their original publication.

6. *Mort à crédit I*, 26.

7. Interview with Poulet, reprinted in *Les Cahiers de l'Herne*, vol. 5, 82.

8. Céline, *Voyage au bout de la nuit*, 454.

9. Julia Kristeva, *Pouvoirs de l'horreur: essai sur l'abjection*, 217: "celui qui *Est* et celui qui *A.*"

10. *Les Beaux Draps*, 70; Kristeva, *Pouvoirs de l'horreur*, 208.

11. At this studio he also met his future wife, Lucette Almanzor. Céline's opportunity to observe dancers at work gives him a particular familiarity not only with ballet plots but with the various group dances and individual variations which structure the classical ballet. Through familiarity with the dancer's backstage preparation for performance, the daily routine of dance class and rehearsal, Céline—like Gautier—writes ballets that comment on the making of ballet itself.

12. Letter to Hindus cited in *Les Cahiers de l'Herne*, vol. 5, 123; cited and discussed in Kristeva, *Pouvoirs de l'horreur*, 194. See also Milton Hindus, *The Crippled Giant: A Literary Relationship with Louis-Ferdinand Céline*.

13. Kristeva, *Pouvoirs de l'horreur*, 170; the passage cited is from *Voyage au bout de la nuit*, in *Romans I*, 489 (my translation).

14. Kristeva, *Pouvoirs de l'horreur*, 210.

15. Céline, *Rigodon*, 225.

16. Sander Gilman, *The Jew's Body*, 2.

17. Ibid., 5.

18. Ibid., 173.

19. Ibid., 202–3. Beyond the interpretation of skin color or other physical characteristics, the identification of Jews as a "mixed race" contributed to their characterization in medical and other discourse as "inferior." Gilman writes: "Within the racial science of the nineteenth century, being 'black' came to signify that the Jews had crossed racial boundaries. The boundaries of race were one of the most powerful social and political divisions evolved in the science of the period. That the Jews, rather than being considered the purest race, are because of their endogenous marriages, an impure race, and therefore, a potentially diseased one. That this impurity is written on their physiognomy. . . . According to Houston Stewart Chamberlain, the Jews are a 'mongrel' (rather than a healthy 'mixed') race, who interbred with Africans during the period of the Alexandrian exile. . . . Jews bear the sign of the black, 'the African character of the Jew, his muzzle-shaped mouth and face removing him from certain other races . . .' as Robert Knox noted at mid-century" (174).

20. Dominique Maingueneau, *Les Livres d'école de la République, 1870–1914*: discours et idéologie, 195.

21. Ibid., 195–99, citing Payot.

22. Ibid., 198, citing Payot.

23. Ibid.

24. Ibid., 200–203, summarizing Payot.

25. Robert A. Nye, *Crime, Madness, and Politics in Modern France: The Medical Concept of Decline*, 330: Nordau's 1892 *Degeneration* "formulated its distinctions from the perspective of modern mental medicine."

26. Nye, *Crime, Madness, and Politics*, 136, discusses Lucien Nass and A. J. Witkowsky, *Le Nu au théâtre*.

27. Nye, *Crime, Madness, and Politics*, 140.

28. Ibid., 331, citing Krafft-Ebing.

29. Nye develops this idea in chap. 5, "Metaphors of Pathology in the Belle Epoque: The Rise of a Medical Model of Cultural Crisis," of *Crime, Madness, and Politics*.

30. Ibid., 143–44.

31. Ibid., 318, citing Maingueneau, *Les Livres*, 295.

32. Ibid., 140n26. Nye notes that the decline of France, charted in myriad studies of the type and the quality of the population, was contrasted with an ideal of France as it used to be and with Germany (141).

33. Ibid., 143.

34. Maingueneau, *Les Livres*, 197, citing Payot: "In the name of the Republic . . . I wish to instruct you of the means to be happy on this earth . . . perfect yourselves [Au nom de la République ... Je veux vous instruire des moyens d'être heureux sur la terre ... perfectionnez-vous]."

35. On the history of the pedagogical mission to tame students' animality, see Nye's discussion (*Crime, Madness, and Politics*, 318); on Céline's praise of an innate animality, see Roussin, "Getting Back from the Other World."

36. Kristeva, *Pouvoirs de l'horreur*, 208.

37. Letter to Hindus reprinted in *Les Cahiers de l'Herne*, vol. 5, 123; discussed in Kristeva, *Pouvoirs de l'horreur*, 194.

38. Among many titles discussed by Nye in chap. 9, "Sport, Regeneration, and National Revival," of *Crime, Madness, and Politics* are Pierre de Coubertin, *Essai de psychologie sportive*; and Philippe Tissié, *L'Evolution de l'education physique en France et en Belgique, 1900–1910*.

39. '*Mea Culpa*' and '*The Life and Work of Ignaz Philip Semmelweis (1818–65)*', 94.

40. Bruno Latour, *Les Microbes*, 25: "Pour suivre l'hygiène dans la *Revue Scientifique*, il est commode de la définir comme un *style*."

41. Ibid., 26.

42. Philippe Roussin, "Getting Back from the Other World," 251. Roussin's full-length study of Céline's medical career and writing appeared too late to be taken into account here.

43. Ibid.

44. Ibid., 254–55.

45. Ibid., 250.

46. "Progrès," in *Oeuvres de Céline*.

47. Roussin, "Getting Back from the Other World," 256, 258, 259.

48. Céline, "Progrès," 276.

49. On the translation and revision of *Bagatelles* in Germany and its use by

the National Socialists, see Christine Sautermeister, "La Traduction allemande de *Bagatelles pour un massacre*."

50. *Les Beaux Draps*, 148; Kristeva, *Pouvoirs de l'horreur*, 210.

51. Foucault, "Right of Death and Power of Life," in *The History of Sexuality: An Introduction*, vol. 1, 139–40.

52. In *Approaching Hysteria*, Mark Micale has noted that views of hysteria linking it to the "social pathologies" also coincide with fin-de-siècle French ethnography's description of hysterias in French colonial territories in Africa and the South Pacific (216).

53. Roussin, "Getting Back from the Other World," 258, 254.

54. I owe this observation to Henri Godard.

55. The height of balletic allegory, this scene recalls the personified appearances of Death in *Mort à crédit*, merging Céline's social realism with the fantastic.

56. In *Poétique de Céline*, Henri Godard has detailed Céline's dislike for these musical forms. But the reference may also be to the American dancer Josephine Baker, who debuted in Paris in the 1925 "Revue Nègre" at the Théâtre des Champs Elysées. During this period, Josephine Baker danced vigorous athletic dances of the type described here, often in minimal costuming and with jungle themes and decor.

57. Letter to Hindus, reprinted in *Les Cahiers de l'Herne*, vol. 5, 113. Cited and discussed in Kristeva, *Pouvoirs de l'horreur*, 225.

58. Letter to Hindus, reprinted in Hindus, *L.-F. Céline tel que je l'ai vu*, 138.

59. Letter to Hindus, reprinted in *Les Cahiers de l'Herne*, vol. 5, 82.

60. Godard, *Les Manuscrits de Céline*, 13, 14, 15. This kind of work seems far from the sort of repetitive rehearsal that Céline would have witnessed in ballet classes. Yet one similiarity can be seen in the fact that the ballerina is taught to consider that she is performing even in a daily class, and to treat the rehearsal as if it were a performance, a task made easier by the presence of visitors like Céline himself. Without this level of concentration and effort, the class or rehearsal is considered useless.

61. Ibid., 18.

62. Céline, "Progrès," 275.

63. *D'un château l'autre*, in *Romans II*, 277. The text of the draft following is reproduced in *Romans II*, 1138.

64. Lucette Destouches performed Fuller's choreographies during her performance career (conversation with the author).

65. Henri Godard has noted that the publication of the pamphlet effectively broke off any hope of using connections, including contacts with ballet administrators, that he had established during his visit there that year.

66. Godard, *Poétique de Céline*, 37.

67. On eating and vomiting in Céline's novels, see, for example, Alain Cresciucci, "Les Nourritures romanesques."

68. Godard, *Poétique de Céline*, 268–75. Godard adds the following note: "Cette dominante rythmique est, en 1936, l'un des principaux griefs que Paul Nizan fait à Mort à Crédit ... allant jusqu'à mettre au passif de Céline l'intuition qu'il a d'un possible rapprochement avec la dé marche de Mallarmé" (269–70).

69. Ibid., 272.

70. *Entretiens avec le Professeur Y*, quoted in Kristeva, *Pouvoirs de l'horreur*, 224.

71. Céline, *Les Beaux Draps*, 171.

72. Godard, *Poétique de Céline*, 272–73, comments on this passage from *Guignol's Band I*, 157.

73. Godard, *Poétique de Céline*, 273.

74. Kristeva, *Pouvoirs de l'horreur*, 171.

75. On male hysteria, see Mark S. Micale, "Charcot and the Idea of Hysteria."

76. Kristeva, *Pouvoirs de l'horreur*, 171.

77. Ibid., 225, 239.

78. On Mallarmé, see Kristeva, *La Révolution du langage poétique*.

79. Michèle Montrelay, *L'Ombre et le nom*: "Par la féminité on entendra l'ensemble des pulsions 'féminines' (orales, anales, vaginales), en tant que celles-ci résistent aux processus de refoulement" (67).

80. See *Semmelweis*, in *Cahiers Céline* 3; trans. as '*Mea Culpa*' *and* '*The Life and Work of Ignaz Philip Semmelweis (1818–65)*'.

81. Kristeva, *Pouvoirs de l'horreur*, 226.

82. Ibid., 227.

83. Ibid., 226.

84. Ibid., 225.

85. Letter to Hindus, dated May 29, 1947, reprinted in *Les Cahiers de l'Herne*, vol. 5, 113. Cited in Kristeva, *Pouvoirs de l'horreur*, 226.

86. *Entretiens avec le Professeur Y*, 71–72.

87. It would be possible to graph onto Céline's opposition of "con" and "vide" the Freud-Jones debate over feminine sexuality. This debate, summarized and commented on by Montrelay, *L'Ombre et le nom*, centers on whether feminine sexuality is organized around concepts of the "phallic" or the "vaginal." Montrelay describes this debate as originating between Freud and Jones, then developing in the work of the next generation of women analysts, including Melanie Klein. Montrelay argues that the volume she is reviewing, *Recherches psychanalytiques nouvelles sur la sexualité féminine*, suggests alternatives to the impasse of this debate.

88. "Les élections de la gauche je trouve se font encore plus au bistrot que les élections de la droite, sans parti pris. Jamais les bistrots n'ont connu d'affluences comparables à celle que le vaut 'les 40 heures.' Le peuple? Jamais tant de loisirs, jamais tant picolé ... Les 350.000 bistrots de France ont tout remplacé dans la vie des masses ... l'église, les chants, les danses populaires, les légendes,

etc. ... les 'grands vinicoles et distillateurs' doivent la plus merveilleuses de chan-
delles au gouvernement 'Boom Bloum' pour les miraculeuses quarante heures et
l'accroissement inouï des pouvoirs vinassiers des foules [Without taking sides, I
think the elections won by the left are decided in the bistros more than those
won by the right. The bistros have never had anything like the good business the
'40-hour-work-week' has given them. The people? Never before so much free
time, and so much drinking. The 350,000 bistros of France have replaced everything else in the life of the masses ... church ... song ... popular dancing ... fairy
tales, etc. ... the 'great wine-growers and distillers' owe the most marvellous of
erections to the 'Boom Bloum' government for the miraculous 40-hour-week
and the unheard-of rise in the plonk-power of the crowds]" *Bagatelles pour un
massacre*, 146–47.

89. Mikkel Borch-Jacobsen, *The Freudian Subject*, 28.

90. Ibid., 45.

91. Freud, *Interpretation of Dreams* (*Standard Edition*, vols. 4 and 5), 149–50,
cited and discussed by Borch-Jakobson, *Freudian Subject*, 50.

92. Godard, *Poétique de Céline*, 287.

93. Although, as noted above, Céline was surrounded by dancers all his life,
and Lucette Destouches gave dance lessons in the house they shared at Meudon
where Céline often spoke with her students.

94. See Isabelle Blondiaux, *Une écriture psychotique: Louis-Ferdinand Céline*.

95. H. E. Kaminski, *Céline en chemise brune ou le mal du présent* (1938),
83–84. This text is also cited and discussed in Blondiaux, "Louis-Ferdinand Céline et le diagnostic de paranoia," 79.

96. Yves Pagès, "Les Crises d'identité du racisme Célinien: entre prédications xénophobes et désir d'exil," 278, cites H. Meige, *Etude sur certains névropathes voyageurs: le juif errant de la Salpêtrière*, 23: "une sorte de prototype des Is-
réalites névropathes pérégrinant de par le monde."

97. Blondiaux, "Louis-Ferdinand Céline et le diagnostic de paranoia."

98. Ibid., 86: "si pathologie paranoiaque il y a, Céline semble bien davantage
l'agir qu'être agi par elle et ce, que le point de vue adopté soit medical ou littéraire."

99. Ibid., 82.

100. Ibid., 86: "un éventuel recours de ce médecin-écrivain aux données
d'un savoir constitué sur la pathologie mentale plutôt qu'à celles d'une expéri-
ence personelle ineffable."

101. Ibid., 87.

102. Jean-Louis Sourgen, "La Danse amère de Céline," reports this electrical
treatment (304). Yves Pagès, "The 'Modest Proposal' of Doctor Destouches,"
finds this experience with medicine as foundational for Destouches's choice of
medicine as a profession: "Ici naît la vocation du docteur Destouches, au contact
d'un acteur privilégié de l'Hygiène de Guerre. . . . En Céline, c'est l'ancien

combattant qui connaît le mieux *les grandes manoeuvres de la main d'oeuvre*, c'est le mutilé qui inspire la vocation théorique du médecin" (201).

103. Roussin, "Getting Back from the Other World," 254.

104. Fredric Jameson, "Céline and Innocence," 318.

105. Ibid., 319.

106. Blondiaux, *Une écriture psychotique*, 11.

107. *Voyage au bout de la nuit*, 7, 10; cited ibid., 18.

108. Roussin, "Getting Back from the Other World," 258.

109. Roussin describes *Voyage*'s motif of the physican's duty to keep secrets (ibid.).

110. Alice Kaplan and Philippe Roussin, "Céline's Modernity," 434.

111. *Entretiens avec le Professeur Y*, 19, 21, 27; cited and discussed in Kaplin and Roussin, "Céline's Modernity," 428.

112. Kaplin and Roussin, "Céline's Modernity," 440.

113. Roussin, "Getting Back from the Other World," 255.

Bibliography

Almeras, Philippe. *Les Idées de Céline*. Paris: Bibliothéque de littérature française contemporaine de l'Université de Paris, 1987.

Apter, Emily. "Figura Serpentinata: Visual Seduction and the Colonial Gaze." In Margaret Cohen and Christopher Prendergast, eds., *Spectacles of Realism: Gender, Body, Genre*. Minneapolis: University of Minnesota Press, 1995.

Ariès, Philippe. *The Hour of Our Death*. New York: Alfred A. Knopf, 1981.

Armstrong, David. "Bodies of Knowledge / Knowledge of Bodies." In Colin Jones and Roy Porter, eds., *Reassessing Foucault: Power, Medicine and the Body*. London: Routledge, 1994.

Asendorf, Christoph. *Batteries of Life: On the History of Things and Their Perception in Modernity*. Berkeley: University of California Press, 1993.

Badouin, A. "Quelques souvenirs de la Salpêtrière." *Paris médicale* 26 (1935): 517–20.

Barish, Jonas. *The Anti-Theatrical Prejudice*. Berkeley: University of California Press, 1981.

Bataille, Georges. *Manet*. Geneva: Skira, 1983.

Baudelaire, Charles. *L'Art romantique*. Paris: Editions de la Nouvelle Revue Française, 1923.

———. *Oeuvres complètes*. Paris: Seuil, 1968.

———. *The Painter of Modern Life and Other Essays*. Trans. Johnathon Mayne. London: Phaidon, 1964.

Beaumont, Cyril. *The Romantic Ballet as Seen by Théophile Gautier*. London: C. W. Beaumont, 1932.

———. *The Ballet Called Giselle*. London: Dance Books, 1996 [1944].

Beizer, Janet. *Ventriloquized Bodies: Narratives of Hysteria in Nineteenth-Century France*. Ithaca, N.Y.: Cornell University Press, 1994.

Bellet, Roger. *L'Encre et le ciel*. Paris: Champ Vallon, 1987.

Benjamin, Walter. *Illuminations*. New York: Schocken Books, 1969.

Benveniste, Emile. *Problèmes de linguistique générale*, vol. 1. Paris: Gallimard, 1966.

Bernard, Claude. *An Introduction to the Study of Experimental Method.* Foreword by I. Bernard Cohen. New York: Dover, 1957 [1856].

Bersani, Leo. *The Death of Stéphane Mallarmé.* Cambridge: Cambridge University Press, 1982.

Binet, Alfred. *The Psychology of Reasoning Based on Experimental Research in Hypnosis.* London, 1899.

Binney, Edwin, III. *Les Ballets de Théophile Gautier.* Paris: Nizet, 1965.

Blanc-Fontenille, M. "Effets de l'electrisation statique sur quelques phénomènes hystériques." In *Le Progrès médical*, Feb. 19, 1887.

Blanchot, Maurice. "Le Mythe de Mallarmé." In Blanchot, *La Part du feu.* Paris: Gallimard, 1949.

———. "Parler, ce n'est pas voir." In Blanchot, *L'Entretien infini.* Paris: Gallimard, 1969.

Blondiaux, Isabelle. *Une écriture psychotique: Louis-Ferdinand Céline.* Paris: Nizet, 1985.

———. "Louis-Ferdinand Céline et le diagnostic de paranoia." In *Actes du Colloque International L.-F. Céline 1992.* Tusson: Du Lérot, 1993.

Boethius. *The Consolation of Philosophy.* Trans. Richard Green. New York: Macmillan, 1962.

Book-Senninger, Claude. *Théophile Gautier: auteur dramatique.* Paris: Nizet, 1972.

Borch-Jacobsen, Mikkel. *The Freudian Subject.* Trans. Catherine Porter. Stanford, Calif.: Stanford University Press, 1988.

Bracegirdle, Brian. *A History of Microtechnique.* Ithaca, N.Y.: Cornell University Press, 1978.

Breuer, Josef, and Sigmund Freud. *Studies on Hysteria.* Trans. James Strachey. New York: Basic Books, n.d. [1893].

Brooks, Peter. *The Melodramatic Imagination: Balzac, Henry James, Melodrama, and the Mode of Excess.* New York: Columbia University Press, 1985.

Butler, Judith. *Gender Trouble: Feminism and the Subversion of Identity.* New York: Routledge, 1992.

Bynum, W. F., Roy Porter, and Michael Shepherd, eds. *The Anatomy of Madness: Essays in the History of Psychiatry*, vol. 1. London and New York: Tavistock Publications, 1985.

Canguilhem, Georges. *The Normal and the Pathological.* New York: Zone, 1989.

Case, Sue-Ellen. "Performing Lesbian in the Space of Technology: Part I." *Theatre Journal* 47 (1995): 1–18.

Céline, Louis-Ferdinand. *Bagatelles pour un massacre.* Paris: Denoël, 1937.

———. *Ballets sans musique, sans personne, sans rien.* Paris: Gallimard, 1959.

———. *Les Beaux Draps.* Paris: Nouvelles Editions Françaises, 1941.

———. *Les Cahiers de l'Herne*, vol. 5. Paris: Editions de l'Herne, 1965.

———. *D'un château l'autre.* In *Romans II.* Paris: Gallimard, Bibliothèque de la Pléiade, 1974.

————. *Guignol's Band I.* In *Romans III.* Paris: Gallimard, 1988.

————. *'Mea Culpa' and 'The Life and Work of Ignaz Philip Semmelweis (1818–65)'.* Trans. Robert Allerton Parker. New York: Howard Fertig, 1979.

————. *Mort à crédit I.* Paris: Gallimard, 1952.

————. "Progrès." In *Oeuvres de Céline.* Paris: Club de l'Honnête Homme, 1981.

————. *Rigodon.* Paris: Gallimard, 1969.

————. *Romans I.* Paris: Gallimard, Bibliothèque de la Pléiade, 1981.

————. *Romans II.* Paris: Gallimard, Bibliothèque de la Pléiade, 1974.

————. *Semmelweis.* In *Cahiers Céline 3.* Paris: Gallimard, 1977.

————. *Le Style contre les idées.* Brussels: Editions Complexes, 1987.

————. *Voyage au bout de la nuit.* Paris: Gallimard, 1952.

Charcot, Jean-Martin. *Charcot the Clinician: The Tuesday Lessons. Excerpts from nine case presentations on general neurology delivered at the Salpêtrière Hospital in 1887–88 by Jean-Martin Charcot.* Trans. with commentary by Christopher G. Goetz. New York: Raven Press, 1987.

————. "Polyclinique." In *Leçons du mardi à la Salpêtrière I, 1887–88.* Rare book collection, UCLA.

————. "Préface." In Paul Richer, *Etudes cliniques sur la grande hystérie ou hystéro-epilepsie.* Paris: Delahaye et Lecrosnier, 1885.

Cixous, Hélène. *Portrait de Dora.* Paris: Des femmes, 1986.

Clark, T. J. *The Painter of Modern Life: Paris in the Art of Manet and His Followers.* Princeton: Princeton University Press, 1984.

Copeland, Roger, and Marshall Cohen, eds. *What Is Dance? Readings in Theory and Criticism.* New York: Oxford University Press, 1983.

Corbin, Alain. *Les Filles de noces: misère sexuelle et prostitution aux 19ème et 20ème siècles.* Paris: Aubier, 1978.

————. *Women for Hire: Prostitution and Sexuality in France after 1850.* Trans. Alan Sheridan. Cambridge, Mass.: Harvard University Press, 1990.

Cresciucci, Alain. "Les Nourritures romanesques." In *Actes du Colloque International L.-F. Céline 1988.* Tusson: Du Lérot, 1989.

Davies, Gardner. *Mallarmé et le rêve d'Hérodiade.* Paris: J. Corti, 1978.

Day, Philip Stephen. *Le Miroir allégorique de Louis-Ferdinand Céline.* Paris: Klincksieck, 1974.

de Boigne, Charles. *Petits Mémoires de l'Opéra.* Paris: Librairie Nouvelle, 1857. Collection of the Bibliothèque Nationale de France.

de Coubertin, Pierre. *Essai de psychologie sportive.* Lausanne and Paris, 1913.

Deleuze, Gilles, and Félix Guattari. *Anti-Oedipus: Capitalism and Schizophrenia.* Trans. Robert Hurley, Mark Seem, and Helen R. Lane. Minneapolis: University of Minnesota Press, 1983.

de Marneffe, Daphne. "Looking and Listening: The Construction of Clinical Knowledge in Charcot and Freud." *Signs* 17 (Autumn 1991): 71–111.

Derrida, Jacques. "La Double Séance." In *La Dissémination*. Paris: Seuil, 1972.

———. *Eperons: les styles de Nietzsche*. Paris: Flammarion, 1978.

———. *Khôra*. Paris, Galilée, 1993.

Didi-Huberman, Georges. *L'Invention de l'hystérie: Charcot et l'iconographie photographique de la Salpêtrière*. Paris: Editions Macula, 1982.

Dowbiggin, Ian. "Degeneration and Hereditarianism in French Mental Medicine." In W. F. Bynum, Roy Porter, and Michael Shepherd, eds., *The Anatomy of Madness: Essays in the History of Psychiatry*, vol. 1. London and New York: Tavistock Publications, 1985.

Duchenne de Boulogne, G.-B. *The Mechanism of Human Facial Expression*. Ed. and trans. R. Andrew Cuthbertson. Cambridge: Cambridge University Press, 1990.

Dufay, Pierre. *Le Pantalon féminin*. Paris: Charles Carrington, 1906.

Foster, Susan. *Choreography and Narrative*. Indiana: Indiana University Press, 1996.

———. *Reading Dancing: Bodies and Subjects in Contemporary American Dance*. Berkeley: University of California Press, 1986.

Foucault, Michel. *The Birth of the Clinic: An Archeology of Medical Perception*. Trans. Alan Sheridan. New York: Pantheon, 1973.

———. *Histoire de la folie à l'âge classique*. Paris: Gallimard, 1972.

———. "The Incitement to Discourse." From *The History of Sexuality*, reprinted in Paul Rabinow, ed., *The Foucault Reader*. New York: Pantheon, 1984.

———. *Madness and Civilization: A History of Insanity in the Age of Reason*. New York: Random House, Vintage Books, 1973.

———. *Les Mots et les choses*. Paris: Gallimard, 1966.

———. *Naissance de la clinique*. Paris: Presses Universitaires de France, 1972 [1963].

———. *The Order of Things: An Archeology of the Human Sciences*. New York: Random House, 1973.

———. "Right of Death and Power of Life." In *The History of Sexuality: An Introduction*, vol. 1. New York: Vintage Books, 1978.

Franko, Mark. *Dance as Text: Ideologies of the Baroque Body*. Cambridge: Cambridge University Press, 1993.

———. "Double Bodies: Androgyny and Power in the Performances of Louis XIV." *TDR* 38 (Winter 1994): 71–82.

Freud, Sigmund. "Charcot." In Peter Gay, ed., *The Freud Reader*. New York: Norton, 1989.

———. *Five Lectures on Psychoanalysis*. New York: Norton, 1989.

———. "Fragment of an Analysis of a Case of Hysteria: 'Dora.'" In Peter Gay, ed., *The Freud Reader*. New York: Norton, 1989.

———. *Standard Edition of the Complete Psychological Works of Freud*. Ed. James Strachey. London: Hogarth Press, 1962.

Fuller, Loie. *Fifteen Years of a Dancer's Life, with Some Account of Her Distinguished Friends.* London: Herbert Jenkins, 1913.

Gann, A. "La genèse de *La Péri*." In *Théophile Gautier: l'art et l'artiste. Actes du Colloque International*, vol. 1. Montpellier: Société Théophile Gautier, 1983.

Garafola, Lynn. "The Travesty Dancer in Nineteenth-Century Ballet." *Dance Research Journal* 17, no. 2, and 18, no. 1 (1985–86): 35–40.

Garelik, Rhonda. "Electric Salome: Loie Fuller at the Exposition Universelle in 1900." In J. Ellen Gainor, ed., *Theater and Imperialism.* New York: Routledge, 1995.

Gautier, Théophile. *Emaux et Camées.* 1852. Collection Bibliothèque Nationale de France.

———. "Giselle ou les Wilis." Paris: Librairie de l'Opéra, 1841. Collection of the Bibliothèque Nationale de France.

———. *L'Histoire de l'art dramatique en France depuis 25 ans.* Leipzig: Hetzel, 1899.

———. *Oeuvres érotiques: poésies libertines; lettres à la Présidente.* Paris: Arcanes, 1953.

———. *Souvenirs de théâtre: d'art et de critique.* Paris: Charpentier, 1883.

———. *Théâtre: mystères, comédies, et ballets.* Paris: Charpentier, 1872.

Gilbert, Sandra M., and Susan Gubar. *The Madwoman in the Attic.* New Haven: Yale University Press, 1979.

Gilman, Sander. "The Image of the Hysteric." In Sander Gilman et al., *Hysteria Beyond Freud.* Berkeley: University of California Press, 1993.

———. *The Jew's Body.* New York: Routledge, 1991.

Ginzburg, Carlo. "Clues: Morelli, Freud, and Sherlock Holmes." In Umberto Eco and Thomas A. Sebeok, eds., *The Sign of Three.* Bloomington: Indiana University Press, 1983.

———. *Ecstasies: Deciphering the Witches' Sabbath.* Trans. Raymond Rosenthal. New York: Random House, 1991.

Girard, René. *Deceit, Desire, and the Novel.* Trans. Yvonne Freccero. Baltimore: Johns Hopkins University Press, 1965.

———. "Scandal and the Dance." *New Literary History* 15 (1983–84): 311–24.

———. *The Scapegoat.* Baltimore: Johns Hopkins University Press, 1986.

———. *Violence and the Sacred.* Baltimore: Johns Hopkins University Press, 1977.

Godard, Henri. *Les manuscrits de Céline et leurs leçons.* Tusson: Du Lérot, 1988.

———. *Poétique de Céline.* Paris: Gallimard, 1985.

Goellner, Ellen W., and Jacqueline Shea Murphy. "Introduction: Movement Movements." In *Bodies of the Text: Dance as Theory, Literature as Dance.* New Brunswick, N.J.: Rutgers University Press, 1995.

Goldstein, Jan. *Console and Classify: The French Psychiatric Profession in the Nineteenth Century.* Cambridge: Cambridge University Press, 1987.

Gould, Evelyn. *Virtual Theater from Diderot to Mallarmé*. Baltimore: Johns Hopkins University Press, 1989.

"Grise-aile: parodie de 'Giselle ou les Wilis.'" In the *Musée Philipon: périodique dit Album de Tout le Monde*. Collection of the Bibliothèque de l'Opéra de Paris.

Guest, Ivor. "Dandies and Dancers." *Dance Perspectives* 37 (Spring 1969): 1–49.

———. "Parodies of *Giselle* on the English Stage, 1841–1871." *Theater Notebook* 9, no. 2 (Jan.–Mar. 1955): 38–46.

———. *The Romantic Ballet in Paris*. London: Sir Isaac Pitman and Sons, 1966.

Harrington, Anne. *Medicine, Mind, and the Double Brain: A Study in Nineteenth-Century Thought*. Princeton: Princeton University Press, 1987.

———. "Metals and Magnets in Medicine: Hysteria, Hypnosis, and Medical Culture in Fin-de-Siècle Paris." *Psychological Medicine* 18, no. 1 (Feb. 1988): 21–38.

Harsin, Jill. *Policing Prostitution in Nineteenth-Century Paris*. Princeton: Princeton University Press, 1985.

Hindus, Milton. *Céline tel que je l'ai vu*. Paris: Editions de l'Herne, 1969.

———. *The Crippled Giant: A Literary Relationship with Louis-Ferdinand Céline*. Hanover, N.H.: University Press of New England, 1986.

Hollier, Denis, ed. *A New History of French Literature*. Cambridge, Mass.: Harvard University Press, 1989.

Huet, Marie-Hélène. *Rehearsing the Revolution*. Trans. Robert Hurley. Berkeley: University of California Press, 1982.

Hugo, Victor. *Hernani*. With a "Notice" and "Documentation Thématique" by Pierre Richard. Paris: Classiques Larousse, 1971.

Huot, Sylviane. *Le Mythe d'Hérodiade chez Mallarmé: genèse et évolution*. Paris: Nizet, 1977.

Huysmans, J.-K. *Against Nature*. Trans. Robert Baldick. Harmondsworth, Eng.: Penguin Books, 1959.

Irigaray, Luce. *Speculum de l'autre femme*. Paris: Minuit, 1974.

Jameson, Fredric. "Céline and Innocence." In *Céline, USA*, a special issue of the *South Atlantic Quarterly* 93, no. 2 (Spring 1994): 311–19.

Janet, Pierre. *Psychological Healing*. New York, 1925.

Johnson, Barbara. "The Dream of Stone." In Denis Hollier, ed., *A New History of French Literature*. Cambridge, Mass.: Harvard University Press, 1989.

———. *A World of Difference*. Baltimore: Johns Hopkins University Press, 1987.

Jones, Ernest. *The Life and Work of Sigmund Freud*. New York: Penguin Books, 1961.

Jordanova, Ludmilla. *Sexual Visions: Images of Gender in Science and Medicine Between the Eighteenth and the Twentieth Centuries*. Madison: University of Wisconsin Press, 1989.

Journal des débats politiques et littéraires. Paris, 1832, 1840.

Juilland, Alphonse. "Elisabeth Craig vous parle." In *Actes du Colloque International L.-F. Céline 1988*. Charente: Tusson, 1989.

Kahane, Martin, ed. *Le Foyer de la danse*. Paris: La Réunion des Musées Nationaux, 1988.

Kaminski, H. E. *Céline en chemise brune ou le mal du présent*. Paris: Champs Libre, 1983 [1938].

Kaplan, Alice, and Philippe Roussin. "Céline's Modernity." In *Céline, USA*, a special issue of the *South Atlantic Quarterly* 93, no. 2 (Spring 1994): 421–44.

Kendall, Elizabeth. *Where She Danced: The Birth of American Art-Dance*. Berkeley: University of California Press, 1979.

Kermode, Frank. *Romantic Image*. New York: Chilmark Press, 1957.

———. "Poet and Dancer Before Diaghilev." In Roger Copeland and Marshall Cohhen, eds., *What Is Dance? Readings in Theory and Criticism*. New York: Oxford University Press, 1983.

King, Helen. "Once upon a Text: Hysteria from Hippocrates." In Sander Gilman et al., *Hysteria Beyond Freud*. Berkeley: University of California Press, 1993.

King, Lester S. "Medical Philosophy, 1836–44." In Lloyd G. Stevenson and Robert P. Multhauf, eds., *Medicine, Science, and Culture: Historical Essays in Honor of Owsei Temkin*. Baltimore: Johns Hopkins University Press, 1968.

Kofman, Sarah. *L'Enigme de la femme: la femme dans le texte de Freud*. Paris: Galilée, 1980.

———. *The Enigma of Woman: Woman in Freud's Writings*. Trans. Catherine Porter. Ithaca, N.Y.: Cornell University Press, 1985.

Koritz, Amy. *Gendering Bodies / Performing Art*. Ann Arbor: University of Michigan Press, 1995.

Kristeva, Julia. *La Révolution du langage poétique*. Paris: Seuil, 1974.

———. *Pouvoirs de l'horreur: essai sur l'abjection*. Paris: Seuil, 1980.

———. *Powers of Horror: Essays on the Abject*. Trans. Leon Roudiez. New York: Columbia University Press, 1982.

Lacan, Jacques. *Ecrits*. Trans. Alan Sheridan. New York: Norton, 1977.

———. *The Four Fundamental Concepts of Psychoanalysis*. London: Penguin Books, 1979.

———. "Dieu et la jouissance de *la* femme." In *Le Séminaire*, vol. 20: *Encore*. Paris: Seuil, 1975.

Lacoue-Labarthe, Philippe. *Musica ficta: figures de Wagner*. Paris: Bourgois, 1991.

———. *Musica Ficta: Figures of Wagner*. Trans. Felicia McCarren. Stanford, Calif.: Stanford University Press, 1994.

Latour, Bruno. *Les Microbes: guerre et paix*. Paris: Métailié, 1984.

Legendre, Pierre. *La Passion d'être un autre: étude pour la danse*. Paris: Seuil, 1978.

Lellouch, Alain. "La Méthode de J.-M. Charcot, 1825–93." *History and Philosophy of the Life Sciences* 11, no. 1 (1989): 43–69.

Lenoir, Timothy. "Models and Instruments in the Development of Electro-physiology, 1845–1912." *Historical Studies in the Physical Sciences* 17 (1986): 1–54.

Le Progrès médical. Feb.–Mar. 1887.

Lista, Giovanni. *Loie Fuller: danseuse de la belle époque.* Paris: Somogy Editions d'Art—Editions Stock, 1994.

Loux, Francoise. "Popular Culture and Knowledge of the Body." In Roy Porter and Andrew Wear, eds., *Problems and Methods in the History of Medicine.* London: Croom Helm, 1987.

Maingueneau, Dominique. *Les Livres d'école de la République, 1870–1914: discours et idéologie.* Paris: Le Sycomore, 1979.

Malaurie, Jean. "J.-B. Charcot: Father of French Polar Research." *Polar Record* 25 (1989): 191–96.

Mallarmé, Stéphane. *Corréspondance I, 1862–1871.* Ed. Henri Mondor. Paris: Gallimard, 1959.

———. *Corréspondance II, 1871–1885.* Ed. Henri Mondor and Lloyd James Austin. Paris: Gallimard, 1965.

———. *Corréspondance III, 1886–1889.* Ed. Henri Mondor and Lloyd James Austin. Paris: Gallimard, 1969.

———. *Les Noces d'Hérodiade: mystère.* Ed. Gardener Davies. Paris: Gallimard, 1959.

———. *Oeuvres complètes.* Paris: Gallimard, Bibliothèque de la Pléiade, 1945.

———. *Oeuvres complètes.* Vol. 1: *Poésies.* Paris: Flammarion, 1983.

Martin, Carol, ed. *A Sourcebook of Feminist Theatre and Performance.* New York: Routledge, 1996.

Marx, Karl. *Capital,* vol. 1. In Robert C. Tucker, ed., *The Marx-Engels Reader.* New York: Norton, 1978.

———. *The German Ideology,* part 1. In Robert C. Tucker, ed., *The Marx-Engels Reader.* New York: Norton, 1978.

Matlock, Jann. *Scenes of Seduction: Prostitution, Hysteria, and Reading Difference in Nineteenth-Century France.* New York: Columbia University Press, 1994.

Meltzer, Françoise. *Salome and the Dance of Writing: Portraits of Mimesis in Literature.* Chicago: University of Chicago Press, 1987.

Micale, Mark S. *Approaching Hysteria: Disease and Its Interpretation.* Princeton: Princeton University Press, 1995.

———. "Charcot and the Idea of Hysteria in the Male: Gender, Mental Science, and Medical Diagnosis in Late Nineteenth-Century France." *Medical History* 34, no. 4 (Oct. 1990): 363–411.

Mondor, Henri. *Mallarmé: documents iconographiques.* Vésenaz-Genève: Pierre Cailler, 1947.

Montrelay, Michèle. *L'Ombre et le nom: sur la féminité.* Paris: Minuit, 1977.

Morus, Iwan. "Marketing the Machine: The Construction of Electrotherapeutics as Viable Medicine in Early Victorian England." *Medical History* 36 (1992): 34–52.

Muray, Philippe. *Céline*. Paris: Seuil, 1981.

Mure, G. R. C. *An Introduction to Hegel*. London: Oxford University Press, 1940.

Nye, Robert A. *Crime, Madness, and Politics in Modern France: The Medical Concept of Decline*. Princeton: Princeton University Press, 1984.

Owen, A. R. G. *Hysteria, Hypnosis and Healing: The Work of J.-M. Charcot*. London: Dennis Dobson, 1971.

Pagès, Yves. "Les Crises d'identité du racisme Célinien: entre prédications xénophobes et désir d'exil." In *Actes du Colloque International L.-F. Céline 1992*. Tusson: Du Lérot, 1993.

———. "The 'Modest Proposal' of Doctor Destouches." In *Actes du Colloque International L.-F. Céline 1990*. Tusson: Du Lérot, 1991.

Parent-Duchâtelet, Alexandre. *De la prostitution dans la ville de Paris*. 2 vols. 3d ed. Paris: J. B. Baillière, 1857 [1836].

Pastori, Jean-Pierre. *La Danse: du ballet de coeur au ballet blanc*. Paris: Découvertes Gallimard, 1996.

Perrot, Philippe. *Les Dessus et les dessous de la bourgeoisie: une histoire du vêtement au dix-neuvième siècle*. Brussels: Editions Complexes, 1981.

Phelan, Peggy. "Dance and the History of Hysteria." In Susan Leigh Foster, ed., *Corporealities: Dancing Knowledge, Culture, and Power*. New York: Routledge, 1996.

Pitres, A. *Leçons cliniques sur l'hystérie et l'hypnotisme faites à l'Hôpital Saint-André de Bordeaux*, vol. 1. Paris, 1891.

Plato. *The Republic*. Trans. and with notes and introduction by Frances MacDonald Cornford. New York: Oxford University Press, 1980.

Porter, Roy. "The Body and the Mind, the Doctor and the Patient: Negotiating Hysteria." In Sander Gilman et al., *Hysteria Beyond Freud*. Berkeley: University of California Press, 1993.

Quéant, G. *Encyclopédie du théâtre contemporain*, vol. I. Paris: Collection du Théâtre de France, 1957.

Quétel, Claude. *History of Syphilis*. Trans. Judith Braddock and Brian Pike. Cambridge: Polity Press, 1990.

———. *Le Mal de Naples*. Paris: Seghers, 1986.

Rabinbach, Anson. "Neurasthenia and Modernity." In Jonathon Crary and Sanford Kwinter, eds., *Incorporations*. New York: Zone Books, 1992.

———. *The Human Motor: Energy, Fatigue, and the Origins of Modernity*. Berkeley: University of California Press, 1992.

Reiser, Stanley Joel. *Medicine and the Reign of Technology*. Cambridge: Cambridge University Press, 1978.

Rey, Roselyne. *The History of Pain*. Trans. Louise Elliot Wallace, J. A. Cadden, and S. W. Cadden. Cambridge, Mass.: Harvard University Press, 1995.

————. *Histoire de la douleur*. Paris: La Découverte, 1993.

Ricci, James V. *One Hundred Years of Gynaecology, 1800–1900*. Philadelphia: Blakiston, 1945.

Richard, Jean-Pierre. *L'Univers imaginaire de Mallarmé*. Paris: Seuil, 1961.

Richer, Paul. *Etudes cliniques sur la grande hystérie ou hystéro-epilepsie: Préface de J.-M. Charcot*. Paris: Delahaye et Lecrosnier, 1885.

Ricoeur, Paul. *Du texte à l'action*. Paris: Seuil, 1986.

————. *Hermeneutics and the Human Sciences: Essays on Language, Action, and Interpretation*. Trans. and ed. John B. Thompson. Cambridge: Cambridge University Press, 1981.

————. *La Métaphore vive*. Paris: Seuil, 1975.

Roach, Joseph. *The Player's Passion: Studies in the Science of Acting*. Ann Arbor: University of Michigan Press, 1993.

Robinson, Paul. *Freud and His Critics*. Berkeley: University of California Press, 1993.

Rose, Jacqueline. *Sexuality in the Field of Vision*. London: Verso, 1986.

Roussin, Philippe. "Getting Back from the Other World: From Doctor to Author." *Céline, USA*, a special issue of the *South Atlantic Quarterly* 93, no. 2 (Spring 1994): 243–64.

Sabatier, Robert. *Histoire de la poésie française: la poésie du 19ème siècle*. Vol. 1: *Les Romantismes*. Paris: Albin Michel, 1977.

Saussure, Ferdinand de. *Cours de linguistique générale: Saussure's Third Course of Lectures on General Linguisitcs, 1910–1911*. Trans. Roy Harris. New York: Pergamon Press, 1993.

Sautermeister, Christine. "La Traduction allemande de *Bagatelles pour un massacre*." In *Actes du Colloque International L.-F. Céline 1988*. Tusson: Du Lérot, 1989.

Schivelbusch, Wolfgang. *Disenchanted Night: The Industrialization of Light in the Nineteenth Century*. Berkeley: University of California Press, 1988.

Schwartz, Hillel. "Torque: The New Kinaesthetic of the Twentieth Century." In Jonathan Crary and Sanford Kwinter, eds., *Incorporations*. New York: Zone Books, 1992.

Screech, M. A. "Good Madness in Christendom." In W. F. Bynum, Roy Porter, and Michael Shepherd, eds., *The Anatomy of Madness: Essays in the History of Psychiatry*, vol. 1, 25–39. London and New York: Tavistock Publications, 1985.

Second, Albéric. *Les Petits Mystères de l'Opéra*. Paris: G. Kugelman, Bernard-Latte, 1844.

Serres, Michel. *Genèse*. Paris: Grasset, 1982.

————. *Rome*. Paris: Grasset, 1983.

————. *Rome: The Book of Foundations*. Trans. Felicia McCarren. Stanford, Calif.: Stanford University Press, 1991.

Seymour, Bruce. *Lola Montez: A Life*. New Haven: Yale University Press, 1996.

Shakespeare, William. *The Riverside Shakespeare*. Ed. G. Blakemore Evans. Boston: Houghton Mifflin, 1974.

Showalter, Elaine. *The Female Malady: Women, Madness, and English Culture, 1830–1950*. New York: Penguin, 1985.

Sieburth, Richard. "Poetry and Obscenity: Baudelaire and Swinburne." In *Proceedings of the 10th Congress of the International Comparative Literature Association 1982*, vol. 2. New York: Garland, 1985.

Silverman, Kaja. *The Acoustic Mirror: The Female Voice in Psychoanalysis and Cinema*. Bloomington: University of Indiana Press, 1988.

Smith, Albert. *The Natural History of the Ballet Girl*. London: Dance Books, 1996 [1847].

Smith, Marian. "What Killed Giselle?" *Dance Chronicle* 13, no. 1 (1990): 68–81.

Solomon-Godeau, Abigail. "The Legs of the Countess." *October* 39 (Winter 1986): 65–108.

Sourgen, Jean-Louis. "La Danse amère de Céline." In *Actes du Colloque International L.-F. Céline 1992*. Tusson: Du Lérot, 1993.

Sperber, Dan. *Rethinking Symbolism*. Cambridge: Cambridge University Press, 1975.

Stallybrass, Peter, and Allon White. *The Politics and Poetics of Transgression*. Ithaca, N.Y.: Cornell University Press, 1986.

Stendhal. *Racine et Shakespeare*. Preface by Henri Martineau. Paris, 1928.

Sugano, Marion Zwerling. *The Poetics of the Occasion: Mallarmé and the Poetry of Circumstance*. Stanford, Calif.: Stanford University Press, 1992.

Terdiman, Richard. *Present Past: Modernity and the Memory Crisis*. Ithaca, N.Y.: Cornell University Press, 1993.

Thomas, Helen. *Dance, Modernity and Culture: Explorations in the Sociology of Dance*. London: Routledge, 1995.

Tissié, Philippe. *L'Evolution de l'education physique en France et en Belgique, 1900–1910*. Pau, 1911.

Todorov, Tzvetan. *Théories du symbole*. Paris: Seuil, 1977.

Verdy, Violette. *Giselle: A Role for a Lifetime*. New York: Marcel Dekker, 1977.

Véron, Louis-Désiré. *Mémoires d'un bourgeois de Paris*, vol. 3. Paris: Hetzel, 1856.

————. *Mémoires d'un bourgeois de Paris*. Ed. Pierre Josserand. Paris: Guy le Prat, 1945.

Walkowitz, Judith. *Prostitution and Victorian Society*. Cambridge: Cambridge University Press, 1980.

Warner, John Harley. "Science in Medicine." In *Osiris*, 2d ser., 1 (1985): *Historical Writing in American Science*.

Wilde, Oscar. *Letters*. Ed. Rupert Hart-Davis. New York: Harcourt, Brace, 1961.

————. *Salomé*. Paris: Limited Editions Club, 1938.

————. *Salome*. Trans. Alfred Bruce Douglas. New York: Dover, 1967.

Williams, Linda. *Hard Core: Power, Pleasure, and the "Frenzy of the Visible."* Berkeley: University of California Press, 1989.

Witkowsky, A. J. *Le Nu au théâtre*. Paris, 1909.

Index

In this index an "f" after a number indicates a separate reference on the next page, and an "ff" indicates separate references on the next two pages. A continuous discussion over two or more pages is indicated by a span of page numbers. *Passim* is used for a cluster of references in close but not consecutive sequence.

Library of Congress Cataloging-in-Publication Data

McCarren, Felicia M.

   Dance pathologies : performance, poetics, medicine / Felicia
McCarren.

      p.   cm. — (Writing science)

   Includes bibliographical references (p.) and index.

   ISBN 0-8047-2989-1 (cl.) — ISBN 0-8047-3524-7 (pbk.)

   1. Dance—Psychological aspects—History—19th century.
2. Mental illness—History—19th century. 4. Pathology—
History—19th century. 4. Women dancers—History—19th
century. 5. Poetics. 6. Giselle (Choreographical work)
7. Céline, Louis-Ferdinand, 1894–1961. Bagatelles pour un
massacre. I. Title. II. Series.

GV1588.5.M33 1998

792.8'01'9—dc21   98-11386

                                     CIP

∞ This book is printed on acid-free, recycled paper.

Original printing 1998

Last figure below indicates year of this printing:

07 06 05 04 03 02 01 00 99 98